CHARLES S. PEIRCE:
LOGIC AND THE CLASSIFICATION OF THE SCIENCES

C.S. Peirce, the American philosopher and a principal figure in the development of the modern study of semiotics, struggled, mostly during his later years, to work out a systematic method for classifying sciences. By doing this, he hoped to define more clearly the various tasks of these sciences by showing how their individual effects are interrelated and how these effects, considered in their interrelations, establish pragmatic meanings for each individual science. Much of his work was centred on the meaning and function of logic in relation to other areas of human knowledge. By rightly defining the work of logic, Peirce argued, the work of the other sciences could be pursued with more rigorous reasoning.

Beverley Kent closely examines the published and unpublished writings of Peirce and carefully attends to the chronological development of his systems of classification; she thereby shows for the first time in the scholarly literature how seeming contradictions in Peirce's evolving classification are really part of an increasingly clear position. Logic (or "normative semiotic"), Peirce came to understand, is actually dependent on ethics and aesthetics for its principles. Kent shows how Peirce's working out of the classification of logic in relation to other sciences is a clue to the significant differences between his early and late philosophy and, perhaps even more important, to a reading of his more general claims for a philosophy of "pragmaticism."

This work will be of interest to readers of Peirce and American philosophy, to historians of logic and semiotics, and to those more generally interested in the history of systems of knowledge-classification.

Beverley Kent is in the department of philosophy at St Cloud State University in Minnesota.

CHARLES S. PEIRCE
Logic and the Classification
of the Sciences

Beverley Kent

McGill-Queen's University Press
Kingston and Montreal

Canadian Cataloguing in Publication Data

Kent, Beverley E.
Charles S. Peirce
Includes bibliographical references and index.
ISBN 0-7735-0562-8
1. Peirce, Charles S. (Charles Sanders), 1839–1914.
2. Logic. I. Title.
B945.P44K45 1987   191   c86-094482-4

Contents

Contents

Figures

As to Plato, unless we are content to treat the only complete collection of the works of any Greek philosopher that we possess as a mere repertory of gems of thought, as most readers are content to do; but wish to view them as they are so superlatively worthy of being viewed as the record of the entire development of thought of a great thinker, then everything depends upon the chronology of the dialogues.

C.S. Peirce, Papers, 434.33-4, 1902.

Preface

Peirce held that all reasoning is diagrammatic. Signs or symbols are used to exhibit the logical characteristics of mental representations. Logic studies the general laws of signs of all kinds to control thought in order to attain truth. This study Peirce called "normative semiotic." What he meant by logic or normative semiotic must be seen within the context of a complex diagram having the three-dimensionality of a lattice, a diagram that represents his classification of the sciences.

Peirce's classification of the sciences is based on the logic of relatives and is intended to display the conceivable effects of a science, in other words to outline its pragmatic meaning. The classification is also intended to vindicate his universal categories. Thus it is crucial to understanding both Peirce's pragmaticism and his architectonic.

Most of Peirce's writings on the classification of the sciences are in unpublished and as yet generally inaccessible manuscripts; few scholars refer to this major source. Of the more accessible writings, many lack chronological ordering and convey the impression that Peirce held contradictory doctrines. The result has often been systematic misrepresentation.

Most authors have declined to take seriously Peirce's assertion that logic is dependent on ethics and aesthetics for principles. Yet in his later writings Peirce rarely began a discussion of logic without prefacing it with that claim.

Almost all of Peirce's investigations into classifying the sciences were written between 1889 and 1903 and this work therefore focuses on the later writings. To give some background to these endeavours, I begin with a survey of relevant contemporary developments and Peirce's earlier philosophy.

Peirce was primarily concerned with the place of logic within the scheme because he was anxious to discourage prevalent tendencies to collapse logic into mathematics or to found it on psychology. Therefore I survey his criticisms of those attempts. I examine what Peirce understood by "science" and his characterization of a natural classification; I then analyse his various classification schemes with a view to identifying the advances made with each successive attempt. This turns out to be very revealing and provides an avenue for understanding the important differences between Peirce's early and late philosophy, and also leads to a clearer understanding of what Peirce meant by logic or normative semiotic. Finally, I look at the implication that this normative semiotic has for pragmaticism and at Peirce's claim that he had developed a more adequate and more thoroughly grounded doctrine.

My principal concern has been to make my interpretation of Peirce's thought convincing. For this reason I include several references in support of a given contention in the hope that, by doing so, readers will recognize that it is not a one-time (and perhaps ill-considered) assertion on Peirce's part, but is probably the product of some reflection.

It will be obvious that I have aimed at understanding and explaining Peirce's views rather than criticizing them. Nevertheless, it should not be assumed that I find these views beyond criticism, or even that I accept any given conclusion that I attribute to Peirce. Too often in the past he has been criticized without being fully heard, much less understood. My attempt at a sympathetic analysis is offered in redress.

The primary source for Peirce's published writings is the eight-volume *Collected Papers of Charles Sanders Peirce*. In referring to the *Collected Papers* I observe the conventional decimal notation for indicating volume and paragraph number, and I follow this with the date as listed in volume 8 of the *Collected Papers*; for example, "5.136, 1903" indicates paragraph 136 of volume 5, dated 1903. My source for the unpublished papers, The Charles S. Peirce Papers, is the microfilm of the manuscript collection located in the Houghton Library at Harvard University; decimal notation for these papers is used to refer to manuscript number and page number. The source for dates and reference format in this instance is Richard S. Robin's *Annotated Catalogue of the Papers of Charles S. Peirce* and his "The Peirce Papers: A Supplementary Catalogue." Accordingly, "329.20, 1904" indicates page 20 of manuscript 329 dated 1904. The following procedure has been adopted to simplify the numerous dating practices:

1 (5.136, 1903) is from a work dated by Peirce. Everyone is agreed that it was written or published in 1903.

2 (329.20, c. 1904) is from a work known to be published about 1904. There is good external evidence and scholarly consensus.

3 (856.9, [1911]) is a work dated by me or accepted by me as being 1911. The evidence is good but it is inferred (either by me or by scholarly consensus) as 1911.

4 (677.1, [c. 1911]) is dated by me (or believed by me following the evidence brought forward by other scholars) as about 1911.

5 (602.5, [c. 1903–8]) is dated by me (or accepted by me following the evidence available) as occurring within, or encompassed by, the specified dates.

6 (735.12, n.d.) indicates that no date is known to me.

Pagination and numbering of the manuscripts also present anomalies as follows:

1 (318.76^3, c. 1907). Superscripts indicate alternate sequences; thus this refers to page 76 in the third sequence following the main sequence of manuscript 318.

2 (339.151r, 1898) indicates lettered page sequences in the manuscript (either by Peirce himself or by scholars subsequently).

3 (451.Add2, 1903) refers to an additional page inserted or the page adjacent to page 2.

4 (1345 [fragment], [1896]) refers to pages that do not fit into any readily assignable sequence.

5 (L463, 1905) designates a letter from Peirce's correspondence.

6 (s97.208, n.d.; 427(s).120, 1903) are references to the supplementary films of microfilm.

Dating is of considerable significance to an understanding of Peirce's developing thought. Generally, I have given equal weight to published and unpublished manuscripts and to early and late drafts. After all, Peirce did not select and arrange the standard *Collected Papers*, nor was he able to publish all he wrote. Rather than rely on the selections now in print, I have tried to make my reading as inclusive as possible. Moreover, as far as the various drafts are concerned, I have often found that the less polished versions convey considerable illumination. Peirce's avowed practice was to write alternative drafts after a lapse of time and without reference to the earlier version; a third draft would combine and critically compare the insights of the first two (5.146, 1903; 311.11–16, 1903; 312.46, 1903), so that where no third version occurs the first two drafts may be equally legitimate. Where chronology is particularly important (as in chapter 4, section 3 below) it is usually irrelevant in what form the data occurred, for my concern is to show the development of Peirce's thought. Allowance for mistakes in drafts should be made, of course, and by indicating the date where possible and the sequence where appropriate, I give the reader the opportunity to assess this likelihood. I trust any errors will thereby be reduced to a minimum.

My references to writings other than Peirce's *Collected Papers* and unpublished manuscripts are given in the endnotes and bibliography.

Acknowledgments

I am grateful to Professor Don Roberts who has provided the invaluable criticism that could be obtained only from a scholar of his calibre; his enthusiasm for the project was very encouraging. Special thanks go to Professor Max Fisch for suggestions that (I suspect) he alone is in a position to supply. I also wish to thank Professors Jan Narveson and Terence Penelhum, who made many salutary observations. Professors Myron Anderson, John Dienhart, and David Boyer, Professors Emeriti Marvin Thompson and John Phillips, all of St Cloud State University, have offered helpful criticisms on recent additions and revisions. Professors Hannah Gay, James Van Evra, William Abbott and Dean Wallace Watson have offered to these later additions valuable suggestions for which I am most grateful. Special acknowledgment is due to William W. Barker and Patricia Cavanagh for their careful editorial work; and to Carey Merten and Keith Ewing, who collaborated with me on the diagrams that attempt to represent Peirce's suggestion for a stereoscopic model of his classification of the sciences. Figure 5 is by the Graphics Department at St Cloud State University and Figures 1, 2, 3, 4, and 6 are by Lennie E. Briese.

The Department of Philosophy, Harvard University, has kindly given permission to quote and refer to the Peirce papers; and the editor of the *Transactions of the Charles S. Peirce Papers* has willingly allowed me to reprint modified versions of two articles that originally appeared in the *Transactions*. These are "Peirce's Esthetics: A New Look" and "Objective Logic in Peirce's Thought," published in volumes 12 and 13 (1976 and 1977) respectively.

This book has been published with the help of a grant from the Canadian Federation for the Humanities, using funds provided by the

Social Sciences and Humanities Research Council of Canada. I deeply appreciate their important contribution.

I also wish to thank both the anonymous readers of the Federation and the publisher. My last acknowledgment is reserved for Professor David Fate Norton, who provided such insightful editorial direction.

CHARLES S. PEIRCE:
LOGIC AND THE CLASSIFICATION
OF THE SCIENCES

I

Introduction

Einstein thought in images. Was he left-handed?

Peirce was ambidextrous. He is said to have astounded his students by writing a logical problem on the blackboard with one hand and the answer with the other – simultaneously.[1] Peirce thought in visual diagrams (619.8, 1909; 632.6:1, 1909).

Einstein probably was not congenitally left-handed. It seems that neither hemisphere of his brain was dominant, enabling him to make linguistic demands on the imaging hemisphere – as left-handed persons are required to do in our right-hand-oriented society.[2] But whether social pressure or the "natural lottery" occasioned diagrammatic thought, neither Einstein nor Peirce relied upon such fickle tutors. Einstein began using his thought experiments (*Gedankenexperimente*) at sixteen, and Peirce began training himself to think in diagrams when a young man, finding it a great advance over algebraic thinking. There is, indeed, a remarkable similarity in their analyses of this thought process: both men emphasized the elements of reiteration and association in imagery; both maintained that inquiry advances in reaction to experiences that conflict with established thought patterns and, in doing so, generate surprise or wonder. The result in Peirce's terms is the "eradication of doubt," the "production of belief," the "settlement of opinion." Einstein referred to it as a "continuous flight from wonder."[3] Both men traced their own creative initiatives to systematized diagrammatic thought.

1. DIAGRAMMATIC THOUGHT IN PEIRCE'S PHILOSOPHY

Beginning with a suggestion from Berkeley's work on vision, Peirce conceived the possibility of forming habits from imaginary practice (620.17, 1909). He claimed that by exercising the imagination, we can visualize the occurrence of a stimulus and mentally rehearse the results of different responses. That which appears most satisfactory will influence actual behaviour as effectively as a habit produced by reiteration in the outside world.[4] From this Peirce was led to pragmatism, conceived as a philosophy in which thinking involves manipulating diagrams in order to examine questions; that is to say, problems would be expressed in diagrams and analysis would proceed by executing transformations upon those diagrams. This requires a formal structure, which Peirce provided by integrating diagrammatic thinking and topology into a system of logical diagrams – his existential graphs. This is puzzling, and I shall venture some clarification.

Topology was not yet set theoretical. This infant study, on Peirce's account, was an imaging activity: "the study of the continuous connections and defects of continuity of loci which are free to be distorted in any way so long as the integrity of the connections and separations of all their parts is maintained" (4.219, 1897). Just as topology (thus conceived) focuses on pure hypotheses and ignores the properties of objective space, so a diagram (in Peirce's sense) is an icon of the *form* of the relations as distinct from the actual relations of its objects.

What is the integrating factor linking topology with diagrammatic thinking to produce the existential graphs? The distinctive aspect of this topology is that the integrity of the relevant connections and separations is maintained, that is, continuities remain continuous and connectives remain conjoined throughout all transitions of even highly plastic distortions and expansions. Similarly, the existential graphs diagram the form of the relations in a uniform schema enabling exact experiments to be performed such that throughout all the transformations, the premisses entrain the conclusions.

Peirce's objective was to have the operation of thinking literally laid open to view – a moving picture of thought. He believed that these existential graphs would allow logical relationships to be displayed in such an iconic way as to yield solutions to problems that had defied analysis through algebraic logics.

Peirce discovered yet another method of thinking, which he expected to be even more potent than his existential graphs – that of "stereoscopic moving pictures." He was prevented from developing the idea, he tells us, because it required expensive apparatus quite beyond his means.[5]

Even so, Peirce may have been reaching for just this kind of thought in his tinctured existential graphs, which extended his logical diagrams to include modality.[6]

Three-dimensional imagery is also found in Peirce's natural classification of the sciences: Comte's hierarchical ordering in terms of decreasing generality becomes, in Peirce's scheme, a series of steps in which the sciences at the top provide principles for those below. This is not a single linear staircase, but a series of ladders related in a three-dimensional array so as to exhibit the more significant relations of logical dependence among the sciences. The whole assemblage might be envisioned as a lattice – yet another area of diagrammatic thought advanced by Peirce.

2. THE IMPORTANCE OF LOGIC

Peirce's genius extended into an extraordinary variety of disciplines. In our age of specialization, this might be viewed as a dispersal of energies, but the unifying factor in this diversity was his interest in methodology. For Peirce, methodology was a study of methodeutic, a branch of logic. In his own eyes he was a logician and, indeed, logic is pivotal to his philosophy. A clear idea of what he understood by logic is therefore necessary when approaching his philosophy. His notion of logic must be viewed in relation to other sciences, and is most clearly explained in his natural classification of the sciences.

A considerable volume of material (largely neglected by scholars) concerning Peirce's classification of the sciences is located in the unpublished manuscripts. Because until recently the published writings lacked chronological ordering, they gave the impression that Peirce espoused contradictory doctrines. Since logic forms the core of his doctrine, a misunderstanding of its role is likely to affect interpretation of other aspects of his work. Until an adequate account of logic in its relation to other sciences is available, there remains a lacuna in Peirce scholarship.

3. PEIRCE THE MAN

1. *Genius Thwarted*

If Peirce was an original thinker, why did he fail to receive widespread recognition while he lived? That question has received no definitive answer, though there has been speculation.

Benjamin Peirce was already Professor of Mathematics and Astronomy at Harvard University when, on 10 September 1839, his second son, Charles Sanders, was born.[7] Benjamin personally supervised his son's education and encouraged him to think analytically and scientifically.

By the time he was twelve years old, Charles had built his own chemistry laboratory. At that age he also came upon his brother's copy of Whately's *Logic* and mastered it in a week. At sixteen (while at college) he was studying Schiller's *Aesthetische Briefe* and Kant's *Kritik der reinen Vernunft*. The *Kritik* impressed him to such a degree that he learned it almost by heart (1.4, c. 1897). In his youth, he and his father spent long evenings discussing the mathematical problems with which his father was wrestling.

Peirce's university career showed – for a child prodigy – a relatively modest academic distinction. He received an MA from Harvard in 1862 and a BSC in chemistry *summa cum laude* in the first class to graduate from the Lawrence Scientific School in 1863. While an aide at the United States Coast and Geodetic Survey in 1859 he gained experience in the methods of scientific investigation. For six months in the early 1860s he studied techniques of classification with Louis Agassiz.

In 1862 he married a member of the New England social elite, Harriet Melusina Fay, a woman of ability and insight who subsequently gained renown as a feminist writer and organizer.

His father frequently boasted of his son's genius, reportedly imbuing the young Peirce with an arrogance that made it impossible for others to work with him. This is said to explain his inability to obtain a tenured position at Harvard or at any other university. Alternatively, his exclusion from academic institutions is attributed to the impropriety of divorcing his wife in 1883 to marry the Frenchwoman Juliette Froissy (Mme Pourtalai).[8] He did lecture at Johns Hopkins University from 1879 to 1884, but his position was terminated abruptly following receipt of certain "information" concerning Peirce. The reasons were not disclosed to him and his dismissal remains a mystery. Thereafter he was unable to obtain a university position. He worked with the U.S. Coast Survey until he was forced to resign in 1891 and from then lived in dire poverty and intellectual isolation. Evidently he had poor judgment in financial matters and his numerous ventures invariably ended in disappointment. He is said to have been an unsystematic writer, to have published little and, in his last years, to have been incapable of completing any of the many projects he had embarked upon.[9]

The image conveyed is of an irrascible, antisocial, hypercritical, overbearing, disorganized, unprepossessing individual.

His writings reveal a different character: here he appears to be confident, witty, engaging, generous, highly critical of himself, and fair in his criticism of others. Future biographers may explain the discrepancy between Peirce the author and Peirce the social (or antisocial) being. Although much remains undisclosed, some of the facts of his life do seem to lessen that disparity: we know, for example, that the first Mrs. Peirce was not abandoned by Peirce, but that she had left him seven years before he divorced and remarried. He had by then shown symptoms of a nervous disorder which was to recur throughout his life and which may explain much of his conduct. Retrospective diagnosis suggests that Peirce may have suffered from a conversion hysteria characterized by immaturity, impulsiveness, and withdrawal from problems.[10]

Peirce's modest university record is usually explained by his extra-currricular activities with his friend, Horatio Paine. Joseph L. Brent, a historian, has referred to their revels and escapades. He cites a letter from Martyn Paine to President Walker, dated 24 March 1857, concerning his nephew Horatio. Paine asked the Harvard president to persuade Horatio to sever relations with his "intimate" and drinking partner, Charles Peirce, as the two "'only administer temptations to each other'."[11] Yet the two friends clearly shared strong intellectual interests as well as high spirits. Max Fisch, the Peirce scholar, has noted that Horatio Paine and Charles Peirce became "intimate friends" when they found themselves neighbours as a result of an alphabetical seating order. Fisch wrote, "John Weiss's translation of *The Aesthetic Letters* of Friedrich Schiller ... interested them more than anything they were required to read in college, and they 'spent every afternoon for long months upon it, picking the matter to pieces as well as we boys knew how to do.'" After Schiller they went on to study Kant's *Critique*.[12]

While today many may see Peirce's actions as the expression of an independence of spirit equal to that of his thought, many of his contemporaries interpreted his actions as a flouting of convention. Unfortunately for Charles, those who disapproved included Charles William Eliot and Simon Newcomb, both of whom later became powerful and sabotaged his career. However, until his death in 1880, his father was able to protect Peirce from much of their influence.

The antipathy with Eliot may have begun in Peirce's sophomore year. He was a student in Eliot's chemistry class; and the records show that he was fined one dollar for cutting up his instructor's bench.[13] Of course, Eliot may have been frustrated in his own career by the influence of the self-styled "Scientific Lazzaroni" who had opposed his advancement, including his candidacy for the Harvard presidency; one of the prime movers of that group was Benjamin Peirce.[14] Even so, Eliot finally became president of Harvard and retained that position for the remainder of Charles Peirce's career.

Simon Newcomb, head of the Naval Observatory, appears to have been more disinterested in his opposition to Peirce, but no less effective. It was Newcomb who conveyed the mysterious "information" to President Gilman that occasioned the non-renewal of Peirce's contract at Johns Hopkins in 1884.[15]

In the winter of 1871-2 Peirce started the Metaphysical Club in Cambridge, where William James, Oliver Wendell Holmes, Jr., and Chauncy Wright were among the lawyers, scientists, and philosophers who met informally to exchange ideas. Until 1875, while Peirce still resided in Boston, meetings were held frequently, perhaps once a fortnight. At Johns Hopkins University he again founded a Metaphysical Club; it survived but a year after he ceased to animate it (1879-85). He was elected to the New York Mathematical Society in 1891. Membership included Thomas Fiske, Edward Stabler, Harold Jacoby, and Carl Steinmetz. Far from being antisocial, Peirce enlivened and frequently occasioned, discourse with his peers. Thomas Fiske wrote:

Conspicuous among those who attended the meetings of the Society in the early nineties was the famous logician Charles S. Peirce. His dramatic manner, his reckless disregard of accuracy in "unimportant" details, his clever newspaper articles (in *The Evening Post* and *The New York Times*) on the activities of the young Society, interested and amused us all ... He was always hard up, living partly on what he could borrow from friends, partly on what he got from odd jobs like writing for the newspapers. He seemed equally brilliant whether under the influence of liquor or otherwise. His company was prized by the various organizations to which he belonged; and so he was never dropped from membership even though he failed to pay his dues.[16]

Peirce had given university lectures on the British logicians at Harvard in the winter of 1869-70 and on evenings when he could not take measurements at the observatory, his students would call at his home for studies in Kant's *Critique*. (One student found this association of Kant's work with clouds and blizzards very appropriate.)[17]

Several of his students at Johns Hopkins attest to Peirce's influence and to their devotion. Christine Ladd-Franklin, the first American woman prominent in modern psychology, was a frequent correspondent. Of the Johns Hopkins experience, Joseph Jastrow wrote:

In those days there was gathered in Baltimore a group of scholars and productive intellectual workers that would have been exceptional in any college community. Their names would suggest the notable contributions of American scholarship in their generation. Yet among them the impression of Mr. Peirce stands forth most prominently *primus inter pares*. The impression that I retain of his analyses of logical and philosophical problems is that of observing a plummet line descending through troubled waters foot by foot, sounding the depths, avoiding the weeds and the shoals, and reaching an undiscovered bottom; for to the student many of the problems in a controversial sea seemed bottomless. It was not argument, but discovery.[18]

And W.P. Montague was downright effusive: "For Peirce himself I had a kind of worship. While his intellect was cold and clear, his metaphysical imagination was capricious, scintillating, and unbridled, and his whole personality was so rich and mysterious that he seemed a being apart, a super-man. I would rather have been like him than like anyone else I ever met."[19] There is considerable evidence, then, that Peirce was an effective and even an inspiring teacher.

Although his scientific contributions in several areas were acknowledged both nationally and internationally, and his work as philosopher and logician was also known, Peirce did not gain the prominence needed to overcome the forces that barred him from academic institutions.

2. The Vicissitudes of Peirce's Career

The u.s. Coast Survey's reputation as America's finest scientific institution owed much to Peirce's genius.[20] In addition to his geodetic work, he made innovations in astronomy while he was assisting at the Harvard College Observatory, which co-operated with the Survey. Yet difficulties arose for Peirce when his father ceased to direct either operation. Eliot suspended his salary in 1870, although Peirce had been charged with doing observatory work in Europe. He also opposed Peirce's bid for the directorship of the observatory, and subsequently tried to terminate his connection there altogether, ultimately succeeding when Joseph Winlock, the incumbent director, died.[21]

Meanwhile, the Coast Survey was subjected to political machinations during Grover Cleveland's presidency. Peirce and other government scientists had enjoyed considerable freedom while J.E. Hilgard was superintendent, but they were unable to counter his alcohol-induced mismanagement. When Hilgard was finally replaced by F.M. Thorn (a lawyer and politician), that freedom was severely curtailed. Peirce's discoveries were ignored, his reports were denied publication by the superintendent, and obsolete equipment was purchased in spite of his remonstrations. Of the scientists in the Survey, Peirce alone publicly denounced the Cleveland Democrats' overt antagonism towards science.[22] In such circumstances he had no recourse but to resign. His resignation was not conveyed to the Secretary, however, and only after six more discouraging and frustrating years, did he actually quit. In 1889 Newcomb gave an adverse assessment of Peirce's gravimetric report to Superintendent T.C. Mendenhall, leading to his dismissal from the Survey, which thereafter, slid from prominence in the scientific community.

Peirce missed out on opportunities to publish, sometimes because he would not accede to modifications with which he disagreed. Frequently he was unable to find a publisher for work that was completed or nearly completed.[23] Always he was beset with personal and financial problems.

After he left the Coast Survey, Peirce resorted to writing (often anonymously) countless reviews and articles on a variety of subjects for newspapers and journals such as *The Nation* and *The Monist*. He already had defined more than five thousand terms for the *Century Dictionary* in the areas of mathematics, mechanics, astronomy, weights and measures, logic, and metaphysics. Subsequently he contributed to the *Dictionary of Philosophy and Psychology* and prepared many papers for the National Academy of Sciences. He was a remarkable linguist; from his own account, he was able to read Arabic and ancient Egyptian, and he constantly used Latin and Greek. His proficiency in the commoner modern European languages and his wide expertise in the sciences made him an invaluable translator for the Smithsonian Institution. Yet all this miscellaneous writing must have obtruded on his other work, making it difficult for him to spend long periods of time on his major projects. Nor did it earn him enough money.

In 1902 he was unable to obtain a grant from the Carnegie Foundation for the production of his work on logic and he also failed in his efforts to return to the Coast Survey as Inspector of Standards. Both applications had met the intervention of Newcomb.[24] He was so beleaguered by creditors[25] that his financial difficulties caused anxiety as well as interruption. His house was in need of expensive repairs, he needed special "luxuries" for his wife's illness, and since they could not afford help, Peirce had to undertake the household chores. From 1909 until his death in 1914 he was obliged to take a grain of morphine each day to control the pain he experienced from cancer. Only the benevolence of William James and other friends alleviated the poverty of his last years.

Lacking the benefit of interaction with students and colleagues, either directly or in print, Peirce had to find his own errors.[26] He carried out this task sedulously – criticizing, reformulating, and developing his ideas – virtually without encouragement or recognition. Earlier, his facility with languages had given him access to primary sources, and so to scientific developments in Europe, sometimes years before his fellow Americans. But in later years his remote home near Milford, Pennsylvania, aggravated his intellectual isolation, making it impossible for him to obtain the books he needed. There were times when Peirce had to part with his own books and was indebted to his brother for buying them back for him.[27] He often had to set aside projects because he could not refer to the works he needed. On 18 May 1901, he wrote to George A. Plimpton, a prominent civic leader, begging him to procure two needed books; he promised to review one of them and to reimburse the purchaser with the proceeds.[28] In a letter to Lady Welby, dated 20 May 1911, he wrote that he had not seen a new book or memoir for three years.

Everything seemed to contrive to prevent him from completing his major projects. His frustration at not being able to do so was tragic for him, and unfortunate for philosophy. Peirce might have done with assurance what others today are still trying to do.

3. Influence and Influences

Peirce unhesitatingly acknowledged his debt to the great philosophers and scientists of the past. Kant's philosophy, in particular, influenced him profoundly. Nevertheless, he could be a powerful critic of these luminaries, for example, of Descartes, Berkeley, Kant, and Mill. From his perspective of scholastic realism[29] he was critical of the positivists, Comte, Pearson, Mach, and Poincaré.

During his five-year association with J.J. Sylvester and others in the Mathematics Department at Johns Hopkins University, Peirce honed his own mathematical knowledge. The problem of continuity had led him to a thorough study of topology and of infinities. Klein, Listing, Möbius, Lobachevski, Clifford, Cayley, Cantor, and Halsted all had an impact on his thought.

Peirce directly influenced Jastrow, Ladd-Franklin, Dewey, Royce, Russell, Whitehead, and Ramsey. More recently, Popper, Quine, Sellars, and Putnam have acknowledged their indebtedness to him. It has often been said that he was too far ahead of his time to receive widespread contemporary recognition. Certainly, most of his initiatives went unrecognized and his importance was not acknowledged. Many later developments in philosophy were anticipated and explored in depth by Peirce, perhaps confirming his dictum that truth will be worked out at last, if not in one way then in another.[30]

Peirce was a competent historian of science and his writings in philosophy are both profound and original. The following list of some of his other achievements is a reminder of the impact of his work in a wide variety of disciplines:

In 1870 he had expanded and modified Boolean algebra and extended it to the logic of relatives.

He devised the matrix form for truth tables and provided a proof of its completeness.

He made pioneer contributions to the foundations of mathematics.

His is the first-known description of an electrical switching machine for logic.

Influenced by Wilhelm Wundt, he was the first to advance experimental psychology in the United States.

He applied the calculus approach to Cournot's work and so prefigured mathematical economics.

He invented a pendulum, superseding the Repsold version, for determining the intensity of gravity.

He advanced the endeavour to determine the form of the Milky Way.

He hypothesized a twist in space analogous to the Möbius strip.

He anticipated Michelson in determining the length of a meter from a wavelength of light.

He developed a quincuncial map projection and researched topological mapping.

The interconnectedness of Peirce's thought, ranging over a vast array of disciplines and ideas, was the source of much of his originality. Yet it had negative aspects. When he wrote on a given topic, other connected ideas would frequently obtrude, hindering him from presenting his work in an integrated form.

Many of his innovations resulted from adapting the methods of one science to the problems of another. Peirce's philosophical writings are permeated with examples of this approach, which he advocated as an investigative procedure. Peirce contended that a thorough study of the history of science such as he had undertaken would provide the groundwork for this method and would give an understanding of the philosophy of science.[31] He attempted to reconstruct the thought processes of the scientist he was researching, believing that there was a lesson in logic to be learned from this approach. Indeed, it confirmed his opinion that the best thinking was the outcome of imaginary experiments performed upon visual images. Because he considered it the task of logic to provide ways of constructing suitable images, he developed his system of logic diagrams, what he called his "existential graphs." This iconic system of schematic shapes was designed to provide concrete diagrams on which to experiment.

4. REACTION TO PEIRCE'S CLASSIFICATION OF THE SCIENCES

Of Peirce's contributions to philosophy, pragmatism is the most widely known. Again, method is paramount. Pragmatism was the outcome of discussions in the Metaphysical Club in Cambridge, Massachusetts. Peirce gave the theory its first expression in 1870, but this account was not promulgated. His best-known statement of the pragmatic method is found in "How to Make Our Ideas Clear," which appeared in 1878. Here is found his maxim, his rule for attaining the third grade of clearness of apprehension:[32] "Consider what effects, that might conceivably have practical bearings, we conceive the object of our conception to have. Then, our conception of these effects is the whole of our conception of the object" (5.402, 1878).

In 1898 William James propelled the term "pragmatism" into the popular sphere through his lecture, "Philosophical Conceptions." To honour his friend Peirce, the ever-generous James referred to his own quite different theory as "pragmatism" and credited Peirce with its invention. James's version did have affinities with Peirce's early philosophy. Yet by 1898 Peirce's pragmatic theory was intimately bound with the logic of relatives, whereas James's theory concerned belief as it affects the life of an individual. According to James, the truth of an idea is a function of the practical effects it has on the individual; although truth is always provisional, it is valuable as an instrument for action.

Peirce was anxious to dissociate himself from James's view. He renamed his own theory "pragmaticism" to indicate that it is a variant of the more general theory; and he submitted it to renewed investigation. While this 1878 statement remained substantially unchanged, what he understood by it underwent significant modification.

At the turn of the century a number of unresolved ideas in Peirce's studies began to coalesce, with implications for pragmaticism. These developments culminated in a new architectonic involving a classification of the sciences. Indeed, they are made clear when seen with his positioning of logic within the classification of the sciences - his vehicle for conveying the meaning of logic in its third grade of clearness. The classification demonstrates relations of a given science to various other sciences and indicates some of the conceivable effects. Ultimately, Peirce regarded logic as one of the three normative sciences (the other two being ethics and aesthetics). He adopted several different views on his way to this position and, because he never ceased to review his ideas, there is a danger that one of the interim positions might be taken as definitive. Hence careful attention should be given to the order in which these developments occurred.

If Peirce's work was unduly neglected, it was not because he published little. On the contrary - and despite the hostility to his views - he published a vast amount,[33] although very little of it was available in a consolidated form, and his significant writings remained unpublished. By 1935 the first six volumes of the *Collected Papers* had been issued and the available material was augmented markedly in a systematic form. Organizing the manuscripts was an immense project that would have daunted even an experienced editor, and the editors of those volumes were inexperienced. Understandably, their work suffered. They culled from innumerable manuscripts and neglected to take account of chronology. Nowhere is this more misleading than in Peirce's research into the meaning of logic as it is exhibited in its relations to other sciences.

The transitional version of the classification featured prominently in the *Collected Papers* under the heading "A Detailed Classification of the Sciences" (1.203–83) is from section 1, chapter 2 of the "Minute Logic" and is dated 1902. Subsequently, Peirce modified the general layout of the scheme in such a way as to bring his classification into accord with his three universal categories. Since Peirce always considered philosophy to be a theorectical science (as distinct from the sciences of review and the practical sciences), the position of the theoretical sciences within the scheme is of particular importance; but he later made further changes. The subdivisions of philosophy in the published 1902 classification were unlike those which Peirce later affirmed and regularly cited (see 1.278–82, c. 1902).

In addition, Peirce was still uncertain of the location of ethics and aesthetics within his scheme. Their positioning is of paramount concern precisely because of the connection Peirce claims that these disciplines have with logic. In his early classification schemes, Peirce had considered ethics a practical science, separating it from philosophy altogether. In 1902 he was still debating whether or not ethics and aesthetics were also theoretical sciences. It was only after some vacillation that he concluded that these three sciences together comprise the normative sciences, his mid-division of philosophy.

Prior to 1903, Peirce's classification scheme was in its gestation stage. He continued to ponder the relationships, modifying and refining them until as late as 1913. The editors of the *Collected Papers* acknowledge that about 1903 "Peirce came to recognize the nature of the Normative Sciences" (1.573note). Yet in volume 1, where the section on the normative sciences is found, the "Introduction" is dated 1906, chapters 2, 3, and 4 are from the period 1902–3, and chapter 5, which concludes the discussion, is dated 1898. Unfortunately, this inverts the order of Peirce's thought. Only the introductory chapter, the first four paragraphs of chapter 3, and all of chapter 4 represent his more considered account. Such mismatching of manuscripts is in large measure responsible for the confusion found in studies concerning this aspect of Peirce's thought.

If the extant Peirce documents are to be regarded as "the record of the entire development of thought of a great thinker," then Peirce's injunction that "everything depends on the chronology" should be accepted.[34] Certainly such ordering ought not to be ignored. When it is observed, the misconceptions of earlier writers may be resolved; and many of the alleged discrepancies and contradictions will be regarded as developments in the thought of a philosopher who submitted his own ideas to incessant criticism, and who was able to abandon a view when he became dissatisfied with it.

Ultimately, Peirce held that logic depends on the other two normative sciences for its principles; a claim that led many scholars to take this late development in Peirce's thought less than seriously. Of those who have examined Peirce's writings on the normative sciences, scarcely any have attempted to sort out the confusion resulting from the disorder of the published materials. Those who have done so have usually compounded the confusion and dismissed unresolved dilemmas as inconsistencies in Peirce's thought. The majority has disregarded the manuscripts. They have complained that Peirce's writings on the subject are too few and sketchy, and some have gone so far as to declare that these are, in any case, the works of an author in his dotage.[35]

Peirce saw himself engaged in the unflagging pursuit of truth, and he expressed the hope that others would carry on his work. He believed that he was at his philosophical finest in the last period of his life, and there are grounds for agreeing with him. His thought undoubtedly retained its vigour into his last years. The volume of material in the *Collected Papers* vindicates the claim of some Peirce scholars that relevant passages are few, but a large number of manuscripts do include discussions of the normative sciences. The microfilm publication of the Peirce papers, along with Robin's *Annotated Catalogue*, has made those manuscripts accessible; the new *Writings of Charles S. Peirce* will further facilitate access, particularly since the edition is chronologically ordered.

Apart from his original contributions to mathematics and logic, Peirce was well versed and innovative in other sciences such as astronomy, chemistry, and psychology, and he was a competent historian of the sciences. When he made statements about the place of logic and philosophy within the sciences, they were not simply the pronouncements of a theorizing philosopher, but observations informed by a detailed, firsthand knowledge of mathematics and several sciences. His views on these topics warrant a thoroughgoing examination to correct distortions and to allow presentation of his ideas in a clear light. If his views on classification are found wanting by contemporary standards, the study of them is nonetheless a gateway to the understanding of his philosophy, which does remain of contemporary importance.

5. PEIRCE'S OBJECTIVES IN CLASSIFYING THE SCIENCES

Why should Peirce have thought it necessary to classify the sciences? He believed that a classification would vindicate his categories by providing them with an architectonic within which they might be tested. It would show where philosophy and its subdivisions fitted in with other intellectual pursuits: it would reveal just how his own ideas of logic and of philosophy differed from accepted views; and, most importantly, it would indicate what kind of science logic must be. He believed that a clear understanding of logic required an examination of its relation to other sciences. A classification scheme would function as a diagram to exhibit those relations most perspicuously.

For a period of ten years from 1903, Peirce rarely discussed logic without first explaining its relationship to other theoretical inquiries. More cursory accounts relate logic to other normative sciences, leaving the wider context unstated, and many scholars have neglected the overall classification, which would enable them to fully understand his concept of logic.

Logic is the dominant concern of the classification for at least one other reason: Peirce thought that recognition of the relation it holds to other sciences would rescue it from attenuation or, worse, from absorption into some other discipline. He was particularly anxious to quash prevalent tendencies to collapse logic into mathematics, or to found it on psychology or on metaphysics or on one of the other disciplines that he identified as underlying the logical studies of his contemporaries. The classification would guard against the hazards of attempting to resolve problems of metaphysics and special sciences without thoroughly considering the nature of the reasoning to be used and the basis of its validity. Clearly there is a need to follow Peirce in an examination of what logic is not. This is pursued in chapter 3.

One does not change classifications easily. Peirce's early consideration of a classification in terms of genus and species based on a subject-predicate logic was superseded by schemes based on the logic of relatives. As developed by Peirce, the logic of relatives concerns systems in which things (in this case sciences) may be connected in any kind of relation. A classification in terms of genus and species operates primarily on the single relation of similarity. Without this limitation, classification is able to display the conceivable effects of a science. Demonstrating those effects is tantamount to outlining the pragmatic meaning of a science, which for Peirce was the most complete way of conveying his understanding of that science.

Classification is itself the business of a science, but which science? Peirce regarded logic as a classificatory science, but he took a similar position about the sciences of review (which systematize the discoveries of the theoretical sciences). At first glance it is uncertain whether logic or review is intended as the proper arena for the inquiry into a classification of the sciences. As it turns out, both have a role in the procedure.

It is also necessary to determine what is being classified. Sciences, of course. Yet what is a science? From his investigation into this question, presented in chapter 4, Peirce concluded that a science is best understood in terms of the activity of those whose lives are animated by the desire to seek truth. Science is seen, then, as a living or continuing activity, and the way is opened for what Peirce called a "natural" classification.

Early in his investigation Peirce adopted a Comtean principle as his central governing idea. Crudely stated, this is the view that sciences form a hierarchy in which the higher sciences supply principles to the lower, while the lower ones furnish data to the higher.[36] Yet the principles governing Peirce's scheme usually have remained either unacknowledged or misinterpreted.

Peirce's experiments with different classifications progress in small steps towards a scheme that he found satisfactory. In chapter 4, using the Peirce manuscripts, a chronological account of that development is reconstructed with the goal of identifying the advances made with each successive proposal. As a result, the reasons for Peirce's more determinate classification are revealed. Confusion, which has been the consequence of treating those various positions as if *all* were Peirce's considered view, can be eliminated.

This procedure reveals that Peirce recognized the relation of logic to ethics and aesthetics only after a protracted inquiry. Futhermore, he permitted the formal differentiating principle – that which governs the breakdown of the sciences – to surface largely of its own accord. One of the early schemes was based on the three categories that Peirce had developed previously. Fearing that his trichotomy might be misleading him, he set it aside and developed alternative schemes, only to find himself ineluctably led back. Even so, it was some time before he conceded that the resulting divisions conformed to his categories.

The science of logic that emerges from these investigations is a normative study. This normative logic, examined in chapter 5, does not include an inquiry into formal logic, which Peirce held to be a mathematical study. He also warned that his aesthetics and ethics are not quite the disciplines they are traditionally taken to be. There may be some difficulty in abandoning the customary understanding of these disciplines, in spite of Peirce's claim. Alternative names for these sciences might have clarified his theory, and Peirce offered an assortment.[37] But even these are not totally different from aesthetics and ethics as traditionally studied; they represent the most general level of investigations conducted in those areas, a level often neglected.[38] As such, their examination does not use the principles investigated in the normative study of logic, but may proceed with deductive logic and a *logica utens* (the theory possessed prior to the scientific inquiry). When this is recognized, Peirce's claim that logic depends on the preceding normative sciences for its principles may be more readily accepted.

At one time Peirce considered criticism or "critic" (as he called the discipline that examines the general conditions for discriminating between good and bad reasoning, and between strong and weak probable reasoning) to be the whole of logic. Eventually he extended the scope of the science to encompass general laws of signs of all kinds. In this general sense logic is best characterized as "semiotic," and normative semiotic is "logic as the science of the principles of how thought ought to be controlled, so far as it may be subject to self-control, in the interest of truth" (655.26, 1910). I propose to elucidate that statement and to explore the development in Peirce's thought that led him to the position it expresses. But first I examine the wider context in which that study was pursued.

II

Preludes to Peirce's Classification

It was not until 1889 that Peirce began a systematic search for a satisfactory classification of the sciences. This task was precipitated by some aspects of his own philosophy, but it was also related to more pervasive concerns in nineteenth-century philosophical thought.

Starting with the early Greeks, classification schemes were devised to bring clarity to the diversity of phenomena found in nature. Philosophers and scientists recognized almost from the outset that classifications have both a practical and theoretical purpose. Many early writers sought schemes that would facilitate identification in the ordering of collections. The emphasis later shifted to indexing information for storage and retrieval in museums and libraries. By contrast, a classification of objects by causation or by origin was found to be more suggestive and to enable wide-ranging generalizations even though governed by many constraints: these classifications aim at revealing connections and analogies between the different areas of knowledge in order to give a comprehensive picture of reality. If a scheme of this kind is presupposed by those pursuing a range of disciplines, it could have a significant impact on their study.

The long-standing interest in classification quickened in the seventeenth and eighteenth centuries so that by the nineteenth century countless schemes were being advanced. Many of these were little more than catalogues providing a record of knowledge as it existed at the time they were devised, but there were classifications of a more useful kind as well.

Peirce's papers reflect an awareness of both historical and contemporary developments.[1] These will be discussed before proceeding to look at pertinent refinements that occurred as Peirce advanced his own philosophy.

1. CLASSIFICATION PRIOR TO PEIRCE

1. Early Classification

The extant writings of the Pythagoreans reveal a burgeoning interest in classification influenced by their conviction that there is an inner harmony in nature's diversity. Phythagoras held that geometry, arithmetic, and music would unravel the mysteries of number and harmony. Plato adopted the procedure of moving from vague, general ideas to specific, clear ideas by tracing the progressive division of each idea or "Form" into those immediately below it. Platonic Forms are unchanging ideal objects by reference to which the changing objects of experience are ordered. Aristotle dispensed with Platonic Forms and replaced the relationship of participation with that of essential attributes and their instantiation. His procedure consisted of indicating a simple or compound attribute shared by other kinds of things, and then indicating another attribute not shared by the remainder. In this way he identified the specific difference that distinguished one kind from others of the same genus. Thus he made a separation between genus and species (as Plato had not). Moreover, he assumed that the correct choice of genus and differentia was not dependent on convention but on the nature of reality itself. Indeed, he thought that classification was the gateway to knowledge and reality. His arrangement of the sciences was in accordance with their relation to theory, action, or production: philosophy was placed first among the theoretical sciences, ahead of physics; ethics and politics comprised the practical sciences; and aesthetics fell into a third group, poetic sciences. Aristotle's pupil, Demetrius of Phalerum, who helped organize the library in Alexandria, introduced divisions and subdivisions of knowledge to accommodate specialization within a science.

The Greeks were not alone in their early recognition of the value of classification. In China, classification appeared in encyclopaedic works and in dictionaries from the Han dynasty (although they probably originated even earlier). They were used as teaching devices and as a means of examining candidates for official positions.

In India the *Dharmaśastra*, or Treatises of the Correct Order, date back to the first century AD. Later encyclopaedic works were produced in Sanskrit until by the nineteenth century new classifications abounded in most of the Indian languages.

The method and approach of ancient Rome is reflected in Marcus Terentius Varro's classification of the first century AD, which listed grammar, dialectic, rhetoric, geometry, arithmetic, astrology, music, medicine, and architecture. Subsequently Pliny's *Natural History* provided an impressive though more narrowly conceived system.

The Arabs preserved and augmented Greek science and, after the seventh century, introduced it to Spain whence it filtered into the rest of Europe. Its classification schemes were contributed by Avicenna, Al Farabi, and Ibn Qutaibah, whose work included an essay on classification. But it was the third-century Neoplatonist, Porphyry, who produced one of the most influential systems. It became known as the "ladder of Porphyry" and recurred in various forms throughout the Middle Ages. Porphyry combined Aristotle's theory of predicables with Plato's method of division and produced a sequence that anticipated modern evolutionary ordering. Using the category of substance as illustration, he diagrammed the relationship between this basic category which is a genus and not a species, the less general terms which are both species and genera, and the differentia which identify the divisions, down to the narrowest species which contains individuals only. This conception in both general and specific theoretical classifications persisted for centuries:

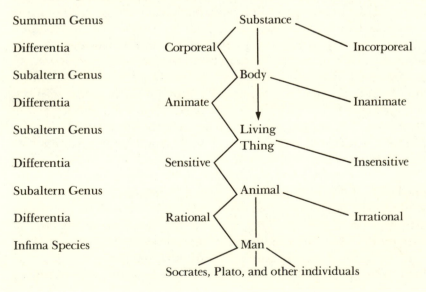

Summum Genus		Substance
Differentia	Corporeal	Incorporeal
Subaltern Genus		Body
Differentia	Animate	Inanimate
Subaltern Genus		Living Thing
Differentia	Sensitive	Insensitive
Subaltern Genus		Animal
Differentia	Rational	Irrational
Infima Species		Man

Socrates, Plato, and other individuals

2. *General Theoretical Classification*

With the possible exception of the work of Peter Ramus, no significant change in the procedure of recording the state of knowledge occurred until the seventeenth century. Francis Bacon based his classification on the subjective criteria of the faculties of the soul. These he identified as memory, imagination, and reason, which respectively yield history, poetry, and philosophy. He believed that the empirical method would reveal individual causes and, more importantly, would show the interrelations of the sciences that he claimed formed an organic whole. Since "first philosophy" contained axioms common to various sciences, laws of reasoning, and certain general concepts, it provided the foundation of the sciences. But Bacon's scheme was not a linear sequence. He claimed that the sciences, like the branches of a tree, emanate from the single root of primary philosophy.[2] Even in the eighteenth century Bacon's scheme remained pre-eminent, adopted by Diderot and D'Alembert as the basis of the French *Encyclopédie*.

Thomas Hobbes drew up an elaborate scheme based on the separation of knowledge into facts (history) and consequences (science). Sciences in turn were divided into natural philosophy, including eighteen special sciences, and civil philosophy, which he limited largely to his own work.[3]

Newton's discoveries gave momentum to the development of mechanical philosophy, and physics advanced at an impressive pace. Predominant thinking assumed a closed mechanical and material order in nature governed by unyielding deterministic laws. In this ambience the Kantian view, that general formulations are leading principles to guide scientific inquiry, gained little acceptance. However, if the sciences were to be reduced to mathematics or physics, it was important somehow to arrange the sciences into a sequence reflecting this reduction. There were many new sciences that needed to be integrated. The impetus to find a satisfactory classification system was renewed.

During the nineteenth century most classifiers were differentiating between sciences of nature and sciences of the mind. One classification, developed early in the century, was the work of Jeremy Bentham, whose elaborate system was based on the principle of dichotomy. Peirce was to make use of some of the unusual terminology that Bentham had devised.

Coleridge and Hegel were among the many authors of systems of an encyclopaedic kind. Hegel's system is overwhelming in its magnitude and intriguing in its conception, which is wed to his dialectic. Peirce tried to emulate Hegel's procedure of classifying things according to their matter, but found his own efforts only marginally more satisfactory, and abandoned the task.

The most notable classification after Bacon's was developed by the French positivist Auguste Comte. He was influenced by Turgot, Condorcet, and Saint-Simon, who were seeking a foundation on which to rebuild a society that they believed had become intellectually and morally bankrupt. Comte sought to achieve this in his *Cours de philosophie positive* (1830). The economist A.R.J. Turgot had sought unity and relatedness within knowledge by ordering it, convinced that scientific study would reveal their interconnectedness. He formulated the concept within the sciences of a hierarchy, which developed through three stages. Comte took up these ideas and ultimately regarded the stages as a fundamental law. The mathematician Jean-Antoine Condorcet had applied mathematical probabilities to the social sciences, yet Comte chose to ignore that part of his work. He was impressed instead by Condorcet's idea of humans progressing from barbarism towards physical, intellectual, and moral perfection. The influence of Claude-Henri Saint-Simon was probably more diffuse and certainly more immediate for Comte, who had been his secretary from 1760 to 1825. However, Saint-Simon did not fully understand the scientific method. Neither did he recognize the importance of chemistry and biology or their relations to other sciences. This was an intolerable limitation for Comte, whose whole philosophy centred on the primacy of the sciences and their interrelatedness.[4]

Comte objected to encyclopaedic classifications based on the different faculties of the mind, such as the schemes of Bacon and D'Alembert. Even if the distinctions claimed were real, he argued, human understanding requires the use of several faculties at once. And because all other classifications suffer from serious defects, he felt that the whole business of classification had been vilified, and that only those who were ignorant of the sciences persisted in it. Yet taxonomy had shown that "classification must proceed from a direct study of the objects to be classified, and must be determined by the real affinities and natural connections that they present."[5] Comte's diagnosis was that all previous classifiers had encountered a dearth of uniformity among the sciences; some studies remained theological and others metaphysical, and only when all became positivistic could coherence be attained. He observed that this had then been virtually achieved, and so classification had finally become possible. He repudiated metaphysical, speculative, and critical reasoning on the grounds that they made no contribution to knowledge. Mathematical analysis alone was to be applied to all natural and social phenomena. In this way ever greater generality was to be pursued until the most abstract of disciplnes reached the most abstract of generalities and principles.

Comte proposed two basic principles of positivism. The first states that each branch of learning passes through three theoretical stages: it begins in a religious or fictitious stage, progresses through a metaphysical or abstract stage, and ultimately becomes a science. His second principle focuses on the last stage, where disciplines attain the level of positivistic thought: it states that there is a natural order of sciences such that each depends upon the laws and methods of the preceding science. Mathematics heads the hierarchy, Comte claimed, while sociology would follow biology into the last stage, where a pattern of knowledge could be expected to emerge. From this, the existence and characteristics of elements that were as yet unknown could be predicted, providing a means to construct an orderly society.[6] A tabulation of the several sciences proceeding through the three stages would thereby give a hierarchical scheme reflecting the historical order in which they were developed, and also the natural and logical dependence of the sciences that follow. Comte proposed that the classification of the sciences would serve as a sensible guide for education as well as a framework for a philosophy of science.[7] Classification, then, is integral to his philosophy. Here is his system in its two developments:

Form of 1830	*Form of 1851*
Mathematics	Natural Philosophy
Astronomy	Cosmology
Physics	Mathematics
Chemistry	Astronomy
Physiology	Physics
Social Physics	Chemistry
	Biology
	Social philosophy

John Stuart Mill and Herbert Spencer were among those who wrote critical notices of the *Cours,* and thereby popularized the work in England. Mill promoted it; Spencer decried it. Spencer considered Comte's divisions to be incomplete and theoretically unsound. For him, a serial arrangement of the sciences was vicious; the system reflected both unsound logic and unsound history.[8]

Mill countered Spencer's criticisms as Emile Littré had done before him. He argued that Comte's and Spencer's distinctions between abstract and concrete sciences mean quite different things. When Comte referred to concrete sciences he had in mind those relating to beings or objects; abstract sciences relate to events. For Spencer, on the other hand, an abstract science is one in which truths are merely ideal, without a referent in the real world. Chemistry and biology are concrete sciences in Spencer's account, because the senses confirm the scientific propositions about them. Without committing himself to either position, Mill argued that Spencer's view classifies truths "according to an unimportant difference in the manner in which we come to know them."[9] Sciences in which some truths are known directly and others indirectly would be splintered by such a procedure. In his apology for Comte's theory, Mill argued that a given science cannot establish its own truths until those of the preceding sciences have been established. Consequently, the order in which sciences are developed must follow the ordering indicated by the hierarchy. This does not mean that preceding sciences must be perfected before lower sciences can begin. Spencer overlooked the empirical stage at which Comte believed it possible for a science to develop independently of that which preceded it. Mill thought Spencer had not made a convincing case against Comte, although he granted the criticism that astronomy did not occupy a satisfactory position in Comte's scheme.[10]

Although Peirce repeatedly inveighed against positivism, he was not deterred from adopting and modifying Comte's principle of classification. He remarked that "naturally more important and regular than the dynamical action of one science upon another is the rational government of one by another which Auguste Comte convincingly showed ought to be made the basis of a classification of some sciences" (601(s).9, 1906).

Others also had reservations about some methods of classification. Sir William Hamilton, for example, observed the ambivalence with which classifiers had treated logic: "by the Platonists logic was regarded both as a part, and as the instrument, of philosophy; – by the

Aristotelians, (Aristotle himself is silent), as an instrument, but as a part, of philosophy; – by the Stoics, as forming one of the three parts of philosophy."[11] Thereafter logic was often classified as an art or as a practical science. Richard Whately is one who took it to be a science insofar as it analyses the process of reasoning, but an art in that it provides practical rules of inference. Hamilton thought that the result of this was even more confusing; he limited his own classification to the sciences of the mind, and equated philosophy with mental science, deeming logic (together with aesthetics and ethics) to be a psychological study. Beginning with the idea that consciousness yields facts, laws, and results, he arrived at three basic divisions:

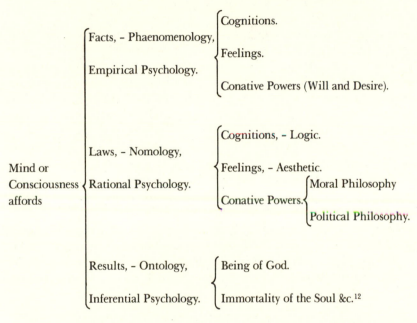

Mind or Consciousness affords

Facts, – Phaenomenology, Empirical Psychology.
- Cognitions.
- Feelings.
- Conative Powers (Will and Desire).

Laws, – Nomology, Rational Psychology.
- Cognitions, – Logic.
- Feelings, – Aesthetic.
- Conative Powers.
  - Moral Philosophy
  - Political Philosophy.

Results, – Ontology, Inferential Psychology.
- Being of God.
- Immortality of the Soul &c.[12]

William Whewell believed that if a classification was to have vital significance, it would need to include moral, political, and metaphysical studies along with physics; it would reveal the measure of our ability to determine truth, and expose any analogies existing between physics, mathematics, and other less rigorous sciences. Nevertheless, he confined himself to a classification of sciences. His procedure was to analyse the objects classified in order to discover the natural and fundamental ideas that inform them. His starting point was the history of sciences. In his arrangement each science involved the fundamental idea appropriate to it, as well as the ideas of those preceding it. The hierarchy had the following broad headings:

1. Pure Mathematical Sciences
2. Pure Motional Sciences
3. Mechanical Sciences
4. Secondary Mechanical Sciences (Physics)
5. Analytico-Mechanical Sciences (Physics)
6. Analytical Science
7. Analytico-Classificatory Sciences
8. Classificatory Sciences
9. Organical Sciences
10. (Metaphysics)
11. Palaetiological Sciences[13]

This arrangement was designed to identify transition points to other sciences and to allow speculation on those disciplines; it suggests analogous ways in which they might be pursued and ordered. In fact, metaphysics is equated with psychology and separates clearly related sciences such as zoology (8), botany (8), and biology (9) on the one hand, and geology (11) and distribution of plants and animals (11) on the other.

In 1856 the American W.D. Wilson used Aristotle's division of theoretical and practical sciences and productive arts (logic is not included). Each was said to divide naturally into two departments, although it is not clear how he determined that his sequence was natural.

Spencer dissociated himself from Comte in producing a classification for which he denied that any natural series was possible. His scheme recaptured Bacon's idea of the sciences branching out from a common root, and had a three-fold division:

I Abstract sciences (including logic and mathematics)
II Abstract-concrete sciences (including mechanics, chemistry, and physics)
III Concrete science (for example, astronomy, biology, and sociology).[14]

Wilhelm Wundt wrote original work in many fields and hence might be expected to have considered the problem of the relations of the sciences. He certainly recognized the significance of classification, and he regarded philosophy as the universal science on which all others depended. Philosophy, he claimed, has two main divisions:

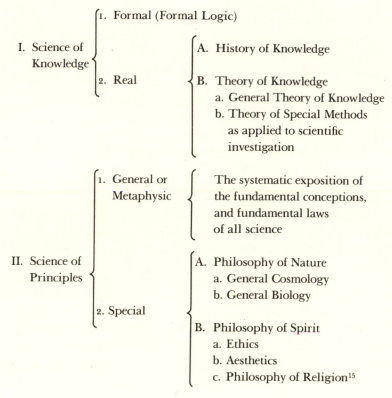

I. Science of Knowledge
  1. Formal (Formal Logic)
  2. Real
    A. History of Knowledge
    B. Theory of Knowledge
      a. General Theory of Knowledge
      b. Theory of Special Methods as applied to scientific investigation

II. Science of Principles
  1. General or Metaphysic
    The systematic exposition of the fundamental conceptions, and fundamental laws of all science
  2. Special
    A. Philosophy of Nature
      a. General Cosmology
      b. General Biology
    B. Philosophy of Spirit
      a. Ethics
      b. Aesthetics
      c. Philosophy of Religion[15]

Karl Pearson examined the schemes of Bacon, Comte, and Spencer before presenting his own. He granted that the pursuit of some sciences may require a prior study of other sciences, but he thought that this did not imply a hierarchical ordering like that of Comte. Instead, he endorsed Bacon's tree, but adopted Spencer's divisions into abstract and concrete sciences. Pearson advocated the historical resumé approach and disavowed what he called the "transcendental exegesis of final causes." Accordingly, he thought that a group of scientists would be more successful than philosophers in achieving an adequate, albeit ephemeral, scheme.[16]

Although Peirce had reviewed *The Grammar of Science* for the *Nation*, he found Pearson's approach so antithetical to his own that he contrasted it with a different classification (also of 1892), devised by the American D.G. Brinton. Peirce also criticized Brinton's scheme for its artificiality and for the way in which it confused final and efficient causation (1.264-7, 1902).

There was no evidence of agreement on a proper procedure among the many classifications being produced. Some opted for the encyclopaedic approach; others were content with an artificial system. Such classifications may have practical value when grouping items in encyclopaedias and dictionaries or when arranging the contents of textbooks, but they are of little value to scientists who need a scheme displaying the real connections among sciences. Many systems were governed by the objects being classified, meaning that some schemes were not confined to sciences but included a multiplicity of categories. Those who aimed at a natural classification were trying to discover the causal interrelation of natural objects, but they were not in agreement about the proper procedure. Many who aspired to a natural classification of sciences had no clear idea of what constituted a science, so that even when the major divisions were in accordance with a principle, the allocations to those divisions could be quite arbitrary. Very often such fundamental divisions, logical in themselves, were governed by the preconceptions of a particular philosophical or scientific theory.

As Hamilton had noted, there was no unanimity regarding the appropriate category for the discipline of logic either. Given the important advances occurring in that field, and Peirce's interest and involvement in it, it is understandable that he made a thoroughgoing reassessment for himself.

3. Specific Classification

The taxonomy of biologists is one area of classification that needs to be looked at in some detail for its relevance to both general classification and Peirce's reassessment. Taxonomy had its origins in the pervasive desire to understand the profusion of life surrounding us. The habit of arranging things according to likeness and unlikeness is in itself a rudimentary form of this classification. When the exquisite patterns exhibited by particular organisms recur, the idea of design in nature surfaces. Animals and plants form a hierarchy and an interconnectedness of species; and yet species themselves remain constant. The one explanation for this regularity, which almost universally presents itself, is that there is an intelligent being ordering the universe. Having granted this, the observed order itself seems to provide evidence that such a being exists, and with this circular argument the hypothesis has become orthodoxy.

By the middle of the eighteenth century, natural theologians had so successfully promulgated the concept of design in nature that it had become the conventional wisdom. For them, science was compatible with the biblical account of divine creation. It was widely believed that distinct and fixed species formed a chain or series of natural classes. However, since this chain of being was not a specific classification scheme, it became less and less able to accommodate the numbers of new plants and animals which were being discovered. An adequate taxonomy was needed and in fact became the preoccupation of continental biologists late in the eighteenth century.[17] But if a classification was to express the plan of the designer of the universe it would need to be a natural system based on real classes. In spite of many attempts throughout the eighteenth and nineteenth centuries, no satisfactory scheme was found.

Newtonian mechanics had spurred the taxonomy of biologists to explain organisms in terms of physico-chemical systems. This led to a constant search for laws; but finding laws to unify the increasingly varied collection of living organisms was difficult. The route to a solution was thought to lie in classification, where the confusing array of phenomena could be given order. Ordering soon became central to the work of the eighteenth- and nineteenth-century naturalists.

In the middle of the eighteenth century, the naturalist Carl Linnaeus developed a hierarchy of class, order, genus, and species. Although he intended a natural scheme, he conceded that his higher taxa were simply conventions that enabled him to get started. Nevertheless, his scheme was an improvement on the unwieldy downward dichotomies that characterized the efforts of earlier taxonomists. Downward classification by logical division had the virtue of accessibility, for it required no training to divide an easily recognizable genus into two species, and it satisfied the prevailing penchant for logical order. Yet the initial choice of characters could lead to radically different outcomes, and even small adjustments might produce an entirely different scheme. In practice, downward classifications were unable to provide a convenient identification revealing a natural order.[18]

Not all biologists sought a natural classification. Georges Louis Buffon ridiculed the attempts of Linnaeus and his followers. He was influenced by the work of Leibniz and Newton, and sought to unify observed diversity by subsuming it under general laws. Whereas Linnaeus was concerned with "essential" characters, and with identifying species, genera, and classes, Buffon focused on individuals – their anatomy, behaviour, and distribution.

In the nineteenth century Georges Cuvier reasserted the importance of a natural downward classification. Cuvier's approach was distinguished by his aim to discover the general principles underlying a natural scheme, and not merely to name species. Jean Baptiste Lamarck concurred on this point. Lamarck valued the business of classifying because he thought that the study of "affinities" was fundamental to progress in the natural sciences, and he was one of the few to infer continuous evolution (a theory of evolution by gradual transformation). The majority of natural scientists continued to address the question of origins by attempting, for example, to account for the fact that God had allowed many creatures to become extinct.

Cuvier was convinced that the distinctness of species was inconsistent with evolutionary change. When he discovered what seemed to be radical discontinuities in the fossils of different geological periods, he posited localized geological revolutions. Cuvier supposed that in due course animals from areas unaffected by disaster migrated to vacated areas, meaning that all living and all extinct animals coexisted at some point. Exploration failed to confirm his thesis, for no fossilized remains of modern animals were to be found; but no links connecting apparently disparate species were found either.

Other catastrophists avoided this difficulty. Extinction, they argued, provided an opportunity for new species to be able to cope with the environment of a new era. Cuvier rejected this explanation because it introduced theology into science. But since he found the theory of evolutionary progression even less palatable, he left the problem unresolved.

William Paley's natural theology predominated in Britain where prevalent thinking posited a supernatural agency that created higher forms of life as the physical environment developed. Using a different approach, German idealists (notably Lorenz Oken and Friedrich Schelling) attributed progress to the unfolding of a rational plan directed towards the ultimate creation – man.

Louis Agassiz, another catastrophist, integrated an idealist philosophy of nature with a belief in divine creation. He claimed that at the end of each geological period, God started over by creating a new species. These new species might resemble the discards of earlier periods just as God's current concepts might reflect ideas used earlier.[19]

Agassiz was invited to America to give the Lowell lectures in 1846, a forum for his scientific acumen and his reassuring creed, as well as his continental charm. Up to five thousand Bostonians heard him on some evenings, and others attended repeat performances arranged to satisfy the demand. His success brought invitations to lecture from all over the eastern states. Thus his explanation of the origin of the world's organisms, with its transcendental interpretations, was disseminated to a wide audience and his welcome was extended far beyond the confines of the university. The American geological elite, who also held catastrophist views, was happy to have them reinforced.

After this auspicious introduction to America, Agassiz was made professor at the Lawrence Scientific School. By 1853, he, along with Benjamin Peirce and others, had formed the informal yet powerful alliance of "Scientific Lazzaroni" mentioned earlier.

Because Agassiz wanted to incorporate ever more lavish embellishments, his eagerly awaited *Essay on Classification* was postponed until 1857. The naturalists James Dwight Dana and Asa Gray were among those disappointed to find that, after their long wait, the work offered nothing substantially new. Gray found it so sterile as to be an impediment to further inquiry. In June 1858, he wrote to R. W. Church of his own interest in writing on quite different views of the principles of classification. In fact he challenged Agassiz's assumptions more than once with the aim of permitting a fair discussion of the ideas expressed in Darwin's forthcoming work.[20]

The *Origin of the Species* appeared just two years after the *Essay*. Charles Darwin recognized the biological significance of continuous or individual variation. He hypothesized that species are not constant, but change and grade into one another, making it necessary to view the extension of species as variable, involving borderline cases. He also hypothesized that genetic variations are inherited, one species descending from another through organic reproduction. This meant that classification by species would need to be based on the frequency distribution of certain characters exhibited within populations of animals. The idea was inimical to the theories confidently affirmed by Agassiz for many years, but since he had been instrumental in bringing these issues into the public domain, and since Americans wanted him, as their authority, to pronounce on the new work, he felt an obligation to assess it. He opposed it emphatically, of course, but without success,[21] and with the acceptance of Darwinian ideas among scientists, his scientific following dwindled.

Yet Chauncy Wright, William James, and Charles Peirce had all
benefited from studying taxonomy with Louis Agassiz. On a number
of occasions Peirce acknowledged the usefulness of that training to
his own work.[22]

Peirce recorded that he was surveying in the wilds of Louisiana
when the *Origin of the Species* arrived in America. On his return
to the East he found Chauncy Wright enthusiastically endorsing the
new work. Wright had initially subscribed to the philosophy of Sir
William Hamilton. He and Peirce had enjoyed frequent and protracted
discussions about the philosophy of Hamilton and also of Kant. On
reading John Stuart Mill's writings, however, Wright was so impressed
that he redirected his allegiance to utilitarianism and to Mill. Peirce
pointed out that approval of Darwin could not mesh well with Wright's
new commitment to Mill's associationalism (5.64, 1903).[23]

What was the difficulty that Peirce had identified but that had escaped
his friend? Peirce believed that Darwin's evolutionary view, which was
based on positive observation, could not be fully explained in terms
of mechanical action. In the same vein he had frequently decried the
use of science to support individualism, phenomenalism, sensation-
alism, and materialism, all of which he grouped under nominalism
and traced back to Ockham. This is an important observation on
Peirce's part, but to understand it more fully, it will be useful to consider
Darwin's approach.

Mindful of the fate of Robert Chambers's *Vestiges of the Natural
History of Creation* (1844), Charles Darwin was careful to present
his theory in a guise that conformed to prevailing scientific standards.
His initial training had been in the catastrophist tradition, but he
went on to read Charles Lyell's *Principles of Geology* (1830–3), and
in one revision of Comte's *Cours* he found additional encouragement
to consider all phenomena as subject to unvarying natural laws. He
knew and respected both Herschel and Whewell and wanted these
"senior" scientists to approve of his work.[24] Accordingly, he contrived
to present his theory in a way that would meet their approval. To
this end he proposed hypotheses and referred to consequences as
deductions. Still he needed a mechanism to explain scientific change.
This he found in Malthus's population studies, but with one important
modification: he reversed Malthus's conclusion in that he saw struggle
instigating change, where Malthus had seen it precluding change. Yet
it was his methodology that attracted Darwin. Malthus had used a
deductive approach, presenting his ideas as laws, in a form consistent

with Herschel-Whewell canons.[25] Using Herschel's procedure, Darwin argued from the known (artificial selection in domestic breeding) to the unknown (natural selection); and using Whewell's method of consilience, he showed that natural selection, together with his other mechanisms, was applicable to such varied fields as behaviour studies, palaeontology, anatomy, and embryology; and that all of these studies could be explained by one basic mechanism, as a consilient theory requires.[26]

Later, when he was criticized on the basis of one method, Darwin would respond by appealing to the other method. If his analogy from artificial selection was questioned, he would appeal to the breadth of the explanation provided by natural selection, claiming that it was the centre of a consilience. Thus he was able to deflect criticism by capitalizing on his initial scrupulousness.

Nevertheless, one Cambridge scholar, William Hopkins, offered a more stringent argument in 1860. He understood and approved the hypothetico-deductive method, but argued that many of Darwin's factual claims could not be deduced from the hypothesis of natural selection; at best Darwin could assert their probable occurrence. On this basis, he rejected Darwin's theory.[27]

Peirce also perceived the difficulty, but his response was to reject the methodology. He cited Helmholtz, Liebig, and Darwin among those who had ostensibly presupposed deterministic principles but practised statistical explanations. He thought that they needed to recognize that science was not as "nominalistic" as they believed (8.38, 1871). Indeed, he asserted more than once that evolution and mechanical necessity were diametrically opposed (6.298–9, 1893; 5.64, 1903).

Peirce had already recognized the need for a more adequate theory; for example, he found that right- and left-handed molecular screw-structures of "optically active" substances were absolutely inexplicable by mechanical action. That failure, he held, was enough to demolish the "corpuscular philosophy."[28] Accordingly, he sought a viable alternative that looked beyond the mechanistic garb in which Darwin had identified his theory's allegiance to statistical probabilities. He recorded that his early suggestion that Darwin had taken a hint from Malthus's treatise was "authoritatively denied," although subsequently admitted (5.364 note 1, 1903). Peirce noted that a precedent for the statistical method had occurred eight years prior to the *Origin* when R.J.E. Clausius and J.C. Maxwell used the approach in the kinetic theory of gases. Peirce himself had used the method in the theory of measurement. He noted that "Darwin, while unable to say what the operation of variation and natural selection in any individual case will be, demonstrates that in the long run they will, or would, adapt animals to their circumstances. Whether or not existing animal forms are due to such action, or what position the theory ought to take, forms the subject of a discussion in which questions of fact and questions of logic are curiously interlaced" (5.364, 1877; see also 7.66, 1882; and 6.11, 1891). The importance of statistics for the logic of probability was only just being developed by Augustus De Morgan, George Boole, and by Peirce himself.

Not surprisingly, Peirce deplored uncritical applications of Darwin's theory outside the field of biology, and the practice of using science in support of individualism. Herbert Spencer is his prime example of one who explained evolution on mechanical principles and who concluded that survival of the fittest applied to individuals without recognizing that what is fit for the species may well be unfit for the individual.

Thus Peirce did not accept Darwin's theory unreservedly. He thought that it described one of several processes of evolution, but he was more interested in evolution as it related to the development of science, which Darwin did not pursue. Peirce held that the aim of science is truth and that this is approachable in the indefinite long run through hypothesis and experiment. The objectivity of that pursuit would be undermined if practical and technological considerations were to obtrude. This anti-instrumentalism may seem odd to the reader since the terms "pragmatism" and "instrumentalism" are now frequently used interchangeably. Nevertheless no discrepancy exists between Peirce's pragmatism and his anti-instrumentalism; in fact they highlight his crucial disagreement with such Darwinian instrumentalists as Karl Pearson, William James, John Dewey, and Ernst Mach. Peirce had already accepted the assumption shared by those four, *"that a theory of biological evolution should apply to human cultural evolution*, including the evolution of science."[29] Thus he could not dismiss the instrumentalist description of the scientific method and at the same time embrace the Darwinian account of biological evolution in its entirety. Instead, he augmented natural selection with Lamarckian and catastrophist views and related all three to his universal categories.

The *Origin of the Species* was relevant to general classification as well as to taxonomy. For two thousand years the dominant concept in theoretical classifications, both general and specific, had been the equation of absolute permanency with perfection; change and origin indicated imperfection. The orthodox view held that variations within species were accidental occurrences to be lost in the succeeding generation; individuals might depart from specific norms, but the species would remain constant. The ideas of purpose, of fixed form, and of final cause informed the central principle of knowledge and of nature. Darwin not only rejected the assumption, he reversed it with his claim that origin and transience were integral to the nature of things. Ernst Mayr remarks that with Darwin's theory of common descent,

the metaphysical interpretation of classification was replaced by a scientific one ... It became the primary function of classification to delimit taxa and construct a hierarchy of higher taxa which permitted the greatest number of valid generalizations. This was based on the assumption that members of a taxon, sharing a common heritage as descendants from a common ancestor, will have more characters in common with each other than with species not so related.[30]

Peirce appears to have been alone in applying the Darwinian suggestions to general classification. He recognized that sciences are not rigidly defined; that borderline studies might require arbitrary distinctions and subsequent revision as new sciences emerge and others become obsolete. A classification capable of incorporating these changes would have to be an evolving one.[31]

Aside from a few early attempts at schemes based on the single relation of similarity and dissimilarity, Peirce's classification derives from research into the logic of relatives and from his method of thinking in diagrams. He explicitly rejected a classification based on similarities and differences in a manuscript entitled "Why I am a Pragmatist?":

My classification of the sciences purports to be a natural classification such as the taxonomical biologists draw up; and here, less for the sake of the opinion itself than for the illustration it affords of my method of thinking, I wish to express my dissent from a certain form of reasoning that is universal among the taxonomists. Namely, they are in the habit of taking two forms that appear to be markedly different, and if they can find specimens to bridge the interval between them with a "series" in which successive members show hardly any perceptible difference, they say that these two forms belong to the same natural species and that there is but a single natural class to which all the specimens belong. But I say, on the contrary, that it may be a hard fact of nature that a whole consists of three or more different divisions, and yet it may be a pure matter of arbitrary election to which of these three divisions almost any individual member shall be regarded as belonging. I will prove this by an example. Let us imagine a flat piece of dough, such as would make a cruller or doughnut if it were fried; and imagine this piece to have two holes in it, thus:

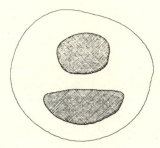

Now by moulding the dough, *without joining any parts that are separate or separating any parts that are joined*, we can give the dough an endless variety of shapes, such as these.

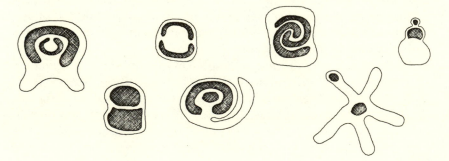

But in all cases, there will be two holes which make the dough to consist of three parts, the part between the holes, the part between one hole and the outside boundary of the dough, and the part between the other hole and the outside boundary of the dough.[32]   (327.6–8, n.d.)

It had become clear to Peirce that the unswerving dichotomies, the rigid chain of values, and the linear framework of previous classifications were not satisfactory. A classification useful to practising scientists had to take a new direction if it were to reveal the intricate and reciprocal relationships among the sciences. As might be expected of a philosopher interested in relating evolution to the sciences, the classification that Peirce devised was flexible and dynamic.

A development in the specific area of classification in chemistry should be noted. Chemistry was the discipline in which Peirce had trained and, predictably, Dmitrii Mendeleev's classification of chemical elements attracted him. Mendeleev had perfected the periodic classification in a way that exhibited the qualities sought by biologists. By classifying the elements in terms of their atomic weights (the formal component) it was possible to predict their material properties and to indicate those as yet undiscovered elements. It afforded Peirce a fine model for another component of his architectonic; it illustrated that classification by formal aspects can reveal material connections (see, for example, 5.469, 1907).

4. *The State of Logic*

There was little agreement on the position that logic should occupy in a classification scheme, at least partly due to the lack of unanimity among logicians. Since logic is the focal point of Peirce's classification of the sciences, the status of that discipline should be considered from a historical perspective. It was, after all, Peirce's favourite study and he was in the forefront of developments in mathematical logic. Nevertheless, he was concerned that logic might be absorbed by mathematics altogether.

Of the continental logicians, Peirce respected Grassmann and Schröder but deplored the psychologism of others (8.41, c. 1885; but see also 3.432, 1896), and apparently was unaware of Frege. But what had gone before? I.M. Bocheński claimed that Bolzano, Peirce, and Peano (Schröder should be added) were the first genuine historians of logic:

Most historians of logic in the 17th, 18th and 19th centuries treat of ontological, epistemological and psychological problems rather than of logical ones. Furthermore, everything in this period, with few exceptions, is so conditioned by the then prevailing prejudices that we may count the whole period as part of the pre-history of our science. These prejudices are essentially three:
1.   First, everyone was convinced that formalism has very little to do with

genuine logic. Hence investigations of formal logic either passed unnoticed or were contemptuously treated as quite subsidiary.

2.   Second, and in part because of the prejudice already mentioned, the scholastic period was treated as a *media tempestas,* a "dark middle age" altogether lacking in science. But as the Scholastics were in possession of a highly developed formal logic, people sought in history either for quite different "logics" from that of Aristotle (not only those of Noe and Epictetus, as Ramus had done, but even, after his time, that of Ramus himself), or at least for a supposedly better interpretation of him, which put the whole investigation on the wrong track.

3.   Finally, of equal influence was a strange belief in the linear development of every science, logic included. Hence there was a permanent inclination to rank inferior "modern" books higher than works of genius from older classical writers.[33]

With the history of logic in this unsatisfactory state, Peirce was obliged to explore the field himself.[34]

However, a text that had introduced Peirce to the subject at an early age had, he declared, made a considerable impression on him. Was Richard Whately's *Elements of Logic* (1826) also an "inferior modern work"?

Typically, this early encounter with Whately's *Logic* is cited as evidence of the young Peirce's precocity; but it is probable that it influenced him very differently than any other contemporary text on syllogistic reasoning might have.[35] Whately had responded to the British Aristotelian tradition, which had existed for centuries, as well as to criticisms that had been fermenting for more than two hundred years. He thought that both critics and logicians were mistaken about the nature of the study – that they had confused the discipline of logic with the areas of its application. Logic, he claimed, was a science and not merely an art or a tool. Others before him had described it as a science (Richard Kirwan for example), but they had in mind a study of the broad Aristotelian variety, while Whately intended a theoretical study in the modern sense. Consequently, Whately had a significantly different view of the basic components of logic and its relation to other disciplines. Mill, Boole, and De Morgan, along with Peirce, referred to Whately as their starting points.

Peirce's use of the work of De Morgan and Boole in his refinement of the logic of relations sent his own philosophy in a direction that required a new classification of the sciences for its consummation.[36]

Exigencies developed in Peirce's philosophy that made research into the classification of the sciences his preoccupation for more than a decade.

2. PERSPECTIVES ON PEIRCE'S PHILOSOPHY

Peirce moved from the subjective, practice-oriented, and individualist perspective of his early philosophy to the objective, theoretical, and abstract system of his later work, which required the classification of the sciences for its completion.

Curiously, the most frequently read philosophical papers from the Peirce opus have been the "Fixation of Belief" (5.358–87, 1877) and "How to Make Our Ideas Clear" (5.388–410, 1878), which are fundamentally of that earlier period. They reflect only a small part of his crucial development. The 1898 lectures of William James, which were successful in popularizing pragmatism, also interpret that earlier perspective. Peirce's profoundly revised and more cogent views have had a comparatively minor impact, largely because the evolution of Peirce's thought has been ignored.

Peirce's transformation and many of the concomitant problems and their solutions are discussed in Flower and Murphey's *A History of Philosophy in America*,[37] parts of which will be drawn upon in the following outline.

1. The Early Categories

With his thorough grounding in the *Critique of Pure Reason*, it is not surprising that Peirce took Kant's thesis as his point of departure: all knowledge begins with the manifold of sense brought into unity. But he encountered difficulties with Kant's principle of architectonic according to which universal categories are to be derived from logic. Peirce concluded that Kant's logical base for his fundamental categories was mistaken leading him, in 1862, to embark on an intensive study of the logic of the scholastics (1.560–1, c. 1905). His paper, "On a New List of Categories" (1.545–59, 1867), was the outcome. In it, Peirce analysed propositions in terms of a subject-predicate logic. He accepted Kant's theory insofar as it refers to possible experience, but he did not accept noumena (Kant's "things-in-themselves") because, he argued, the concept of incognizables is self-contradictory.

Peirce maintained that all thought is in signs, each cognition caused by a previous cognition. He denied *both* that we have any intuitions *and* that any cognition relates immediately to a transcendental object. He also eschewed the procedure that the British sense-datum theorists were to adopt, of positing sense-data as the immediately given in awareness; this was to espouse idealism.

Yet Peirce also called himself a realist. How did he arrive at a real object in this context? He shunned the route of defining the real as the cause of cognition, and instead took the opposite approach: the real is the final result of cognition. He argued that the existence of objects is an hypothesis needed to explain the coherence of our experience. It is inferred by hypothetical reasoning; and if it is a hypothesis, then the real must be general.

All cognitions, Peirce maintained, result from inference: if there are reals that have effects on us, these effects must be neural responses; accordingly, there is no first cognition. He did not flinch from the apparently infinite regress involved in this approach, because he believed that it was not vicious.

In this attempt to combine realism with phenomenalism, the real is a possible sensation and it *will* occur in the future. (If it does not become actual then it cannot be known, and there are no incognizables.) But the real is not simply a set of phenomena, because the future is infinite. Possibility can be actualized in every instant without ever exhausting itself. Thus the real is not the incognizable cause of cognition; it is the ultimate outcome of cognition – the agreement that a community of investigators will arrive at in the infinitely distant future.

Flower and Murphey tell us that Peirce's argument in the "New List" was that the unification of the manifold,

was achieved through the sign relation, and he had then explicated the sign relation in such a way as to show that the sign necessarily involved triple reference to an object, an interpreting representation, and an abstraction. On this basis, Peirce elaborated a cognitive theory and a theory of reality which amount to an attempt to construct an extreme realism on the basis of a semiotic idealism. The human mind thus becomes identified with its phenomenal manifestation, the sign, and the Universal Mind with its phenomenal manifestation, the community; and the real object is defined as that which is postulated in the proposition which is the limit of an infinite series of investigations.[38]

Relational terms were important to the theory of categories. Peirce's interest in them was whetted by De Morgan's studies in the logic of relations. In retrospect, Peirce estimated that he had received a copy of that work in 1866, but had not assimilated De Morgan's ideas at the time of the "New List" (1.562, c. 1905). In 1870 he completed a paper on the logic of relatives[39] which made use of the work of De Morgan and Boole as well as work that his father, Benjamin Peirce, was publishing concurrently. With the advances developed in his paper the logical foundation of his categories was undermined.

In the "New List" Peirce had characterized his three categories as *qualities* (which are non-relative characters), *relations* (dyadic relations) and *representations* (plural relations) (1.565, c. 1899; 1.561, c. 1905).[40] Flower and Murphey remark:

Peirce had there assumed the traditional subject-predicate theory of the proposition, and his method of deriving the categories and of proving their universality rests on that assumption. The "New List" seemed to explain the relation of subject and qualitative predicate by showing that the representative relation connects them. But the logic of relations showed that there are propositions whose predicates are dyadic or triadic relations and which do not involve qualities at all. Hence the question at once arises, how are relations connected to their correlates – and specifically, how is the representative relation connected to its correlates? Nor can this question be answered by postulating another relation between the correlate and the representative relations connected to their correlates – and specifically, how is the reprewas now faced with a complicated logical problem to which he had in 1870 no immediate answer and which threatened the categorical foundations of his system.[41]

Peirce reported that it took him twenty-five years to reach a provisional conclusion (provisional because, like all universal science, it remained open to doubt). Nevertheless, he had speedily come to a mathematical demonstration of his categories.[42] Peirce was not simply responding to inadequacies in his earlier views, but was seeking ways to develop an alternative to nominalistic logic.

2. The Categories Reformulated

When relations are taken to be the fundamental components of propositions, meaning is seen as relational and not qualitative. Consider the effect of this on the pragmatic maxim, Peirce's rule for arriving at the most adequate understanding of concepts. In its 1878 form it states, "Consider what effects, that might conceivably have practical bearings, we conceive the object of our conception to have. Then, our conception of these effects is the whole of our conception of the object" (5.402, 1878). Those conditionals relating operations on the object to conceivable effects will be habits. Thus the concept of the object means simply that set of conditionals, or those habits.

Peirce remained satisfied with this initial statement of the maxim, but he had not then elucidated the distinction between a law and the set of all actual instances of the law.[43] This is because he had not yet adopted the view that there are real possibilities - possibilities that may never be actualized.

With the integration of quantifiers into the logic of relatives in 1885,[44] Peirce came a step closer to this position. It allowed him to make a distinction between membership and inclusion; and his category of Firsts could be indicated quantitatively by a variable. Peirce now felt that he could reformulate his theory of the categories, and did so between 1885 (1.369-72, 1.376-8) and 1890 (1.374-5), this time distinguishing a formal and a material aspect.

In this new version Peirce maintained that the logically formal categories are irreducible relations: firsts are monadic, seconds are dyadic, and thirds are triadic relations; none can be reduced further and all higher relations can be reduced to these three. These provide a basis for the classification of signs.

The logically material character of these categories is obtained independently by examining experience in what Peirce called a psychological study. Ultimately he considered it to be a phenomenological study, as will be seen in chapter 4, where the fully developed theory of categories is examined. He identified three fundamental aspects in the phaneron (that is, whatever is or can be before the mind, without discriminating between fact or fancy).

Firstness is quality, but this is not to be understood in the same sense as in the "New List." Here quality is undifferentiated, unanalysable suchness. Secondness is characterized by opposition, action, and reaction. Thirdness is representation, mediation, and (ultimately) continuity.

The inclusion of continuity was the upshot of Peirce's reaction to Cantor's set theory. Peirce disagreed with Cantor's definition of continuity, in which it was implied that geometrical continuity has to be thought of as a set of discrete points.[45] Peirce claimed that Cantor's definition could not be used in topology which, as it was then conceived, was thought to be presupposed by all of geometry (4.219, 1897). He then proposed an alternative definition of a continuum that contains no discrete points. Such a definition is consistent with the theory of real infinitesimals which Peirce wanted to retain.[46] With real infinitesimals, the limit must be contained in the continuum, meaning that there is no limit to the number of distinct individuals just because the continuum is *not* a multitude of distinct individuals. Peirce stated:

there may be a *potential* aggregate of all the possibilities that are consistent with certain general conditions; and this may be such that given any collection of distinct individuals whatsoever, out of that potential aggregate there may be actualized a more multitudinous collection than the given collection. Thus the potential aggregate is, with the strictest exactitude, greater in multitude than any possible multitude of individuals. But being a potential aggregate only, it does not contain any individuals at all. It only contains general conditions which *permit* the determination of individuals. (6.185, 1898)

Continuity is quantitatively defined as the collection of all the possibilities that cohere with the general laws defining them. A qualitative definition is provided by what Peirce referred to as "Kanticity"; something is Kantistic if it is continuous such that every part has itself parts of the same kind.[47] An alternative explanation in terms of points states that something is continuous if between every possible pair of points it is possible to insert another point; which is to say, the law of the excluded middle does not apply. None of the points are actual because the moment a point is indicated the continuity is disrupted. While it is continuous, it has no definite parts and there are no individuals.

The infinite regress in combinatorial relations, as remarked earlier, is ultimately Kantistic (6.164, 1889; 6.165-7, n.d.; and 6.168, 1903). If laws are, in the final analysis, continuous processes, and given Peirce's understanding of continuity, laws are necessarily general. They hold for all instances, including those possible but unactualized.[48]

In 1903 James prevailed upon Eliot to allow Peirce to give a series of lectures at Harvard. At that time his categories were fully developed and he was able to propose a new theory of perception. Its starting point was immediate sense experience: the percept is what is real; it reaches consciousness in a perceptual judgment, which is the interpretation arrived at through the unconscious synthesis of an endless series of percepts. Even so, Peirce could maintain that there is no first intuition. These unconscious inferences, he argued, are beyond our control and cannot be criticized; only after a proposition has been formulated does thinking become conscious and subject to criticism.

Peirce could then say, according to Flower and Murphey, that

the function of knowledge is to give coherence to perceptual experience, so that our hypotheses of real objects are justified only as explaining our perceptions. It is then a legitimate way of formulating the realistic position to say that, if there are real objects which affect us according to the laws of perceptions, then, if inquiry goes on indefinitely, agreement will be reached. But the coming of final agreement is here explicitly a consequence of the reality of objects, and no claim is made that inquiry will go on indefinitely.[49]

In this expanded version the status of both the categories and the architectonic is substantially altered. Peirce's phenomenological inquiry has shown that experience can be seen to have three fundamental aspects that correspond to the three formal categories; but whether these phenomenological categories are universal, whether they are amenable to proof, whether they are of any practical value, remains to be shown. No inductive investigation will be conclusive, of course, but Peirce wanted to demonstrate that the categories provide a basis for empirical science by means of an inductive survey of the sciences. He first attempted this in "A Guess at the Riddle" (1.354-68, 1.373-5, 1.379-416, all c. 1890) and "The Architecture of Theories" (6.7-34, 1891). He showed that the categories are basic to existing sciences but, since he took them to be universal, he wanted to demonstrate that they are fundamental to sciences in the future.[50] More than that, he wanted to illustrate how all sciences relate to one another, thus extending his architectonic to a classification of the sciences. In fact, he had already started experimenting with schemes.

The principle of architectonic states that categories of experience are to be based on logic, suggesting that there is an interdependence among the sciences. Peirce was convinced that a sound metaphysics must be based on logic. Here was a difficulty. Logic was in a perilous state as long as different or confused conceptions of what it was supposed to be abounded. It was important to address this confusion and to furnish a clear idea of the discipline by showing how it related to those other sciences.

With the categories and the classification of sciences now based on the logic of relations, the pragmatic maxim indicated that any given science could be understood in terms of the network of relations to other sciences. As they are interdependent, Peirce could exhibit the principles of that interdependence, and point the way to the conceivable effects of each and every science. Pick a science, and Peirce's scheme should reveal it in its "third grade of clearness," its pragmatic meaning.

For the practitioners of the many young sciences who had reductionist ambitions, such a classification would obviate many uncertainties. Scientists would have at their disposal clear indications of where to seek solutions to their problems. Yet Peirce's classification would not present a scheme defining present and future sciences. Pragmatism, Peirce insisted, "does not undertake to say in what the meanings of all signs consist, but merely to lay down a method of determining the meanings of intellectual concepts" (5.8, c. 1905). Pragmaticism is a dynamic open-ended thesis; the classification of the sciences is not a fixed system because sciences evolve. As new sciences arise and others atrophy, the classification itself would evolve. The image Peirce provided is of a three-dimensional continuum. Just as points can be added or erased at any location, so sciences can be introduced or deleted within the continuum. Indeed, Peirce thought that it ultimately could be undifferentiated as all sciences might eventually resolve into mathematics.

The method of proof of the principles governing the scheme is the same as that of the pragmatic maxim itself: it must be submitted to the test of experience. If the classification is able to incorporate new sciences, if it establishes order that has practical advantages for existing sciences, if scientists find that it enables them to understand their own and other sciences – gaining principles from those above, data from those below, and suggestions from those laterally related – then it has withstood the initial test. If the classification were to evolve through many metamorphoses without substantial modification to the principles, then it might reasonably be accepted with the confidence accorded established scientific laws; that is, it would nevertheless remain open to doubt.

III

Reasons for Classification

Mendeleev's periodic classification was adopted and refined into an invaluable resource for chemistry. Nothing of the kind resulted from the many attempts at classifying the sciences.

A consideration of what sort of discipline Peirce conceived classification of the sciences to be will provide a first step towards a fuller understanding of his reasons for developing a scheme. He thought a classification would reveal the relations between the sciences, but he was primarily interested in one specific science – logic. Many classifiers had not even conferred on it the status of a science. Obviously Peirce was dissatisfied with the confusion surrounding traditional views and this chapter takes stock of his assessment of the state of logic.

1. THE TASK OF CLASSIFICATION

Peirce appeared to be ambivalent as to whether the process of classifying the sciences is the business of logic or the sciences of review. This is not because of indecision or because of a reversal in his thinking, but because these two sciences are concerned with quite different aspects of classification. When this is recognized, his appeal to both sciences appears to be entirely consistent with his scheme. A full vindication of this explanation awaits a study of the scheme's development precisely because the two are so closely connected. Nevertheless, the direction of Peirce's thought can be followed here.

As early as 1866, Peirce regarded the classification of the sciences as a logical procedure (357.26) and he still held this view in 1902 (1.204, c. 1902; see also 1.243, c. 1902; 1343.11, c. 1902; but cf. 1.268, c. 1902). By 1903, however, he was ascribing the classification of the sciences to the sciences of review (1.182, 1903; 1334.18–19, 1905; 601.26[1], [1906]; 675.10, [c.1911]).

Although Peirce did not cease to regard logic as a classificatory science, at one point he considered the study of the pure laws of classification to be prelogical (728.1, n.d.; 729.1, n.d.), by which he may mean mathematical. In a somewhat different sense, the manuscript from which "Detailed Classification of the Sciences" has been taken is also regarded as prelogical. It bears the title "Chapter 2. Prelogical Notions, Section 1. Classification of the Sciences" (427.1, c. 1902). While its "preliminary reflections" may also appeal to mathematics, Peirce probably had in mind an examination aided by *logica utens*, for he subsequently reiterated that classification is a topic for logic and must receive scientific treatment (1.204, c. 1902).

How can classification of the sciences be a topic for logic as well as for the sciences of review? An answer is suggested in two of the 1902 sources in which classification is assigned to logic. In one passage, Peirce explained that logic brings his three categories to light; but they remain vague and uncertain. Moreover, there is no indication that any increase in knowledge is valuable to a natural classification scheme. To escape the "high priori" method, Peirce proposed to shelve the scheme revealed by logical analysis until the "framework" provided by an enumeration of the chief sciences was almost, or even fully, concluded (1343.11–17, c. 1902).[1] In the other passage, a "study of the history of science" is said to be needed for the natural classification of the sciences (1.268, c. 1902). In both cases the sciences of review can provide the appropriate data (for example, 1338.3, [c. 1905–6]). The point here is that logic and the sciences of review are concerned with classification in quite different ways. Just how they differ is made clear by the principles governing Peirce's classification and their positions in that scheme. The sciences of review consider the relations between the sciences, and discern whatever order can be determined, however imperfect. Regularities thus obtained are neither universal nor precise; precision is deliberately avoided so as to find the order that exists in the farrago of observed disciplines (7.84, 1901). Logic, on the other hand, is a theoretical science seeking laws that are universal and more or less precise. It makes no special observations (for example, 7.524, n.d.) and its hypotheses involve the spontaneous operation of the "natural light of reason" (7.84, 1901). Because Peirce insisted on a *natural* classification (one that is thoroughly rational), his classification of the sciences involves a classification of the activities of the scientists (1.268, c. 1902). Those pursuing the sciences of review may undertake enumeration of the sciences, and these will serve as data for the logician; the history of sciences, with a modicum of rationality in its more general aspects, will point them in the right direction (339.169r, 1899). It is the logician's task to seek out the principles determining the method that governs ordering.

It might seem that only the ordering of the sciences (as revealed by the sciences of review) is required for their classification and that the logician's task is futile. This may be the case for the non-scientist, but the actively involved scientist wants to know which sciences relate to their own disciplines, and how. Peirce would not deny that a satisfactory scheme will sooner or later be found, even without the aid of logic. But whatever we learn by alternative methods, something more may be learned through the general laws obtainable from a theoretical study (cf. 2.105–6, c. 1902). The sequence in which the correct solution is approached is important; the order in which different problems are tackled is not (601.17[1], [1906]). A classification scheme based on logic facilitates this by exhibiting the relationship of a particular science to all other sciences.

Pierce's seeming ambivalence was linked to his preoccupations. Until 1902 he was trying to find the appropriate principles for his scheme. Because of his insistence on a *natural* classification, one of the principles involved data obtained by the sciences of review. In 1903 he was reasonably satisfied with his logical investigation, only needing to fit the sciences into his scheme. This was the task of the sciences of review which, at the outset, had only been able to discern regularities through a mass of observations, but which could now appeal to the principles marked out by logical analysis.[2]

2.   PERTINENT LOGICAL DEVELOPMENTS

Peirce believed that the majority of proposed classifications had been based on the very objects of their concern. He found two objections to this procedure: first, some sciences are concerned with a whole spectrum of things; and second, a classification of things rests ultimately on a classification of the sciences (357.25, [1866]).

Traditionally, a thing was thought to be explained when the class under which it is subsumed had been stated. At first Peirce objected to using induction in this way because such a procedure discovers natural classification only. To use Peirce's own example: that neat,

swine, sheep, and deer are ruminants/herbivera is explained by the
fact that all cloven-footed animals are ruminants/herbivera. (357.26,
[1866]; 728.1, n.d.; 729.1, n.d.). He recognized that this procedure would
not suffice for certain sciences; optics, for example, proceeds by
hypothesis; mathematics and law, by deductions (357.26, [1866])[3] So
he attempted to classify the sciences under the rubric of induction,
deduction, and hypothesis on the assumption that a classification of
the sciences is based on a classification of arguments. Every hypothetical
science involves classificatory knowledge, he claimed.

Thus gravitation is founded on Kepler's laws which are inductions in the
proper sense. Classificatory science is founded upon some deductive knowledge
but the matter does not rest here for every deductive science requires a knowledge
of the general principles whose consequences it sea[r]ches out and these are
derived from induction & every induction requires the knowledge of a hypothetic
conclusion. Thus knowledge proceeds in irregular spirals from one of the
three divisions to another and we have here the principle of a new subdivision
of the sciences.   (357.[28] [1866]).

This is insightful, but Peirce did not find it satisfactory. Apparently,
he never attempted another scheme based on a subject-predicate logic.
He soon began to develop the logic of relatives, which disclosed all
kinds of new possibilities.

Ordinary logic allows us to classify according to genus and species,
to a class and its members. The character of a particular genus is
an abstraction realized in its species through its dissimilarities. The
several differences constitute all the ways in which it may be realized.
The two fundamental factors involved in this method of classification
are generalization and the single relation of similarity and dissimilarity.
Peirce asserted that inner associations are based on similarities, while
outer associations involving experience are based on contiguity (see
3.419, 1892; 7.391, 1893). The subject-predicate logic, then, is limited
to inner association. Accordingly, the analyses of pure mathematics
are associations by resemblance (7.392, 1893), as are the analyses of
definitions that characterize the second grade of clearness (835.15, n.d.).

There is no reason for a classification of the sciences to be limited
to inner association. Indeed, the sciences are pre-eminently concerned
with experience, which includes outer associations. For the association
of contiguity, generalization no longer means merely moving to a larger
class, but encompasses an entire system of all those elements linked

to one another in a group of connected relations. This is a move to the logic of relatives. Within a classification based on the logic of relatives, generality *is* continuity (4.5, 1898; 438 [Fragment], 1898).[4] The experimental way of thinking, which is the sphere of natural classification, is no longer simply a matter of contemplating a sample of a class and from that inferring the whole class. (Such a procedure provides information adequate for the interested observer, but is of little value to the scientist.) With the logic of relatives, induction in combination with retroduction[5] "rises from the contemplation of a fragment of a system to the envisagement of the complete system" (4.5, 1898). What once seemed complex may now be augmented and simplified into an integrated whole (4.116, 1893). The result is a classification system that will be of interest to scientists, who will be able to perceive all related sciences with significance for their own disciplines.

Any doubt about this account of the direct connection between Peirce's evolving classification scheme and the logic of relatives should be dispelled by an examination of manuscript 1336 [1892]. Its title is "Philosophy in the Light of the Logic of Relatives" and the content of the manuscript is a discussion of the place of philosophy in an early version of his classification of the sciences.[6]

As already suggested, exhibiting the relations of a given science to various other sciences indicates some of the conceivable effects of that science; the meaning is conveyed in its third grade of clearness.

Peirce's discussion of the three grades of clearness is found in his article "How to Make Our Ideas Clear" (5.388–410, 1878). It withstood most of his own critical appraisal, but he thought that he had not been sufficiently aware of there being three *grades* and not three *stages*.[7] Be that as it may, he reiterated that their differences are qualitative and that they are not meant to supplant one another (1.222, c. 1902; 649.3, 1910). Indeed, they might well be "symmetrically developed" (8.218, c. 1910).

The first grade of clearness is marked by familiarity with a word, such that it can be used readily and confidently, and so that others have a good idea of one's meaning (835.9, n.d.). It involves a recognition of whether or not a given concept applies to a given image. Accordingly, a person who is familiar with a word has a "canonical, typical, or pattern image" of it, and can contrast it with other images (649.11, 1910). One may be able to summon the image on demand, and yet not be able to spell out its meaning.

A person is in possession of a more adequate understanding of a concept when it is possible to "put oneself in readiness to attach to it any of its essential characters that there may be occasion to consider; and this must be done by general signs, not by an image of the object" (4.622, 1908). In this second grade of clearness an abstract, precise definition results from analysing a term or concept in its components. The components are not open to dispute, for they only give the logical relation of the conception being defined to concepts already employed (4.325, c. 1904). Analysis discovers the various broader classes that characterize what is being defined. If more elementary component qualities are found in the analysis, fewer individuals will possess the compound quality. As the classes become more general, our ideas become somewhat less distinct, for the dividing lines are less definite. Ultimately the procedure is confronted with an inexplicable simple idea; or so it was thought prior to the logic of relatives. The logic of relatives demonstrates that even these "simplest" conceptions can be defined effectively. Peirce's view was that there is no such thing as an inexplicable idea (5.207, 1903; 313.24–5, 1903; 835.10–12, n.d.).

The value of words is to communicate. A complete exposition of their function must of course await the determination of the purpose of human beings. If we assume that such a purpose is known, we assume that we already possess the answer to one of the most fundamental questions of philosophy. Yet whatever that purpose might be – in terms of feeling, action, or knowledge – it can only be realized by action. Hence the necessary conditions for action, enumerated abstractly and generally in an analytic definition, are only applicable when the purpose is known. When its purpose is known, as with all artificial things, a thing can be defined (s79.1, n.d.). Since our actions are not general and abstract, "the terms of a definition cannot express the real significance of a word" (835.15, n.d.). The pragmatist, however, realizes that meaning resides in a conditional resolve. "Pragmatic adequacy" is conveyed because the entire intellectual import and value of a word is found in the conceivable consequences, for self-controlled conduct of the acceptance or rejection of that concept (for example, 8.191, c. 1904; see also 3.457, 1897; 313.25–9, 1903; 5.438, 1905; 327.3, n.d.).

In the third grade of clearness, the meaning of a concept lies in general habits of action. According to Peirce, "the most perfect account of a concept that words can convey will consist in a description of the habit which that concept is calculated to produce. But how otherwise can a habit be described than by a description of the kind of action to which it gives rise, with the specification of the conditions and of the motive?" (5.491, c. 1907).

A classification based on the logic of relatives might be expected to indicate the relations that hold between one science and any other. The aims of the science and its relation to other sciences should ascertain its conceivable effects, a description of which is a description of the habit that it is calculated to produce. So Peirce's classification of the sciences should enable any science to be understood in its third grade of clearness.

Peirce referred to the conditional and the future tense in the context of the third grade of clearness. He stated that the meaning of a pure concept rests in future possible instances (288.153, 1905). It is important to recognize the significance of real possibility to Peirce's later formulations; he took every opportunity to redress his failure to recognize this in his 1878 article,[8] and it is integral to the relation between ethics and logic. In "Why I am a Pragmatist" Peirce explained that an examination of the classification of the sciences would be preparation for a deeper understanding of his pragmaticism (327.4-5, n.d.). The classification scheme itself would permit an explanation of any science in its third grade of clearness.

3. PURPOSE

Peirce's primary purpose in developing a classification of the sciences was to display a given science in relation to other sciences in order to exhibit its conceivable effects. The fundamental virtue of a classification scheme is its simplicity, which will also prevent it from displaying the more intricate relations between the sciences (615.29, 1908). Consequently, even a classification scheme under the aegis of the logic of relatives will not give a complete explanation of the sciences, although Peirce expected it to exhibit the principal facts and the real affinities of the different sciences insofar as they are open to investigation (1334.9-10, 1905).

Peirce maintained that all sciences are engaged in the common task of portraying the universe in an "intelligible presentment"; his classification sketched the outline of their composition (601.17^1-18^1, [1906]). Peirce did not presume to think that absence of a classification scheme could prevent discoveries being made sooner or later; the order in which problems are encountered was not at issue. Nonetheless, the classification is not simply a convenience (1338.2, [c. 1905–6]). Although the slow evolutionary process will eventually yield results, to adopt it as procedure (Peirce maintained in a slightly different context) is to apply the "Wild Oats doctrine" which, he thought, "involves unspeakable waste" (8.240, 1904). A systematic study of preceding sciences would hasten a problem in the direction of its final solution (448.47–8, 1903; 601.17[1], [1906]). He thought it essential to progress (8.297, 1904).

Once a science is positioned, the scheme will not only display what sort of science it is, but will reveal which science must be appealed to for principles, which for problems, data, etc., and which to appeal to for alternative methods. Moreover, it will indicate the different standards of certainty for the several sciences. Peirce expected this to have a salutary effect on the economy of time, money, and energy (4.242, c. 1902).

Peirce believed that his classification would reveal how his own ideas differed from accepted views (327.6, n.d.). It would also show where philosophy and its subdivisions fitted into the scheme (602.1, [1903–8]). But primarily Peirce was concerned to show what sort of science logic must be, which required that he first indicate its relation to other sciences (e.g., 2.119, c. 1902; 427.1–2, c. 1902; 283.96, 1905; 1334.3 and .7, 1905; 605.16–17, [1905–6]; 655.13 and .15, 1910; 673.44, c. 1911; 675.9, [c. 1911]). Because of the uncertainy about the appropriate method with which to pursue the difficult discipline of logic, Peirce wanted first to determine the necessity of undertaking the study. Logic seeks to show how truth might be attained; all the other sciences comprise the various divisions of the attempt to reach the truth. Peirce thus thought that a systematic study of logic would result from an examination of its relation to these other sciences, of their relations to one another, and of the assistance they render one another (427.1–2, c. 1902). Until the place of logic has been correctly determined, the method of investigation is uncertain, and whatever affects the method of reasoning infects every other discipline (605.17, [1905–6]; see also 7.158 note 5, 1902).

In 1867 Peirce had defined logic as the "science of the formal laws of the relations of symbols to their objects" (283.96, 1905; see also 1334. Add 40, 1905). Later he believed that a much broader view was needed for logic to survive as a distinct discipline. He was dissatisfied with traditional views of logic in relation to other sciences. To

understand what he thought logic was not can elucidate his own view
of it.

Since Aristotle, many have regarded logic as an organon or tool, denying
it the status of a science. Some who have admitted it among the sciences
do not consider it to be a theoretical discipline and instead number
it among practical sciences or arts. Still others regard it as one of
the sciences of review (605.17, [1905-6]).

1. *Logic as an Organon*

In view of Aristotle's definitions of the disciplines, it did not seem
appropriate to subsume logic under speculative science, practical
science or art. The Aristotelians gave it the name "instrument"
(*organon*) without defining it any more precisely, and the result was
that Aristotle's logical works came to be known as the *Organon* (2.547,
1901). Peirce felt that this was a negative move intended primarily
to indicate what logic was not.

Francis Bacon took up the term in his *Novum Organum* (1620),
as did William Whewell in his *Novum Organum Renovatum* (1858).
Peirce thought that John Venn (in *The Principles of Empirical or
Inductive Logic* of 1889) and his Cambridge colleagues might have
held a somewhat similar view, since for them logic " 'is not an ultimate
science.' " Peirce took this to mean that "it is not a scientifically
established doctrine at all, but a collection of more or less consistent
reflexions"(606.10-11, [1905-6?]).

Beyond noting the problematic nature of the origin of the term
"organon," Peirce does not appear to have made any criticism of the
position, perhaps because he allowed it a certain limited cogency. He
did not wish to deny that a thorough grounding in logic is a useful
asset to any individual, but that this does not make logic an instrument.

2. *Logic Viewed as a Practical Science*

Those who have considered logic to be a practical science, pursued
not simply for its own sake but for another reason, have commanded
the greatest following. Among these Peirce cited the untutored, the
Stoics, the Scholastics who dissented from Duns Scotus, and the

philosophers – particularly the British philosophers – immediately prior to Kant (606.11-12, 1905-6?]).

Just as the evident utility of logic is no reason to consider it merely an instrument, neither is it reason to regard it as a practical discipline. Unlike the curiosity of the pure theoretical scientist, that of the practical scientist *qua* practical scientist does not extend beyond knowledge applicable to one's own particular pursuits.

There are two areas of logic which, Peirce admitted, do appear to have some reference to practice. First, the *doctrine of fallacies*: those who pursue this discipline are rarely interested in critic, which is the central study of logic. Far from involving deliberate thought (the province of logic), fallacies usually arise from inattention, as when one slides from one object thought to another. Though it is somewhat dependent on logic, Peirce considered it to be a study for psychology (4.10, 1905; 606.17, [1905-6?]).

The second area of logic is *methodeutic*. Interest in methodeutic comes from every school of logic, and includes some who have no interest in logic whatsoever. Peirce proposed that some of these were merely ignorant of logic; but the majority lived between 1516 and 1650, when a disdain for it was expressive of a contempt (on the whole appropriate) for Peter of Spain and the *Parva logicalia*.[9] Even the more eminent among them were unsuccessful in developing a methodeutic that could withstand criticism of its most fundamental tenets. Peirce attributed this to their inadequate grasp of logic. Methodeutic investigates the appropriate way to pursue and order an inquiry, and it must be allied with critic in a way that precludes any of the characters of a practical science. But even without that connection with critic, methodeutic must be dissociated from any ulterior purpose: it is assumed that truth will ultimately result; and methodeutic, after all, aims only to resolve whatever the truth may be (606.17-19, [1905-6?]).

3. Logic Regarded as a Science of Review

Although Peirce did not present them, the same kinds of arguments show that logic cannot be one of the sciences of review either. The first section of this chapter illustrates this distinction. The sciences of review are not pursuing truth for its own sake, but neither are they pursuing it for the sake of some practical purpose. Their function is to take the discoveries of the theoretical sciences and make them ready for application not merely by the practical scientist, but by philosophers, educationalists, and even by those interested in amusement (655.17, 1910).

The sciences of review do not discover universal laws. They generalize, arrange, restate, digest, and classify the discoveries of all the theoretical sciences in accordance with principles obtained from them (605.7, [1905-6]; 1338.3 [c. 1905-6]; 601.26¹, [1906]; 326.20, n.d.). Logic is a major source for such principles and therefore cannot be a science of review, but a theoretical discipline. It now remains to decide whether it is a division of mathematics, of philosophy, or of one of the special physical or psychical sciences.

5. ALTERNATIVE BASES FOR LOGIC

Others have proposed a variety of methods for determining principles basic to logic. Peirce identified "several sciences to which logicians often make appeal by arguments which would be circular if they rose to the degree of correctness necessary to that kind of fallacy" (8.242, 1904).[10]

The only way to keep logic inviolate, Pierce thought, was to broaden its scope to include a general theory of signs of all kinds – a theory to include all of their relations and not simply the relation to their objects (1334.[40-1], 1905; see also 283.96, 1905). He was so perturbed by the indifference with which most of his contemporaries viewed logic that he devoted at least one manuscript to investigating how far that apathy was reasonable (624.51, 1909). He thought there was a real danger that logic might collapse into psychology or mathematics (cf. 1334.5-7, 1905), and devoted a great deal of space to analysing the errors of pursuing these two methods. The complexities involved in the very different kinds of appeals that have been made to psychology would make a cursory discussion of the topic confusing. For all of these reasons, it is necessary to fully examine the several appeals made to psychology. The relation of logic to mathematics is more straightforward and will be discussed at length in a later chapter. Appeals to metaphysics, etc., are recurrent and require only a brief look. Their simple statement will illustrate that some appeals are obviously mistaken. One may imitate Peirce in procedure (for example, 448.8, 1903) and call those appeals he opposed "defendent arguments."

According to Peirce's own report, the development of modern psychology led a great many logicians to base their principles on psychology. He found such a procedure understandable since psychology had begun as little more than a "logical analysis of the products of thought" (2.41, c. 1902). Topics for brain physiology were not clearly separated from topics for consciousness; and it seemed to Peirce that psychology was still unsure of its proper domain (2.42, c. 1902). Because it is indefinite, this opinion is difficult to disprove and, in any case, its refutation involves subtle, important distinctions (606.22, [1905–6?]).

Peirce's own view was that questions concerning logic are completely independent of psychology. He considered any confusion of the two disciplines to affect the most fundamental tenets of each. Consequently, a clear understanding of logic cannot be obtained until this elementary confusion is eliminated (751.1, n.d.). Logic is generally independent of psychology, particularly in the more limited sense.

1. Appeal to Psychology: Logic Considered as Critic

Narrowly conceived, the chief aim of logic is to inquire into the general conditions for distinguishing good and bad reasoning, as well as those for distinguishing strong and weak probable reasoning (750.1, n.d.; 751.1, n.d.). This is the task of critic – the central division of logic in Peirce's scheme. It is with reference to this aspect of logic that Peirce identified at least two distinct ways in which various writers on logic have appealed to psychology: first, appeal to the direct dicta of consciousness (a certain logical feeling or taste); and second, appeal to the results of the science of psychology.

Consider the first manoeuvre: appeal to the direct dicta of consciousness. Peirce argued that it might be more appropriate to regard the tendency to treat logic subjectively as an assimilation of logic to aesthetics, since the upholders of this view "are willing that we should like or dislike reasoning, as we might a piece of music" (2.165, c. 1902). It is not strictly correct to regard an appeal to a conviction of feeling as an appeal to the *science* of psychology. Yet it does involve a confusion of the logical question (what are the criteria for distinguishing good reasoning from bad?) with the psychological question (what process does the mind undergo?).

The philosophers who are guilty of this error rest the distinction between good and bad reasoning on a quality of feeling – of logical gratification. Although different authors give this principle different guises, the apparent divergence in doctrines and the varied forms of argument share a common core of confusion (451. Add 2, 1903).

The proposed criterion is that reasoning agreeable to the reasoner's "logical feeling" (*logisches Gefühl*) is good; if it is not, it is bad. The criterion is chosen by defenders of this view on the basis that any criticism of reasoning must be pursued by reasoning and, as one cannot pursue reasonings endlessly, one is bound to accept the termination afforded by the feeling of logicality experienced. The only test for reasoning, according to this doctrine, is that it seems to be good (448.7-8, 1903). If reasoners see all their reasonings as good, there is no way to admit bad reasoning. As long as it exists as reasoning, it is good. If it later seems to be unsound, it immediately ceases to be reasoning. So the distinction between good and bad reasoning is eliminated (451.2-3, 1903).

In reference to this, Peirce remarked that in addition to feelings that "judge" reasonings to be good, there are some that "judge" them to be bad, suggesting that people have a tendency to reason wrongly as well as correctly. If so, the disposition to reason well or ill cannot render the reasoning valid. Indeed, a feeling of logical satisfaction provides no grounds for making an inference: however prone one may be to accept a bad argument, it remains bad. Peirce's view is quite otherwise: reasoning presupposes an objective truth independent of any particular person's opinion of it and is therefore independent of whether or not one is satisfied with it (2.209, 1901).

The principle examined here precludes those who reason sincerely from being mistaken; they could never be illogical. The defendents would be powerless to refute Peirce's sincere argument against them (5.87, 1903), for one feeling is just as admissible as another and the rational feeling of all "reasoners" must be equally trustworthy. It would have to be conceded that contrary feelings yield equally sound logic (283.92-3, 1905).

Peirce's own analysis is that a feeling is such as it is without reference to anything else; in itself it has no influence on anything else (283.91, 1905). If the regular coincidence of a feeling of logical gratification with logical truth has led one to conclude that logical truth and feeling are virtually the same, one would be committing a category mistake. A logical system based on such a premiss allows nothing but feeling to adjudicate between the logically true and the logically false (451.19-21, 1903). In contrast, Peirce believed that genuine criticism is not even possible until reasoning is doubted; and when doubt arises the feeling of satisfaction is immediately dispelled (2.209, 1901; but see below).

Peirce stated that logical feeling as the ultimate criterion for distinguishing good and bad reasoning was the fashionable view for the German logicians of his day. Christoph Sigwart, together with his follower, Ernst Schröder, were singled out as notable advocates.[11] Peirce provided several reasons for holding this subjective view.

First, some believe the subjective view enables them to avoid basing logic on the theory of cognition. The error here is to confuse the theory of cognition appropriate to logic with a similar theory found in psychology.[12]

Second, some contend that correct reasoning is a question of feeling because they have observed that mathematicians (the most exact reasoners), physicists, and naturalists pursue their studies successfully without any regard for theories of reasoning. Peirce replied that this does not show that logic must be based on feeling, but that expertise in reasoning (as in billiards) is best acquired through training and not through mastery of the theory (448.45-6, 1903).

Third, as already mentioned, some believe that the feeling-criterion permits a collapse in a distinction between good and bad reasoning so that logic is reduced to a matter of intellectual taste (2.20, c. 1902; 448.4-9, 1903; 451.2-4, 1903). Peirce had another rebuttal: even if it were granted that a feeling of logicality determines all of our reasoning, comparing those reasonings with ideals formulated by relating our thoughts to facts would maintain the distinction between good and bad reasoning. When discrepancies between a particular reasoning and the logical norm occur, the feeling of logicality would immediately be altered. Only if there could be no subsequent comparison with a logical norm would the distinction between good and bad reasoning be eliminated. Unless conclusions are criticized by comparing them with logical norms, the operation cannot be called reasoning. Reasoning, as opposed to mere association of ideas, means controlled thought, and the only way to control thought is to subject it to critical review. Hence, in any given reasoning, not only is it believed that a particular conclusion is true, but also that a like conclusion would be true in all parallel circumstances (451.12-13, 1903).

There are two components of Peirce's thought that might lead one to suspect that he was sympathetic to the view that he opposed here. In the first place, Peirce did maintain that instinct, although not immune to error, is more reliable than reasoning (2.176-8, c. 1902). This may seem tantamount to giving precedence to a quality of feeling; Peirce's thesis should be carefully qualified. He recognized that tradition and generations of ordinary experience have modified our instinctual responses (6.569-70, c. 1905; 682.50^2, [c. 1913]). He believed that people do not have instincts for every occasion; when they attempt to improve some circumstance, for example, they are driven to invention and so into the hazardous area of reasoning (2.178, c. 1902; see also 5.511, c. 1905). There can be no critic of instinct, because there is no such thing as bad instinct (unless it is from the point of view of something else). Nevertheless, people do reason badly, and reason itself makes such judgments. Peirce considered this to be the single advantage that reasoning has over instinct: it is itself the critic of reasoning (832.[1], n.d.). Clearly, instinct was not intended to replace reasoning in Peirce's system.

Peirce's position on the subject of doubt is less readily dismissed. He stressed that a reasoner perfectly satisfied with a proposition, cannot question it. Pretending to question it is merely pretence, and no genuine doubt is involved. Peirce seems to find that reasoning ultimately involves a feeling of satisfaction. Yet there is a very important distinction between Peirce's position and the one he has criticized. The apparent similarity lies in the ambiguity of the word "ultimate." Sigwart and his followers maintained that logic is ultimately *based* on a feeling of logical conviction; whereas Peirce maintained that, because inquiry ceases at that point, we act *as if* the ultimate purpose of all reasoning is to reach a feeling of satisfaction. But this aim cannot actually be the aim of logic itself. A satisfactory action means that the action is congruent with its aim; and if an action has the aim of being congruent with its aim, it has no aim (330.[6-9], n.d.; 750.1, n.d.; see also 6.485, 1908). What Peirce identifies as the aim of reasoning will be discussed in a later chapter. The defendent view examined here is evidently quite unrelated.

Peirce could not ignore the implications of stating that the purpose of all reasoning is to reach a feeling of satisfaction. If this were so, why should Sigwart's method not be followed, the proposition or set of propositions that feel most satisfactory be chosen? As he did in the "Fixation of Belief," Peirce argued that such an attitude is unable to withstand the social impulse. Sooner or later the equal legitimacy of contrary views would have to be recognized. If a whole community were to agree on a complete set of propositions, if children were indoctrinated, and dissenters were silenced, the purpose of reasoning might seem to be attained; those who inquire would have to be silent. Peirce was convinced that people would sooner or later want to amend their agreement, for he believed that mankind is constitutionally incapable of accepting any arbitrary set of beliefs indefinitely. Even a belief-set carefully devised to conform to the natural temperament of the group would fail. Peirce countered that this "admits the principle of revision of the creed, and yet it supplies nothing better than taste and fashion to guide the revision." But the greatest opponent to its success is experience, which demonstrates that the most lasting preferences develop quite independently of what any individual prefers or wills (750.1-2, n.d.).

The second appeal involving logic considered as critic was to the *results* of the science of psychology. Peirce noted that many logicians see no objection to using propositions in psychology as principles of logic (693a. 154-6, [1904]). The Wolffian logicians (G.B. Büllfinger and L.P. Thümmig) as well as J.S. Mill are among those who maintain that the theoretic grounds for logic are to be taken from psychology (2.39, c. 1902). The arguments in support of this position are that it is uneconomical to refuse to use the results of psychology concerning abstraction and association and that normative rules prescribing how we ought to reason are irrational unless based on how we *must* reason. When the aspect of logic here equated with psychology is removed, a purely normative study that is merely an "ancillary practical art" remains (correction of 2.40, c. 1902). Peirce conceded that there is something akin to psychological association in logic, but insisted that only by studying the two theories seperately, can the connection be determined (2.45, c. 1902), although the relation between the two types of association is of more interest to psychology. Peirce denied that logic is relevant only to the practical application of a theory without being concerned with its development. On the contrary, he considered logic an abstract science with no such experimental basis; its normative character originates in ideals, and not in facts taken from psychology.

Peirce credited J.S. Mill with holding that logic is founded on laws that show how we must think (evidently associational principles).[13] Peirce began his analysis of this position by distinguishing uncontrolled subconscious thought (in which there can be no logical criticism) from conscious thought (for which there are alternative ways of thinking). He thought it unlikely that Mill would make Sigwart's claim, that conscious thought *consists* in an irresistible disposition. If Mill claimed that conscious reasoning somehow compels people to reason the way that they do, he must mean that if they bring all of their knowledge to the task and consider things sufficiently, they must think in the only way possible. But, Peirce continued, when Mill:

asserts that in such a case there is *no other reason* to be given for thinking in a given way than barely that the thinker is under compulsion so to think, is he not applying that Criterion of Inconceivability against which we have heard him fulminate in his finest style? It is true that Mill does not say that there is no other reason in support of the conclusion, but only that there is no other reason why the reasoner ought to accept the conclusion. But this makes no pertinent difference; the arguments against the Criterion apply in this case.[14]   (2.47, c. 1902)

To say that we should be under compulsion here would amount to the claim that the opinion in this instance is true. The corollary is that we ought to think what is true. Such a proposition is supported by the science of psychology only when a psychological fact is being asserted, but Mill would not have claimed that there is a special logic for reasoning about psychological facts.[15] It follows, Peirce argued, that apart from associational compulsions, psychology provides no support whatever for the view that conscious reasoning is compelled in any definitive way; wherever compulsion of thought operates, logic has nothing to say about what we ought to think, but merely recounts the facts (2.47-9, c. 1902).

Peirce concluded that the appeal to psychology for the problem of critic (the branch of logic that studies the conditions for distinguishing good and bad reasoning) is not able to withstand criticism.

2. *Appeal to Psychology: Logic Broadly Conceived*

If logic is considered broadly, it must include the methodeutic problem concerning the method which most speedily leads to the truth. Many logicians, who make no appeal to psychology for their logical principles, nonetheless constantly refer to the findings of psychology when they consider this problem.

These logicians argue that because logic is the theory of reasoning, it can only be performed by a mind; therefore discoveries of psychology are relevant to the theory of reasoning. Peirce responded that anything that could reason independently, including machines (2.56-9, c. 1902), could qualify as mind (283.86-7, 1905): given that there is such a thing as truth, and that logic must determine by which method truth may be most readily attained; and given that truth is, as he contended, independent of what it may be thought to be, this must be true for any intelligence whatsoever. How humans think – their psychological processes – is irrelevant to the logical question. Logic makes no assertion of fact, but only claims that under all possible circumstances of fact a certain method will direct us to the quickest discovery of truth concerning a specific problem (693a.156, [1904]).

For simplicity, and because serious omissions could thus escape notice, Peirce objected to the admission of irrelevant psychological findings to studies in logic (693a. 178, [1904]). He was dissatisfied with their limitation of what constitutes logic, and their propensity to divert the logician from demonstrating the modes of reasoning most conducive to the discovery of truth (634.6–7, 1909).

Having disposed of the view that logic is based in any way on psychology, Peirce urged the contrary. He believed it important to recognize that psychology is dependent on logic for two reasons: because errors in psychology will have repercussions in the normal course of life (unlike, for example, those that infect astronomy); and because they might continue unnoticed and become pernicious (673.8, c. 1911).

Peirce contended that psychology must be based on logic if it is to be anything more than logical analysis (2.51, c. 1902). Psychology is an observational science, requiring the research and experience of specially trained persons, whereas logic is abstract and requires only the common-sense observations available to all mature persons, using facts about the human mind that are well known and beyond doubt (283.60^4, 1905; 606.26–7, [1905–6?]; 5.485, c. 1907; 614.5, 1908).[16] Indeed, Peirce considered it a serious error to base the science of the general on the science of the special (283.85, 1905); for if psychology vouches for the varieties of reasoning that logic approves, all reasoning would remain equivocal until the science of psychology was securely established, including the very reasoning involved in its establishment. In Peirce's vivid imagery, "logic would be saved from falling into the bottomless abyss of falsity only by planting its feet upon the arms of psychology; while psychology would escape the same fate only by clutching the ankles of logic" (634.8, 1909).

3. Appeal to Erkenntnislehre (the Doctrine of Cognition)

Some of the works that appeal to psychology for data or principles may be more specifically distinguished by taking logic to consist in

or be deduced from either of the two disciplines. The first is *Erkenntnislehre* or the investigation of how knowledge is possible (what Kant
calls "the critic of knowledge" or "the critic of cognitive faculties").
This is sometimes called "epistemology," although Peirce said that
the term is etymologically associated with the second term, *Wissen-
schaftslehre*, the science the subject matter of which is the common
presuppositions underlying all sciences, including itself. It differs from
the special sciences in being universal.

Peirce agreed that logic must start with a critic of knowledge, and
he also granted that a theory of cognition was one of the subjects
pursued by psychologists of his day. His dispute was with the view
that the psychological theory of cognition is relevant to logic. He
disagreed, believing that psychological theory terminates at the point
where consciously controlled reasoning starts; whereas logic's connection, however indirect, is with consciously controlled thought alone.

Those who study *Erkenntnislehre* deny that it is psychology. Benno
Erdmann stated that it addresses the question: "What justification is
there for assuming that ideas refer to external objects?", a problem
unrelated to psychology.

It is not the logician's task to determine whether or not there is
a reality, nor has he or she any need of the answer. The logician need
only discover the habits of inference that will lead to positive knowledge
if there should be a reality, or to a semblance of positive knowledge
if there is no reality. Before this is answered, the nature of knowledge
must be discovered (2.60-4, c. 1902). This is the task of speculative
grammar, the first division of logic in Peirce's scheme (see for example,
3.430, 1896; 2.206, 1901; 1.191, 1903; see also pp.175-6 below). Peirce
claimed that the unpsychological *Erkenntnislehre* is the propaedeutic
to logic proper and that it antecedes critic, the second division of logic
(2.83, c. 1902).

4. Appeal to Direct Individual Experience

Because of its affinity with Sigwart's view, it is appropriate to examine
the idea of resting logical principles on direct individual experience.
Peirce wrote that the Abbé Gratry proposed some such method in
La Logique. Logical principles are general, of course, but the only
way for.general principles to be experienced by individuals directly
is by mystical experience. Peirce did not recall Gratry explicitly resting
logical principles on this basis, but he did not doubt that Gratry

"considers every act of inductive reasoning in which one passes from the finite to the infinite – particularly every inference which from observation concludes that there is in certain objects of observation a true continuity which cannot be directly observed – to be due to a direct inspiration of the Holy Spirit" (2.21, c. 1902).[17] When this is generalized, as consistency requires, a logical principle is obtained: all inductive inferences from the particular to the general occur through mystical experience. Peirce warned against confusing this opinion with the traditional view that humankind (and, in particular, human reason) is created in the likeness of God.

If Gratry is correct, every inductive inference from the finite to the infinite will be accompanied by surprise and a sense of struggle, as if the conclusion were forced upon us in spite of ourselves. Peirce held that the shock of surprise in the unanticipated experience is evidence for the encounter (struggle) with the individual existent; but this experience only occurs when it runs counter to inductive inference. This is the distinction that differentiates a vivid imagery from genuine experience. Continuity and generality are observed when a feeling of compulsion and struggle is usually absent (2.21–2, c. 1902).[18]

5. *Appeal to the Inward Light of Reason – Self-Evidence*

Peirce noted that the most rigorous logicians recognize a distinction between logical principles revealed by the Holy Spirit (the view expressed above), and those known by an inward light of reason – *il lume naturale* (2.23, c. 1902). Reference to "light of reason" can be found in the most ancient of documents. Peirce credited it with originating retroduction, the single mode of inference that can lead to new experimental knowledge. Yet he was circumspect. While he found it the only way to account for our relative success in guessing the principles of the universe, he thought that it should be treated with the utmost scepticism and that, until investigated, its hypotheses could only be warranted if accepted as "interrogations" (6.528, 1901; 2.25, c. 1902).

The Aristotelians, however, base the principles of logic on a direct appeal to self-evidence or the light of reason. Aristotle took induction from experience to be the origin of the first principles, and held that the general is directly perceived in the particular. Nonetheless, he believed that the inductive process could not be criticized. (Here Peirce reaffirmed his own conviction that a given process is not entitled to be called "reasoning" unless it is amenable to logical criticism.) The Aristotelians' only proof for the first principles is that they are self-evident.[19]

Descartes is credited with attempting to reinforce the light of reason position by appeal to the "veracity of God" and by his criterion of clearness and distinctness. The latter, Peirce wrote, endeavours "to define the old 'self-evidence' of the axioms of reason" (2.28, c. 1902). Peirce felt that the criterion of inconceivability (see note 14 above) also gave credence to this position.

Kant's transcendental method is yet another way in which instinctive beliefs are supported, according to Peirce. As Kant developed it, the method "consists in showing, by some ingenious argument – different in every case – that the logical analysis of the process which the mind must go through shows that the proposition which is to be defended is involved in the *a priori* conditions of the possibility of practical everyday experience" (2.31, c. 1902). Peirce believed that, had Kant pursued his method, there would have been no *Critique of Pure Reason*, because a logic based on the transcendental method would have been incompatible with the already-established scientific logic that Kant did in fact use. This discrepancy is even more readily apparent in Hegel, although his transcendental method, Peirce wrote, had little in common with that of his predecessor (see 2.32, c. 1902).

One other method reported by Peirce, which is related to Hegel's is also relevant to the appeal to the light of reason. This method involves a sort of inward observation whereby a conception is dialectically and inevitably generalized. The procedure has affinities with the way in which relations in mathematical diagrams are generalized to apply to all diagrams constructed according to the same set of rules. But the dialectic method, on which logic is said to be based, needs no diagrams (2.216, 1901).

6. *Appeal to Usages of Language*

Appeals to ordinary usages of language as the basis for logical principles abound in English texts. Peirce felt that this was often inadvertent. Those who approve the practice generally confine themselves to the small class of Aryan languages, a highly select and largely undifferentiated group. Forays further afield usually end by contorting the more remote languages into the "Procrustean bed of Aryan grammar"

(2.211, 1901; see also 2.69, c. 1902), so that any conclusions drawn are of little value.

Why this method should be pursued at all is difficult to determine. Peirce thought that it seeks to "establish a psychological proposition valid for all minds" (2.211, 1901), connecting it with psychological appeals. In spite of Husserl's claims that his work is uncontaminated with psychology, he appears to follow this line. (4.7, 1905). Peirce thought that Venn's *Principles of Empirical or Inductive Logic* (1889) was marred by "puerilities about words." Among lesser logicians, Carveth Read, Horace William Brindley Joseph, John Neville Keynes and Constance Jones also followed this course (4.7, 1905).[20]

Logic is concerned with the way in which two supposed facts are related. Of course these two supposed facts must be expressed in some manner. Nonetheless, the logicality of reasoning is unaffected by the language in which it is expressed. This is one reason for inventing a completely uniform artificial language, free of psychical and linguistic idiosyncrasies, and capable of expressing any hypothesis whatsoever (735.2^1, n.d.; 751.3, n.d.).

Logicians generally do remark the distinction between logical forms and linguistic expression. Yet the majority of their texts are still permeated with points involving a particular language. The remedy that Peirce pursued (although he was not in need of it, since he had no sympathy for the defendent view) was to examine twenty dissimilar languages. This study revealed that many of the logicians' inferences were not "necessities of thought." He discovered that among the non-Aryan languages, some of these "necessities of thought" had not been thought of at all.

According to the defendent argument it is a "necessity of thought" for a "judgment" to comprise a subject nominative (generally a common noun), the copula ("is"), and a predicate (generally an adjective). Yet Peirce pointed out that Gaelic, surely a language familiar to some of the Scottish logicians, usually avoids the subject nominative by turning the nominative into an oblique case and making it an "object."[21] The predicate too, is not universal, because not all languages are replete with adjectives. Peirce reported that the copula was omitted in writings as recent as those of Aristotle's day. Yet "it is curious to find how late in the development of the different languages the necessity of this 'necessity of thought' came to be recognized, although people had probably not spoken in earlier times entirely without thinking" (693a.186, [1904]). If the defendent logicians were correct, many non-Aryan groups would have had to resort to quite devious methods just to avoid thinking what they must necessarily think.

Peirce concluded that logic has no need of principles from linguistics. Nor has the study of languages contributed usefully. Languages, he maintained, never provided him with any fresh ideas; they only contributed examples of truths that he had previously determined by *a priori* reasoning. The same can be said of texts representing every school of logic. Nonetheless these schools are also represented by other texts the reasoning of which constantly appeals to facts of the language in which it is written, or else of closely related languages (693a.190-2, [1904]).

7. Appeal to the "Stability of Society"

Karl Pearson's writing was socially oriented. He held that good and bad reasoning are a function of their propensity to augment or subvert the stability of the established society. Peirce argued that if it is desirable to perpetuate a given society there will be good reasons for doing so; but to regard this as an *ultimate* aim is absurd. A society might well be so pernicious that its demise would be a good thing even from its members' viewpoint (8.141-3, 1901; 2.71, c. 1902).[22]

8. Appeal to Authority

Medieval logicians respected authority over reasoning as the determinate of truth. When discrepancies arose, they would actually distort the principles of logic and so make them conform to the edicts of the church. Their procedure, Peirce said, was to argue that when a proposition appears to be preposterous it cannot really be so if the church happens to hold it to be true. For example, against all evidence of continuity (an important logical doctrine in Peirce's view), they persisted in an incisive bifurcation between the innocent and the guilty, the wise and the stupid, the chaste and the dissolute, and so on (1.61, [c. 1898]; 735.11², n.d.).

Peirce did not deny the legitimacy of adopting the reasoning of a reliable authority in matters outside one's competence, provided that this procedure is recognized as unscientific (1.30-2, 1869; 2.72-3, c. 1902). In light of this, Peirce thought that "arguments from authority are of no authority in a question of logic" (4.660, 1908).

9. *Appeal to Common Sense*

Peirce allowed that logic may get its first impetus from common sense and even that it might be appropriate to regard common sense as a high authority. Of course, like any other authority, it is to be respected but subjected to thoroughgoing criticism (770.9–10, n.d.). Elsewhere he said that pragmaticism "implies faith in common sense and in instinct, though only as they issue from the cupel-furnace of measured criticism" (6.480, 1908).

Even so, Peirce warned against anything that might be termed a "common sense logic." Common sense is identified with the collective beliefs that inevitably arise in the adults of an ordinary community, given human faculties and the normal course of experience. As its name suggests, common sense is what sane persons think, almost in spite of themselves; logic, in contrast, is essentially the product of self-control, whereby the first impulsive opinion is resisted and that which will be accepted, (given an indefinite time to consider it) is approximated as closely as possible (770.7–10, n.d.; see also 5.369, 1877).

10. *Appeal to Mathematics*

Many "seminary" logicians are said to be under the impression that those who treat logic algebraically understand logic to be a division of mathematics. Peirce wrote that, with the possible exception of George Boole, this is not the view of the logical algebraists at all. Even if it were, it would have no momentous repercussions, because their studies are limited to formal logic which is, according to Peirce, mathematical logic.

Does this make mathematics a branch of logic, or does formal logic need to be dissociated from the science of logic? Peirce considered this a problem for the classification of the sciences (4.134, 1893), and personally took the latter position. Formal logic, he stated, *is* mathematics in that it is restricted to hypotheses. Every science has a mathematical branch and logic is no exception; the mathematical inquiries into formal logic are an important source of principles for logic. But this is the *application* of mathematics and consequently no part of the pure theoretical science of mathematics, which Peirce considered to be the most abstract of all (4.240, .244, and .263, c. 1902).

Peirce gave three reasons for not elevating logic to the same level as mathematics. In the first place, mathematics is completely abstracted from reality and hence its hypotheses are purely ideal in intention. Logic is less abstract: equipped with the investigations of phenomenology, it burgeons into a positive science. Although it makes no special observations of its own, and is limited to the phenomena revealed in ordinary experience, its hypotheses are intended to represent positive fact (15.4-5, [c. 1895]; 1.443, c. 1896; 3.428, 1896; 3.560, 1898; 5.126, 1903; 7.524, n.d.). Secondly, mathematics is purely deductive, whereas logic is not so limited. Indeed, Peirce added, deductive reasoning is not even the major part of logic. Inductive logic, which is more clearly founded on phenomenology, must still seek principles from mathematics (5.126, 1903; 1336.11, [1892]). Thirdly, neither logic nor mathematics is concerned with what is the case; facts utilized by the mathematician are taken up as hypotheses and treated as if they were creations of the imagination. The mathematician is interested in what would be the case, whereas the logician is interested in what ought to be the case – with bringing phenomena into conformity with aims not inherent in them. Logic is a normative science (5.126, 1903; 693a.134, [1904]; 1339.3^1, n.d.).

One of the principal logico-mathematicians of Peirce's day, Richard Dedekind, took the opposite approach and claimed that mathematics should be demoted to a division of logic (4.239, c. 1902; 466.2, 1903; 608.2, [1905-6?]; 1334.4, 1905).[23] This was the logicists' program. Peirce countered that the two disciplines have such widely divergent aims that had Dedekind been as familiar with logic as he was with mathematics he could not have tolerated the opinion. The mathematician is interested in reaching a conclusion as efficiently as possible, seeking methods that allow short cuts and eradicate complications without sacrificing security. Logicians want to discover the fundamental components of reasoning and of thought in general, analysing each small step; their predilection is for splintered and laborious reasoning (4.373, 1901; 4.239, c. 1902; 466.6, 1903; 4.533, 1905; 4.614, 1908).

Peirce was convinced that mathematics is one science that need never appeal to logic to ascertain the validity of its reasoning, "for nothing can be more evident than its own unaided reasonings" (7.524, n.d.; see also 1.417, c. 1896; 693a.134, [1904]). Hence, to base mathematics on logic could only give rise to anomalies.[24]

11. Appeal to Metaphysics

If explicitly asked, the majority of logicians and metaphysicians would not dispute that metaphysics depends on logic. Nevertheless, most works on logic betray a dependence on metaphysics. This, Peirce believed, was true of those who accept traditional logic as well as those who would have liked to dissociate themselves from it; for example, Bacon in his *Novum Organum* (1620), Descartes in his *Discourse on the Method* (1637), and Locke in his *The Conduct of the Understanding* (1706).

Peirce offered two reasons for this. One is that the dependence on logic is strong enough that from knowing people's metaphysics their logic can be readily discovered. (Thus Kant's list of categories more adequately reflects his logic than does his work *Logik*.) In addition he noted the indoctrination from childhood of two metaphysical beliefs that are humankind's most certain propositions: the knowledge of our own existence, and the knowledge of the existence of God. If metaphysics does indeed furnish the most certain knowledge, Peirce would have conceded that logic ought to rest on metaphysics; but in fact, most metaphysical propositions (and especially the two cited here) are doubted or denied by many who have given deep consideration to the problems (693a.142–8, [1904]).

It would be rash to attempt to resolve the intransigent problems of metaphysics without having thoroughly considered the nature of the reasoning to be used, and ignorant of the basis of its validity (283.34, 1905). Peirce felt that the inferences of the metaphysicians, if at all amenable to empirical testing, must be in a "department" of experience wholly different from that in which the premisses are found (1.624, 1898).[25]

Apart from the practice of logical reason, there is the more pressing need for metaphysics to obtain its principles from the theory of logic. Most metaphysical conceptions are simply logical conceptions applied to reality. Consequently, they can only be elucidated through the prior study of logic (3.487, 1897; 1.625, 1898; 2.121, c. 1902; 602.3, 1903–8; 283.35, 1905).[26]

Peirce credited Kant with the principle that metaphysical conceptions should be modelled on the theory of logic, although the opinion also had support in Aristotle; both philosophers founded their list of categories on logical analyses of the proposition. Unfortunately, the *Organon* opens with a metaphysical book, the *Categories*, and ordinarily this is preceded by Porphyry's metaphysical text on the predicables. Many scholastic texts consist in commentaries on the collection in this format and this fostered the tendency to base logic on meta-physics.

Later writings also presuppose special metaphysical systems. Peirce cited the Epicurean logic of Gassendi in *Syntagma philosophicum*, Pt. 1 (1658), *La Logique, ou l'art de penser* of Antoine Arnauld and Pierre Nicole (1662), *Logick* of Isaac Watts (1724), *System der Logik* of S.V.D. Esser (1823), and many others (2.38, c. 1902). He concluded that this insidious procedure was adopted in some measure, by most logicians.

12. Appeal to the History of Science

Many scientific hypotheses eventually collapse under the weight of myriad adjustments and give way to new hypotheses, leading many scientists to conclude that no hypothesis can be regarded as final – that revolutionary coups are to be expected at intervals when the whole establishment of theories will be ousted and a new set of theories will take over. Peirce noted that such scientists also conclude that different types of reasoning characterize different periods of scientific thought (2.150, c. 1902).

If the defendent argument is correct in basing logic on probable reasoning, and if these arguments survive criticism, they are cogent. But the defendent must be quite certain that the historical account is accurate, and a sufficient number of facts must have been gathered to warrant an induction. Several variables must be taken into account; for example, which facts are to be used, and what range of the induction is to be based on those facts? Reasoning based on scientific experience is more hazardous because the reasoner is likely to forget the tenuous nature of the procedure (2.74, c. 1902).

Peirce contended that the history of science has been altogether too brief to constitute the sole basis for a theory of knowledge (2.150, c. 1902).[27] He had no more definite criticism to make of this approach to logic, and even admitted that there has been much of value in the works of Comte and Whewell – three who based logical doctrines on the history of science. Still, Peirce found no reason to expect that such a method could encompass the whole of logic (735.3², n.d.).

Whether or not logic needs to make any assertion concerning matters of fact was for Peirce an open question. If it does not, the appeal to experience is otiose. If it does, that appeal might not be to scientific experience, but to the ordinary universal experience of any mature individual. Peirce believed that such things cannot be doubted; they have practical infallibility in contradistinction to absolute infallibility. (The only assertion that Peirce allowed absolute infallibility is that which maintains that no assertion, save this, is absolutely infallible.) The sort of things known to everyday experience are not subject to genuine doubt, and scientfic facts will not serve the logician who appeals to facts of that nature (2.213-14, 1901).

Two other theories that attempt to support inductive reasoning fail to account for the fact that pure induction (preceded by retroduction) is ampliative. The conclusion goes beyond what is asserted in the premises. Although in quite different ways, both theories seek support for inductions from mathematical reasoning. But if it is at all sound, mathematical reasoning is explicative. It concludes nothing that is not already asserted (at least implicitly) in the premises. With consummate subtlety, J.S. Mill derived inductive conclusions from the (absolute) uniformity of nature; P.S. Laplace, on the other hand, professed to reach inductive conclusions by means of the doctrine of chances, which is thoroughly mathematical (660.1-12, 1910).

Both men have made valuable contributions to knowledge in fields other than logic, and since both theories have some plausibility, their influence has been considerable. Indeed, Peirce believed that Mill's logic in particular had been more influential than any other outside of the universities during most of the nineteenth century. Yet, curiously, no mention of either theory is included in Peirce's two lists. This may be because the appeals are intended to support inductive inference alone, and not the whole of logic; or perhaps because they came later. Elsewhere Peirce wrote extensively on them, particularly on the examination of Mill's procedure.

13. *Inductive Reasoning: Appeal to Uniformity of Nature*

According to John Stuart Mill, the conclusion of an inductive argument follows from its premises because nature acts uniformly. He avoided the expression, "law of nature," but from his use of the term "uniformities" it is unclear if he held any set of phenomena displaying similarities to be a "law." "Uniformity of nature" shifted in Mill's meaning, but usually meant that under the same circumstances the same phenomena will occur.

Although quite different events may occur under very similar conditions (precisely the same conditions are never found) Mill implied that when circumstances are *sufficiently* similar, events are alike. Peirce suggested that Mill might be pinned down further on whether he meant every event or only some events. His inclusion of all kinds of events would mean "that every kind of circumstance contributes to every kind of result" (735.7^2, n.d.) since all events are related, a proposition belied by experience. If he maintained that under sufficiently similar circumstances *some* events will be similar, his claim is scarcely controversial; but it will not support inductive reasoning unless we have a criterion for identifying the appropriate events, and this criterion cannot be the principle itself (735.6^2-7^2, n.d.). Observations exhibiting a peculiarity are not selected and afterwards described as a "law of nature" that they possess that very same peculiarity (872.2^2, 1901; 692.15-17, 1901; see also 6.100, 1901).

Peirce discovered two errors in Mills' procedure: not all uniformities are of the same kind; and there is no evidence to substantiate the supposed law. Mill himself all but recognized the distinction between a resemblance and a law. In his *System of Logic*, he noted that a chemist discovering that a reaction occurs with a piece of gold he is experimenting upon will infer with complete assurance that any piece of gold will react in the same way under the same conditions. On the other hand, Mill continued "not all the instances which have been observed since the beginning of the world in support of the general proposition, that all crows are black would be deemed a sufficient presumption of the truth of the proposition to outweigh the testimony of one unexceptionable witness who should affirm that is some region of the earth not fully explored he had caught and examined a crow, and had found it to be grey."[28]

Peirce felt that Mill's prejudice against admitting the reality of laws blinded him to the distinction thus laid bare. Mill's second case is probably no more than a resemblance, but countless successful predictions would show that in his first case there is an underlying law of nature that is not merely a similarity between particular events, but that influences what *will be* (621.41, 1909): a law essentially refers to an indefinite future.

For Mill to substantiate his claim, he had to show that the uniformity of nature is exact, rigid, and exceptionless; it cannot be simply a chance coincidence, nor can it be an ingenious fabrication of the mind describing a uniformity fully realized in a limited number of past events (8.192, c. 1904). Augustus De Morgan demonstrated that in any given selection of observations innumerable propositions may be devised (without going beyond what is given, Peirce added) that are precisely true for those observations, but that are unlikely to be true for any additional observations selected on the same principle.[29] Even the uniformities that are candidates for laws ("prognostic generalizations of observations," as Peirce on one occasion defined a law of nature [872.2^2-3^2, 1901]) will not serve as a foundation for inductive inference. There is no reason to suppose that a hypothesis, now regarded as a law, is eternal and immutable. Neither is there any reason to believe that any given law is absolute in the sense required by Mill's thesis. Peirce claimed that, "on the contrary, it is presumable that any given law is continually violated in an excessively small measure, and with excessive infrequency in perceptible measure" (660.6, 1910). He found confirmation of this in the prodigious variety of nature and he somewhat cannily suggested that it is even more strongly supported by a law of logic (660.7, 1910; 856.18^1, [1911]). Peirce was of the opinion that exploring the difficult problem of "how far nature does act uniformly" would require a great deal of logical acumen.

14. Inductive Reasoning: Appeal to Doctrine of Inverse Probabilities

Pierre Simon Laplace invoked the doctrine of chances (alternatively called the "calculus of probabilities") to support the probable conclusion of an inductive inference. The doctrine of chances calls for mathematical reasoning alone; it claims only that the state of things represented in the conclusion would be true in any universe in which the premises were true (660.1-4, 1910). When correctly applied, it can give no determinate probability to an inductive conclusion, unless an assumption converts it to a deductive inference (474.114, 1903). This Laplace did, and developed the "Doctrine of Inverse Probabilities" in his *Théorie analytique des probabilités (1812)*.[30] In order to apply this doctrine to a particular event the antecedent probability of the event must be known. When this information is lacking, Laplace assumed that all the values of the probability were "equally possible," meaning "equally probable." Peirce dismissed this on two counts: there is no reason to make this assumption and it leads to contradictory results (8.224, c. 1910; 660.10-11, 1910).

Underlying the defendent argument is a misunderstanding of what is meant by "probability." Laplace allowed his theory to rest on mere likelihood or subjective probability – what he called the *également possible* – and seemed to assume that this was what the mathematicians meant (2.785, 1901; 8.221, c. 1910). With mathematical reasoning, however, the data may be fictitious or factual. The reasoning is unaffected because it merely directs attention and regroups what has been given in the initial data (625.68 and .73, 1909).

Laplace's theory answers well enough for unexceptional problems involving probabilities in games, in life insurance, and in the handling of observations: when the antecedent probability is known or when fictitious occurrences are involved. But in reference to causes it errs. Laplace failed to distinguish between occurrences (events) and real facts: an occurrence is a "slice of the universe," but a fact is only extracted from the universe by an effort of thought; it *is* the element of an event that results from an act of mental discrimination. It would be more correct to talk of the probability of facts, not of events (472.100, 1903). Peirce noted that occurrences do not have causes, while both a cause and its effect are facts (647.9-11, 1910). The most impeccable reasoning cannot conclude a fact from a series of facts with which it has no connection (625.58 and .75, 1909). In dealing with fact it is entirely arbitrary to consider all values of the probability as equally "probable" if essential information is lacking. The Laplaceans attempt to eliminate the arbitrariness of their procedure by insisting that the (equally possible) events be *simple*, which appears to mean "uncompounded." Peirce pointed out that the difference between a simple event and a compound event is not a matter of fact but depends rather on the manner of expressing the problem (474.123-4, and .136-8, 1903; cf. 692.18-20, 1901). Hence arbitrariness is not circumvented.[31] Consider the ramifications of the theory for problems involving judicial testimony and the credibility of witnesses (647.24-6, 1910; 660.9-11, 1910).

Peirce rejected Laplace's amorphous definition of "probability" as totally unsatisfactory. On the contrary, he thought it advisable to begin by restricting the meaning of probability to whatever is required for the doctrine of chances; with this it would be possible to consider the debatable cases and to decide whether the definition need be broadened or if a new term is needed for such cases (660.18-19, 1910). In a preliminary definition, Peirce took probability to be a certain habit or disposition: "It is a *would be* and does not consist in actualities or single events in any multitude finite or infinite. Nevertheless a habit does consist in what *would* happen under certain circumstances if it should remain unchanged throughout an endless series of actual occurrences" (8.225, c. 1910; see also 5.169, 1903; 660.20-3, 1910). Thus it is "a ratio of frequency in the longrun of experience" (472.104, 1903). Laplace, of course, had in mind a single event although he did not indicate which event. The distinction between this, and the aggregate of an enormous number of instances, and the approximate result that should almost certainly be attained in the long run, escaped him (647.7[1], 1910). He placed all under the umbrella of "probability."

15. Miscellaneous Appeals

Peirce mentioned a few other approaches that he disdained to criticize. Indeed, they were not the sort of ploys likely to attain fame and influence.

A procedure attributed by Peirce to theological students is that of first deciding what position to adopt and only then looking for reasons in its defense (778.14, [c. 1909]).

Leonhard Rabus, in his *Logik und Metaphysik* (1868) adopted a position the account of which Peirce confined to a footnote:

Rabus conceives logic to be a branch of anthropology, by which he means what we in this country would call ethnology, in which he makes Ethics the fundamental science, followed immediately by Esthetics. Logic depends upon them, and Psychology completes "Anthropology." But he makes all Anthropology to depend upon Theology. Finally, anthropology is followed by 'Philosophy,' by which he means what I term 'Science of Review.'   (693a.140 note, [1904]).

If Peirce was correct in finding so many prevalent options regarding the proper foundation of logic (as Bocheński thought he was) his concern for the perilous state of that discipline was entirely warranted. He hoped that his classification would prohibit such erroneous views from recurring and might forestall attempts to include logic within the purview of other disciplines.

Successive Attempts at a Natural Classification

Peirce found his early attempts to formulate a viable classification scheme within the limits of a subject-predicate logic unsatisfactory. Investigations into the logic of relatives gave him a new basis and ultimately resulted in a classification incorporating Comte's principle as the central governing idea and his three universal categories as the formal differentiating device. Here an explication of these principles in terms of the present context is preceded by an analysis of the development of Peirce's classification as revealed in the extant writings. Determining just what should be regarded as a science presented a difficulty in those initial inquiries. Moreover, Peirce had come to the conclusion that the only useful scheme would need to be a *natural* classification. Thus the terms "natural" and "science" must first be clarified in order to understand what Peirce meant by a "natural classification of the sciences."

1. THE MEANING OF "SCIENCE"

Peirce rejected a system that defined science in terms of the objects of investigation; and he found definition in terms of a class and its members equally inadmissible since that procedure is restricted to the natural sciences, and excludes disciplines that clearly are sciences (357.25-6, [1866]). Yet later, Peirce's most frequently expressed disagreement with previous classifications was that they embody no positive information: they are classifications of possible sciences.

1. Earlier Conceptions

Because of its complexity and its diversity, science is difficult to characterize: the concept does not lend itself to precise definition. It was more or less argued that the appropriate genus is some sort of knowledge, but Peirce found no unanimity on differentia.

The early Greeks thought that the differentia involved method – the way in which truth is grasped (7.49, [1906]). Institutions such as the Jesuit colleges promulgated the idea of science as *scientia* in the sense of the Greek *epistēmē* meaning "perfect knowledge" or "comprehension," thus limiting the method to a mental activity (283.7, 1905; 1334.11, 1905; 614.6, 1908; 1339.2, n.d.).

Peirce saw nineteenth-century writers taking their cue from Coleridge's *Encyclopaedia Metropolitana* and considering science as a systematized or organized body of knowledge, but without suggesting that the organization be in accordance with principles (7.54, c. 1902; 1339.2, n.d.). Such a procedure could only get at what he called the "exudation" (1.232, c. 1902) or the "fossilized remains" of science (614.6, 1908). Since the task of science is to generalize experience and not merely to describe it, and since generalization leads to "virtual prediction," it cannot be restricted to the past as this view suggests (8.155, 1901).

Peirce found both method and system essential to the definition of science, although methodology more profoundly so. Yet they fail to convey the genuinely informative idea of science as living. Classifying by abstract definition, though adequate for artificial things, is tantamount to a guarantee against producing a natural scheme, particularly when the items to be classified are of the nature of ideas, as occurs with science. Without disparaging analytic definition, Peirce insisted that it would not lead to natural classes. When the classes are marked out and their underlying purposes are clear, abstract definitions for them can be sought (1.222, c. 1902).

Peirce singled out Bacon as one on the right track, in spite of his naïvety. Bacon thought that science required a life dedicated to sedulous inquiry; fittingly, his own life terminated as a consequence of conducting an experiment (7.54, c. 1902).

2. Science as Peirce Conceived It

Peirce proceeded to use the word "science" in the sense of the collective and co-operative activity of all persons and any group of persons whose lives are animated by the desire to find out the truth (615.14, 1908).[1] Unavoidably, he continued to use the term somewhat loosely in its more general sense. In its restricted sense (in which truth is sought for its own sake) it can only apply to the heuretic sciences, the sciences of discovery (675.13[1], [c. 1911]; see also 283.8-9, 1905; 605.11-12, [1905-6]). Yet the sciences of review and the practical sciences are also encompassed by the term. While the practical sciences do seek to discover truth, they differ from the heuretic sciences because their investigations are directed towards satisfying some definite human want. Sciences in Coleridge's sense are what Peirce called the "sciences of review" (283.9, 1905).[2] Their aim is to marshal the fragmented discoveries of the heuretic sciences by generalizing, criticizing, and systematizing them. The various divisions of the sciences of review and the practical sciences will be treated summarily here for the most part. Although in their general role they occupy an important position in the classification of the sciences, it is with the heuretic sciences that Peirce was primarily concerned.

In the restricted sense then, men and women of science form a social group the single passion of which is to learn the truth for its own sake; not for some ulterior purpose, not even for the pleasure of beholding it, but solely with the desire to "penetrate into the reason of things" (1.44, [c. 1898]).

Peirce thought it characteristic of genuine science to be concerned with useless things. Practical problems will get resolved without the work of the scientist, and besides, to divert "these rare minds on such work is like running a steam engine by burning diamonds" (1.76, [c.1898]). Of course some sciences yield results that can be applied at once, but scientists must ignore the utility of their investigations lest they compromise their scientific acumen (1.619, 1898). This is not to say that scientists who devote their lives to their discipline in order to advance humankind fail to be genuine scientists; Peirce meant that in conducting their research scientists must dismiss all such considerations entirely (1344.13-14, n.d.).[3] This gives the lie to the poet's line, "An undevout astronomer is mad,"[4] for astronomers, according to Peirce, have no chance to respond to the awesomeness of the heavens since in all their observations they must be wholly engrossed in their measurements (615.12, 1908).

Although Peirce's only indispensable requirement for an endeavour to *become* a science was the energetic and single-minded pursuit of the truth (s104 [fragment], n.d.; see also 1.235, c. 1902; 7.50, [1906]), he called an endeavour a science only when a group of people were pursuing similar inquiries, in substantial agreement on the most enlightened method, based on all the available information and work accomplished in that field; when they had access to the appropriate enabling conditions such as inherent ability, education, favourable circumstances, equipment, and so on; when their several problems were sufficiently similar for them to understand one another to an extent that with some modest preparation and the same facilities they could pursue the other's investigation with tolerable success; and when zealous co-operation characterized their efforts to advance towards the truth for the enrichment of future generations (655.16, 1910; 675.13[1], [c. 1911]; 1339.3, n.d.). Peirce had a lurid analogy for this last quality: "The spirit in which they work that posterity may know what they never can is rather like that of disciplined troops who advance upon the walls of a fort, with the idea that when the dead are piled high enough those behind will be able to reach the ramparts" (615.12, 1908; see also 6.3, 1898). When they appear to have failed, the lessons learned from that failure amount to virtual success (7.51, [1906]).

Unlike an abstract definition, the foregoing is a definition of science as it is lived. If science is understood to be the concrete pursuits of an actual group of living persons, it will be characterized by persistent growth (1.232, c. 1902). It follows that the limits of a particular science will be blurred; but if they cannot be mapped out clearly, this must be expressed. One consequence that Peirce noted is that distinctions cannot be too minute. A scientific society whose members all belong to other (differing) scientific groups is a case in point (655.17, 1910); analytic definitions may serve, although considerable circumspection must be brought to the task. Peirce suggested that in this way the definitions might "lead us to turn back and see whether our classes ought not to have their boundaries differently drawn. After all, boundary lines in some cases can only be artificial, although the classes are natural" (1.222, c. 1902).

An individual who strikes out upon a completely new line of investigation cannot be termed a scientist within Peirce's meaning of the term, except by followers who may in retrospect discern errors in the pathfinder's procedure. Yet usually a breakthrough will be made by several people at once, because it will only occur when science has attained a particular level in its development. Peirce believed that no one possesses the capacity to solve any chosen, unsolved problem, however narrowly specialized it might be. *"He only finds himself in condition to attack this and that individual problem"* (614.7–10, 1908).[5]

Since co-operation is an essential characteristic here, a specific science must be such as can be undertaken by several inquirers. For Peirce, one science is distinguished from another by the social relations of those who pursue connected inquiries of sufficient range and filiation to absorb the individual investigators for life (7.55, c. 1902; 605.9, [1905-6]; 4.9, 1906). The smallest such group might be located in one laboratory, wherein all investigators communicate their problems and methods freely. They will be sure to have a keen interest in any other groups pursuing closely related problems but using different ideas. Whatever its proportions, the members of a given group will have an understanding and appreciation of each other's activity as no outsider can (605.10, [1905-6]). Their common dexterity in using certain instruments and performing certain experiments, their acquaintance with the writings of other members of the society, and their familiarity with mutual ideas and language (for example, with the conceptions developed by the society) all contribute to the unity of the group (1.236, c. 1902; 1334.12–14, 1905).

Observation of previously unknown phenomena usually initiates the breaking up of sciences into specialties. Peirce felt that this generally occurs as a result of the unusual aptitude of the observer. The scientist might be located in a rare environment, or have access to some unique object or to some superior and costly instrument; by chance an inquirer might happen on some unusual psychical phenomenon, or succeeed in making contact with a hitherto unknown community, or obtain access to unexplored tombs or documents, and so on. Yet this serendipity would be of no use had not the researcher been equipped with the ideas and training to exploit it (605.8–9, [1905-6]).[6]

Peirce thought that we would find the sciences already organized by nature itself. Provided we confine ourselves to sciences already recognized by the scientific community, we may find the natural classes already arrayed in the list of scientific societies and periodicals. Thus we would have the beginnings of a classification scheme. Any further division would require closer examination, of course (1.237, c. 1902).

2. THE NATURE OF THE CLASSIFICATION

1. *Reasons for a Natural Scheme*

Why should Peirce conclude that only a natural classification of the sciences is acceptable? He did not believe that all classification schemes must fulfil this requirement; he berated publishers for departing from a straightforward alphabetical arrangement in the index of a book which, for all its arbitrariness, is quite the most satisfactory form (427.3, c. 1902, omitted at 1.203). This is instructive because it suggests that an important consideration (Peirce called it the only consideration) is the use for which the classification scheme is intended. Hence an artificial scheme might recommend itself for the classification of the sciences when, for example, the diverse purposes of library science are to be met (1.268, c. 1902). The purpose of Peirce's classification was "to embody the chief facts of relationship between the sciences so far as they present themselves to scientific and observational study" (1334.9-10, 1905). This could only be attained with a natural classification.

Peirce cited Richardson's *Classification: Theoretical and Practical*[7] which (without counting the 173 schemes designed for library reference) examines 145 systems, each purporting to be the only genuine natural classification of the sciences. Peirce claimed no less for his own scheme (1.275, c. 1902; 427.3, c. 1902). But logicians could not agree on whether or not a natural classification was possible. Those who dispute the point, Peirce wrote, are misled by their own notion of what a natural scheme might be. They want a natural classification of real classes; yet they proceed to espouse a metaphysical system that denies that there are any real classes in the required sense.

Peirce's claims were more modest and easier to substantiate. He understood "natural" in a "purely experiential sense" (1.204, c. 1902).[8] A natural classification, then, must be limited to natural experiential objects; in no other way could it provide positive information, which it must if it is to be of value. It must maximize the number of significant distinctions over and above those that determine any given place in the scheme (1336.5-6, [1892]).[9]

If this sort of a natural scheme is possible and if the philosophers who have attempted natural classification systems are correct in thinking that there can be only one natural classification of the sciences, how have all these multifarious systems arisen? Comte's explanation appealed to his doctrine of three stages, but Peirce avoided a theory-laden approach: he complained that many of the writers relied on their own discretion in differentiating between sciences, apparently without referring to any objective data, and that there was no agreement as to what constituted a unit of science for classification. Nor was there any uniformity as to where a given science ended and another began, nor yet to what state of scientific development they refer. But even when classification has more or less included the same group of sciences, the classifiers have been concerned to promote a particular philosophy so that the various systems have been regulated by quite different purposes or generating ideas (1343.3–4, c. 1902; 1341.5–6, n.d.).[10] Moreover, many previous classifications of the sciences classified *possible* sciences, setting forth "decrees" for all future sciences (7.56, c. 1902; 1334.10–11, 1905). Since there is no way to experience a "possible" science, such classifications cannot be of natural objects. Peirce's more modest aspirations were to organize the current sciences and (more cautiously) those which are obviously imminent, while assiduously avoiding all obsolete sciences (675.24–5, [c. 1911]; 1339.1, n.d.). If "science" meant "the actual living occupation of an actual group of living men" (1334.11, 1905) there could be no doubt that the objects to be classified were natural. Thus, notwithstanding the many and varied schemes already proposed, Peirce could still hope to produce the one true natural classification of the sciences.

It has been stated earlier that the sciences of review might produce a perfectly satisfactory scheme to facilitate the *application* of the sciences. Given Peirce's understanding of science, this classification ordering the sciences to be found in journals and lists of scientific societies would be of natural objects. A natural classification of the sciences could emerge from this, but even so, it is unlikely to be the scheme Peirce sought, because it would have a different purpose. Although the classification developed by the sciences of review serves a valuable function in the initial formulation of that scheme, it is the business of the logician to find the principles and method governing the ordering of the sciences (see chapter 2, section 1).

2. Characterization of a Natural Classification

According to Peirce,

Every class is constituted and held together by a concept or idea expressed in its definition. Every arrangement of ideas is itself an idea. Consequently, every classification whatever is governed by an idea, however loose and incongruous it may be. A natural classification, that is to say, a birth-al classification, is a classification whose governing idea coincides with the idea which determines the things classified to exist. An idea, so far as it has any relation to life, is a possible purpose.   (1343.11–12, c. 1902)

Hence, the purpose or quasi-purpose determining the existence of the objects to be classified may lead to the natural classification.

All objects that fit a certain description comprise a class. A "natural" or "real" class, however, would need to be one the members of which derive their existence as members from a single final cause.[11] Peirce recognized this to be quite vague, but he also felt that until there is reason to be more exact, vagueness may be an asset.

Such fabricated objects as lamps give immediate access to their purpose in a way that can hardly be expected of natural objects (1.204, c. 1902). Yet classification of artificial objects is none too straightforward even when the purpose is known. For example, when people decided that clothes were needed to protect them from the elements, they soon found that clothes could enhance their appearance, provide camouflage, or frighten their enemies – all "secondary" purposes. In the normal course of events, certain conditions will need to be met if the problem of protecting against sun, rain, and cold is to be solved, which gives rise to "subordinate" purposes. At the outset the purpose may have been quite general and simple; but as it becomes more determinate it becomes more complex (1343.14–15, c. 1902).

The task is complicated when the purpose is unknown, or not even a question of human purposes, as is generally the case with natural objects. (Peirce preferred to refer to "final" or "ideal" cause, because purpose, he said, is merely its conscious modification and thus its more familiar exemplar). The difficulty is not insuperable (1.204, c. 1902). One clue to the significance of a property in this respect is whether or not other important characteristics are revealed as distinctive. It is generally impossible to know the final cause of natural objects with any exactitude.

It would be a mistake to conclude that there are no final causes. That view, Peirce remarked, is on a par with the suggestion that ideas are found in facts, which are devoid of ideas. He saw both claims as wedded to the belief that purpose is the only final cause and that an idea must presuppose a brain. It is not the idea that is dependent on being possessed by a mind, but the mind that is controlled by the idea, for ideas are not "personal creations" or "personal property." By an idea Peirce did not mean "merely something which a person has had in mind, still less a psychical act of thinking"; but "a principle such as may be set before the mind in thought" (1344.11, n.d.). He admitted that an idea must be embodied if it is to have complete being. (Inherence in a mind "affords it opportunity.") Should it fall short of this it would still have potential being, or being *in futuro*, and consequently would not be the total nothingness that would characterize matter (or, indeed, mind) if no ideas controlled it. Without the final causation of law there would be no regularity, and without regularity matter could not even potentially exist. The final cause, then, determines the general character of the result, but not how the result is accomplished. It may come about in a variety of ways (1.211–18, c. 1902; 426.6–7, 1902).[12]

Peirce maintained, as an empirical fact accessible to all, that every idea is able to work out results to some extent. Hence, by stating that the idea governing a natural class determines the existence of the members of that class, he meant that the idea "confers upon them the power of working out results in this world" (1.220, c. 1902).

3. Methods of Attaining a Natural Classification

Peirce thought that the distinctive feature of final cause was that the present is influenced by the future, though not in the direct manner with which the past acts on the present. The laws of nature afford knowledge of the future, but are known only indirectly. Progress is made in faltering steps by means of experiment and thus infinitesimal advances are gained upon the truth (2.86, c. 1902). According to the theory of natural selection, nature operates in the same way and, according to Peirce, final causation is operative in evolution. Moreover, all laws are the results of evolution, for the only law that can grow by its own virtue is the tendency (which everything has) to take habits.[13] "Now since this same tendency is the one sole fundamental law of mind, it follows that the physical evolution works towards ends" (6.101, 1901).[14] Even though it is likely to be the most inaccessible guide, Peirce felt that a classification founded on the *history of evolution and genealogy of objects* was the most reliable approach to it. This is the first of the four ways to attain a natural classification that he cited.

Fortunately, classifying the sciences does not require insight into the secrets of evolutionary advances. Peirce claimed that there is a second way (similar to the approach used by Plato and Aristotle) in which the *purposes and governing ideas* that have brought the sciences into existence are identified (426.3–4, 1902).

The appropriate guide for any given classification system, Peirce maintained, will depend on which one is known. When neither of the above approaches are accessible, that is, when the creating purpose as well as the genesis of things are unknown, a third approach may be adopted. Logical analysis reveals that there is a relation, often numerical, between things and a system of abstract ideas. This is not to say that any numerical classification will do. Only the *universal categories* that are the ideas determining the possibility of things can produce a logical sequence that would be a guide to natural classification. Without a complete understanding of these categories, Peirce thought, it would be wise to leave them aside and so avoid the "high priori" method (1.223, c. 1902; 426.3–4, 1902; 1343.12–17, c. 1902).

Properly interpreted, each of these three approaches should lead to the same classification, but Peirce believed that the "cenopythagorean" categories[15] would emerge in due course, not merely as coincidental, but as "sole and supreme" (426.7, 1902).

A fourth consideration that might lead to a natural classification acts as a supplement to whichever of the above methods is appropriate. It should be accepted that it is frequently impossible to find a clear demarcation between classes, or that there may be a discrepancy of some sort. This will generally be the result of some *accidental occurrence* quite extraneous to the objects themselves, but necessitated for some convenient or economic reason (1.205, c. 1902; 426.4, 1902; 1343.13–14, c. 1902).

Even with a clear understanding of what distinguishes a natural classification, it is difficult to know which idea fulfils the requirements for a natural classification of the sciences. Examining a specific natural classification may clarify this.

The periodic classification pioneered by Mendeleev may have the requisite characteristics. Governing the scheme is the configuration of electrons in the atoms of the elements. The sequence is according to atomic number (the number of electrons in one atom) and the arrangement on the table is according to valency (the number of electrons in the outer shell). An electron configuration determines the existence of the members of a natural class; it designates the period in which the element is located as well as its position there. The elements in the vertical columns exhibit common characteristics and so form groups. Valency determines how the elements relate to each other. The table can thus demonstrate how other characters fall into line.

Perhaps because atomic theory was still in its infancy and the periodic table not fully worked out, Peirce thought that its relevant idea could not be identified, even though the natural classification had been determined.[16] Although Peirce recognized that imperfect regularity was to be expected in classificatory science, he thought that the irregularities that were becoming apparent with new information made atomic *weight* an inadequate governing idea. It took classification by atomic *number* to provide a scheme in which irregularities are tolerable.

Peirce insisted that the description of a natural class must not be determined by its abstract definition but by typical examples of it (1.224, c. 1902). He prescribed a procedure for every investigation: first ascertaining the purpose of the inquiry[17] and, after reviewing earlier attempts at classification, pursuing the method of the inductive sciences (cf. 427.1-2, c. 1902; 299.1, c. 1905). In the broad sense of testing hypotheses by appropriate observation this is experiential; trying one possibility after another (whenever there is some reasonable ground for optimism) until the right idea is identified and embodied in a classification system.

3. ALTERNATIVE SCHEMES

1. Survey of Earlier Attempts

Peirce's method included examination of previous attempts to classify the sciences, the most influential for him being that of Auguste Comte. Peirce adopted Comte's principle but nonetheless rejected his particular ordering. Comte placed astronomy ahead of physics, whereas Peirce considered it merely a historical accident that astronomy had provided the necessary stimulus to physics. He also found it curious that the two disciplines that Comte had pursued (namely, philosophy and geometry) were omitted from his plan, prompting Peirce to call this "a singular argument for his [Comte's] own doctrine that introspection, or self-observation is impossible" (1336.3-4, 10-11, [1892]).[18] Only after he had developed the ideas discussed in the foregoing section did Peirce add the further objection that Comte viewed the sciences as abstractions and so had produced an artificial classification (1334.7-10, 1905).

Various other philosophers (for example, Spencer, Fiske, and Wundt) placed philosophy below the special sciences. Peirce had no serious objection to this, provided that they clearly meant synthetic or cosmic philosophy, belonging to the sciences of review (1334.26, 1905). As noted in chapter 2, D.G. Brinton proposed a classification of "anthropology" that Peirce found unacceptable (1.264-7, c. 1902). Aggasiz proposed a mode of classificaton by final cause, but when zoologists tried to implement it, Peirce recounted, they found they needed to spell out the "idea of the creator" and to have preconceived notions of the various ways in which the idea was worked out (1.571-2, 1910).[19]

Although Peirce adopted Comte's principle early in his inquiry, there is no evidence to suggest that he completed these studies of previous efforts before producing some classifications of his own. Tracing Peirce's succession of classifications reveals the problems with which he wrestled as he developed a satisfactory scheme.

2. *Classification of [1866]*[20]

In the early Lowell lecture, Peirce rejected a classification scheme based solely on induction because it resulted in a natural classification and so excluded certain sciences. The "defect" was remedied by adopting a classification based on a logical procedure that incorporated hypothesis and deduction as well as induction. It yielded the following scheme:

Deductive Sciences

> Mathematics
> Law
> Political Economy

Inductive or Classificatory Sciences

> Natural History or Zoölogy
> Botany and Mineralogy
> Morphology
> Descriptive Astronomy
> Chemistry
> Logic
> Philosophy
> Physiognomy
> Physical Geography (a portion of)

Hypothetical or Causal Sciences

Order 1 (unity of science is unity of hypothesis)	Order 2 (unity is the unity of their object)
Gravitation	History
Mechanics	Geology
Acoustics	Physiology
Optics	

Heat
Electricity, etc.

(357.26-8, [1866])

Peirce felt that this was inchoate and needed a new division: the underlying assumption is that the classification of the sciences should be based on a classification of arguments.

3. Classification of 1878

The same assumption is found in a subsequent attempt; but here Peirce lauded the distinction between hypothesis and induction just because it is conducive to a natural classification.[21] Its important distinction from the earlier attempt is that both sciences and scientists are taken into consideration. The kinds of techniques employed are regarded as the major distinguishing factor, closely followed by the modes of reasoning. Peirce sketched the following scheme:

Classificatory Sciences (purely inductive)

Systematic Botany and Zoölogy
Mineralogy
Chemistry

Sciences of Theory

Astronomy
Pure Physics, etc.

Sciences of Hypothesis

Geology
Biology, etc.

(2.644, 1878)

4. Classification of 1889

The 1889 edition of the *Century Dictionary* is the source of what seems to be the next scheme. It is cited in a *Monist* article of 1896, which might suggest that Peirce did not consider his interim attempts an improvement.[22] On the other hand, Peirce's reference to the scheme in the "Regenerated Logic" involved only the classes that remained unchanged during that time; he may well have thought that the previously published classification would serve.[23] His interest was in countering the view that logic is founded on metaphysics and defending the view that it is founded on mathematics – a science much less open to dispute. Of course he also maintained that metaphysics must be founded on logic.

Philosophy is featured prominently and was Peirce's dominant interest in this scheme. Its governing idea was that employed by Auguste Comte in his classification:[24] to have the sciences arranged according to their abstractness – according to the level of generalization of their objects of investigation. Sciences at the top of the scale provide regulating principles for those below, while the more specialized sciences provide data and problems for those above. If the sciences can indeed be arranged according to this model, the relationships between them are assured. As Peirce argued, "if anything is true of a whole genus of objects, this truth may be adopted as a principle in studying every species of that genus. While whatever is true of a species will form a datum for the discovery of the wider truth which holds of the whole genus" (3.427, 1896 [=1889]).

Here is Peirce's 1889 scheme:

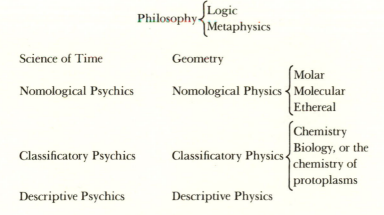

MATHEMATICS

Philosophy {Logic
Metaphysics

Science of Time	Geometry	
Nomological Psychics	Nomological Physics	{Molar, Molecular, Ethereal}
Classificatory Psychics	Classificatory Physics	{Chemistry, Biology, or the chemistry of protoplasms}
Descriptive Psychics	Descriptive Physics	

PRACTICAL SCIENCE

(3.427, 1896)

Mathematics is not a positive science at all and although philosophy is, it has no special objects. No further investigation is required for these two disciplines to occupy their positions. But this is not so for the subdivisions of philosophy. Because metaphysics turns to the generalization of physics for data in a way that logic does not, Peirce claimed that logic is the more abstract science. This argument left him vulnerable to the criticism that logic cannot possibly be classified as the third normative science (as it eventually is) since it is more abstract than any of the preceding divisions of philosophy (ethics, aesthetics, and phenomenology). Peirce overlooked the insights of the earlier schemes: sciences are not satisfactorily distinguished by their objects.

5. Classifications of 1892 and environs

An undated manuscript roughly similar to the above, attacked this difficulty on a different front. Noting the split of the special sciences into psychics and physics, Peirce thought that philosophy, as the science of things in general, might fall into similar divisions. Psychics, he had already suggested (without explanation) should precede physics (3.427, 1896). Metaphysics, as the "philosophy of all things," is said to be less abstract than logic, the "philosophy of learning all truth" (1336.5, [1892]). In addition to their agreement in placing the psychical sciences ahead of physics, these two classifications both include practical sciences.

Mathematics

Philosophy $\begin{cases} \text{Logic} \\ \text{Metaphysics} \end{cases}$

Nomological Psychics {General Psychics   Nomological Physics {General Physics

Classificatory Psychics $\begin{cases} \text{Anthropology} \\ \text{Linguistics} \\ \text{Mythology} \end{cases}$ Classificatory Physics $\begin{cases} \text{Chemistry} \\ \text{Biology} \end{cases}$

Practical Psychics $\begin{cases} \text{Political Economy} \\ \text{Ethics} \\ \text{Poetry, music} \\ \text{Games, etc.} \end{cases}$ Practical Physics $\begin{cases} \text{Engineering} \\ \text{Medicine} \end{cases}$

Descriptive Psychics $\begin{cases} \text{History} \\ \text{Biography} \\ \text{Theology, etc.} \end{cases}$ Descriptive Physics $\begin{cases} \text{Geology} \\ \text{Descriptive} \\ \text{astronomy} \\ \text{Physical} \\ \text{geography, etc.} \end{cases}$

(1336.2-3, [1892])

Here practical sciences and descriptive sciences are interchanged, although Peirce commented that the reverse might be more correct (1336.12, [1892]).. It is difficult to assess the date of this manuscript; it could be as late as 1897 or even 1898. A number of additional subdivisions are given, which are not in the 1889 scheme, and more are claimed to have been worked out. Ethics is one such that is subsumed under the practical sciences. Peirce acknowledged his indebtedness to Comte's principle but criticized his particular ordering of the sciences.

Comte's regulating principle is operative in Peirce's scheme dated February 1892, and the broad divisions following upon philosophy are not very different from Comte's own:

I. **Mathematics** { Pure / Applied

II. **Philosophy** { Logic / Metaphysics

III. **Nomology** { Psychology / General Physics, i.e. { Thermotics, Kinetic energy / attractions, positional energy

IV. **Chemistry** i.e. the science of kinds of matter except ether & protoplasm

V. **Physics of the ether** { Electricity / Optics

VI. **Biology**

VII. **Sociology** { Conduct { Ethics / Theology / Politics / Law / Etiquette } Communication { Art / Language

VIII. **Accounts of particular objects** { Cosmology { Astronomy / Geognosy { { Geography / Meteorology } Geology } Human History

(1347.[4], 13 Feb. 1892)

Ethics, it should be noted, is subsumed under sociology.

An undated manuscript, which presents a scheme differing only in minor details from the foregoing, undermines the previously established basis for placing logic ahead of metaphysics (assuming manuscript 1336 is prior, of course), by revising the order of the psychical and physical sciences. All sciences, Peirce argued, stem from the idea of growth. Physics gets its inception from ideas having to do with nutrition and psychics from those associated with reproduction. Just as lust after food begins earlier than lust after sex in any individual, so the evolution of physics is naturally prior to that of psychic sciences (1337.1–2, n.d.).

The fifth division (physics of the ether) drops out in two other undated manuscripts, one entitled "The Categories; studied with reference to the English Language." In it, ordering in accordance with the degree of generality is retained, but ordering with reference to logical dependence is also recommended (1335.1–2, n.d.). The other manuscript is more detailed and features an innovation that adumbrates a procedure later to be developed more fully (at 1135, [c. 1897]). Subdivisions are given the number of their division together with another number registering their place within it.

1 **Mathematics**
   11 Finite Groups
   12 Number
   13 Continua
2 **Philosophy**
   21 Logic
   22 Metaphysics
      221 Entitative being – quality
      222 Existence – brute insistance
      223 Orderly being – cosmical being
3 **Nomology**
   31 Physics
      311 Time
      312 Space
      313 Mechanics
      314 Gravitation
      315 Heat and elasticity
      316 Light and electricity
   32 Psychology
      321 Feeling
      322 Sense and will
      323 Habit
4 **Chemistry**
5 **Biology**
6 **Organology**

61 Physiology
62 Sociology
7 **Individual history**
71 Material things
711 Astronomy
712 Geognosy
72 Living beings
721 Men
722 Gods and spirits, etc.

(1346.[1–6], [1892])

6. Classifications of 1895

In a manuscript containing a classification that fills out the scheme of 1889, Peirce credited Comte with the principle ordering the sciences according to the abstractness of objects of observation (15.14; see also 15.5-6, [c. 1895]). Logic is considered the more abstract branch of philosophy since it observes "real facts about mental products" while metaphysics studies real objects. The science of time is regarded as psychical (cf. 1346.[1–3], [1892]) and the science of space as physical. Psychics and physics are said to be quite distinct and to have little influence on one another.

1. **Mathematics**
2. **Philosophy**
   2a Logic
   2b Metaphysics

| 3. **Science of time** (psychical) | & | **Science of space** (physical) |
| PSYCHICS | | PHYSICS |

4. **Nomological**

4a General laws of psychics (i.e. Association, etc.)	4a General laws of physics (i.e. Dynamics)
4b Laws of psychics in single individuals (i.e. Psychology)	4b Law of interaction of single particles at sensible distances (i.e. molar physics or the Science of Gravitation)
4c Laws of [psychics] which appear in the study of great agregations (i.e. Nomological Sociology)	4c Laws of interaction of particles studied in the statistical effects of great aggregations (i.e. Molecular Physics or Electrics & Thermics)

4d Inquiry into Spirits (scientific inquiry into whether there are such)

4d Inquiry into physics of Ether or Optics and Electrics

5. Classificatory

5a Description of different kinds of minds and their works (science of character or anthropology, but of lower animals as well)

5a Description of different kinds of matter (i.e. chemistry including crystalline forms)

5b Ethnological psychics (language, manners & customs, governments, etc. of different societies)

5b Sciences of protoplasm (i.e. biology, embracing botany & zoology)

6. Descriptive

6a General History

6a Astronomy

6b Biography including Genealogy

6b Meteorology including Ocean currents & Tides

6c History of intellectual products
   History of Science
   History of Useful Arts
   History of Art & Literature

6c Geology including the Atmosphere & Ocean but not the rapid movements of fluids

6d Geography including the fauna & flora of the Sea

7. Practical Sciences

"which with a few doubtful exceptions, such as Religion . . . and Ethics, equally depend upon the principles of Psychics and of Physics."

(15.14–17 [c. 1895])

Although there is no indication in this manuscript, it is evidently at this time that Peirce first defined science in terms of the activity of the scientist (17.5, [c. 1895]). In a classification scheme from yet another manuscript, dated [c. 1895] (13.2) the Coleridge definition (as an organized body of truth) is rejected in favour of a "group of possible researches after truth." It holds no mention of Comte or of abstract objects, although the relationship of principle-dependence persists. Thus philosophy generally, and logic in particular, are said to be based on mathematics. Logic, Peirce said, has been mathematical from the start. Metaphysics must derive its principles from logic, while the special sciences appeal to metaphysics. The precedence of the psychical sciences over the physical sciences was inserted as an afterthought, and there is no overt recognition that logic's priority over metaphysics no longer rested simply on the abstractness of its objects of observation. Peirce continued to wrestle with this problem.

1. Mathematics
   i. System of two values
   ii. Systems of discrete quantity having more than two values each
   iii. Systems of continuous quantity

2. Philosophy
   i. Logic – philosophy of thought
   ii. Metaphysics – philosophy of being

3. Special observational sciences

Psychical	**Physical**
Nomological	
i. Universal laws of mind, of time, association, fatigue, etc.	i. Universal laws of matter – physical geometry, real properties of space, dynamics, etc.
Classificatory	
ii. Manifestations of mind, such as language, business, worship	ii. Chemistry – crystalline forms Biology – protoplasms
Descriptive	
iii. History, political geography, law, theology, etc.	iii. Astronomy, geography, geology, etc.

4. Arts
(depend on both psychical and physical knowledge; some almost entirely psychical such as rhetoric, ethics, religion, jurisprudence; others almost entirely physical – glassblowing, horology; still others require both – painting, music, etc.)

(13.1–4, [c. 1895])

Although ethics is here classified among the arts, a curious comment suggests that Peirce may have been toying with the idea of subsuming ethics under philosophy. He tells us that "[t]he inquiry whether any given branch of science, such as ethics, belongs to philosophy or to any other division of science is an application of logic" (13.2 [c. 1895]).

7. *Classifications of 1896*

In an undated manuscript (1345, which I estimate as 1896) Peirce renewed his attempt to substantiate the precedence of logic over metaphysics. He tried yet another alternative, fitting the divisions common to both psychical and physical sciences on to philosophy. The three different schemes proposed are remarkable in several ways that indicate that this manuscript fits between the last [c. 1895] manuscript (13) and one dated [c. 1897] (1135), which continues some of the explorations found here. Two things indicate that it succeeds manuscript 13: a suggestion that science is to be defined in terms of the activity of the scientist rather than the objects of investigation; and the inclusion of ethics among the divisions of philosophy. Other innovations are found in its hint that the three categories might be relevant in classifying the sciences, and its recognition of phenomenology, characterized as the "study of *phenomena* with the purpose of identifying their Forms with those which mathematics has studied" (1345.[7], [1896]). Phenomenology would eventually form the first division of philosophy; here it encompasses both philosophy and the special sciences.

Introducing ethics as a subdivision of philosophy indicates that this manuscript succeeded the 1896 *Monist* article, for it is unlikely that Peirce would have published a scheme that did not reflect the alternatives being tested in those divisions since they are important to the *Monist* discussion. Still, that these attempts were very much in question might have 'determined Peirce to revert to the previously published list rather than his 1892 scheme for example; it is, after all, the outline of the first [c. 1895] scheme. If this is the case, it would have been more consistent for Peirce to acknowledge some dissatisfaction. Still other considerations support the suggestion that the manuscript is from 1896 or 1897. On Peirce's own account the connection between logic and ethics was taken up in 1896 or 1897.[25] In a letter to William James, dated 25 November 1902, Peirce remarked that the Cambridge Lectures of 1898 were delivered at a time when he "had not really got to the bottom of it or seen the unity of the whole thing" (8.255, 1902). It was 1901 before he recognized that ethics had any significance for logic, still, the first inkling of this novel element in philosophy must have occurred to him about 1896–7.

This date is worth establishing because several elements were fermenting in Peirce's philosophy at the same time, all relevant to his classification scheme and hence to an understanding of what he meant by logic. Significantly, 1897 is the date of Peirce's discovery (via the logic of relatives, which revealed several kinds of possibility) that real possibility is an essential consequence of pragmatism.[26] Real possibility had critical implications for the relation between logic and ethics and might well have precipitated the inclusion of ethics among the divisions of philosophy. Again, science had only just been defined in terms of the activities of the scientists.

The first of the three schemes presented in the undated manuscript is headed "Encyclopaedia." Peirce designed it to serve the compiler, knowing that it might not suffice for the user. He also announced that all of the sciences were to be divided into *"three* parts,"[27] evidently utilizing his universal categories.

I. **Mathematics**
   1. Geometry
   2. Arithmetic
   3. Theory of finite groups
II. **Empirics or Phenomenology**
   1. Philosophy (study of universal characters of things)
      A. Logic
      B. Metaphysics
   2. Nomology (characters of classes of phenomena)
      A. Psychics
         a. Psychology proper
         b. Anthropology
      B. Physics
         a. Energetics
         b. Chemistry
         c. Biology
   3. Episcopy (description of individual things)
      A. Ergography (the account of the works of intelligent beings)
      B. Empsychography (the account of those beings themselves)
      C. Cosmography (the account of inanimate nature)
III. **Pragmatics**
   1. Ethics (general principles of conduct)
      A. Private
      B. Public
   2. Arts
      A. Private arts

      a. Teleological
      b. of bodily well-being
   B. Sociology or public arts
 3. Policy
   A. Policy toward men
   B. Religion or policy toward superior beings
   C. Policy toward lower animals

(1345.[4–9], [1896])

Peirce dropped applied mathematics because he thought it of little moment to philosophy; the psychical sciences again preceded physics; ethics, as the first division of pragmatics, was concerned with principles; and philosophy is one division that did not get the triadic treatment.

In the second system, the physical and psychical sciences are reversed once more. The sciences were divided according to their degree of abstractness, not that of the objects under investigation. In a colourful and not altogether lucid statement Peirce wrote that they are divided "according to the distance at which they paint nature" into:

1. Mathematics
2. Philosophy
   1. The philosophy of thought: The *Philosophical Trivium*
   2. The philosophy of action: *Ethics*, etc.
   3. The philosophy of being: *Metaphysics*
3. Nomology: general physics and general psychics
4. Natural History, the descriptions of classes
5. Sciences descriptive of individual objects, geography, astronomy, ordinary history, etc.

(1345.[1]¹, [1896])

The "philosophical trivium" supplies a triadic division for philosophy and brings ethics into its province. It should be noted, however, that ethics succeeds logic.

The third scheme is prefaced with comments on the special training and special instruments required to assemble facts in the different sciences, making it desirable to classify them in accordance with the peculiar observations made by each. Peirce recognized that economic factors may give rise to modifications of such a scheme; for example, instead of photographers or spectroscopists engaging in astronomy, astronomers might take up spectroscopy and photography because their

observatories are the more expensive outfit. But the degree of specialization in the objects of observation is more telling and lasting than
the kinds of instruments used, which is reinforced by Comte's view,
that the more specialized sciences must await the findings of the more
general.

I. **Mathematics**
II. **Philosophy**
    A. Logic
    B. Metaphysics
III. **Positive Sciences**
    A. Nomology – Science of Laws
       General Physics
       General Psychology
    B. Systematic Science – Classifications and systems of things
    C. Descriptive Science – individual objects
       Astronomy
       Geography
       History, etc.

(1345.3–4 [fragment], [1896])

Ethics has been dropped without explanation; and both departments
of the special sciences are separated into three inclusive divisions.

8. *Classifications of 1897*

The transition matures in a manuscript entitled "A Classification of
Ideas and Words" in which the categories afford the guiding pattern.
Nonetheless, the overall system remains that of degrees of generality.

    The numbering system of manuscript 1346 is combined with the
categorial ordering latent in manuscript 1345 to produce a fresh
approach.[28] It involves allocating a series of numbers: the first indicates
the most abstract division; the next indicates the widest subdivision,
and so on – rather like numbering the rooms in a building by allocating
a new hundred for each successive floor. In Peirce's scheme, however,
three is the dominant (though not the limiting) number. Zeros are
inserted on occasion to indicate that items are not simply specializations
of those immediately above. As a "provisional method" for working
out a system, it has the advantage that rearrangements may be made
without upsetting the entire scheme (1135.1, [c. 1897]).

The categories were initially derived from the logical analysis of propositions although "they reappear in Protean metamorphoses throughout all thought" (1135.1, [c. 1897]). Peirce described them in a guise that is at least partly phenomenological, even though phenomenology had yet to be assigned its position within philosophy. As it is the business of logic to discover the principles of a classification system, there can be no objection to his use of a logically derived procedure.[29]

Virtually every activity is given a place in this system, and many disciplines are finely anatomized. The first major division in the classification of ideas concerns qualities of feeling and sensible qualities; the second, ideas of common life and experience; and the third, shown here in its broader divisions, concerns the sciences:

3. **SCIENCE**
    31. **Mathematics**, studies hypotheses and their consequences, ignoring facts
        311. Discrete systems
        312. Continuous systems
    32. **Positive Theoretical Science**
        321. Philosophy, science based on familiar experience
            3211. Logic, the philosophy of thought
            3212. Metaphysics, the philosophy of being
            3213. Ethics, the philosophy of purpose (Partly an art. But let it have place here. Esthetics and psychol.)
        322. Catholonomology, the exact science of laws common to all matter and mind
            3221. Chronomology, the exact science of time
            3222. Physical geometry, inquiry into the exactitude of the postulates of geometry
            3223. Etionomology, exact science of laws of causation underlying physics and psychics
        323. Special Sciences
            3231. Psychics
                32311. Nomological psychics
                32312. Classificatory psychics
                32313. Descriptive psychics
            3232. Physics
                32321. Nomological physics
                32322. Classificatory physics
                32323. Descriptive physics

33. **The Arts**

(1135, [c. 1897])

An alternative scheme in this manuscript classifies the divisions of the special sciences as "3231. Physics" "3232. Psychics," indicating that Peirce had not arrived at a definite opinion as to their ordering. His tentative placement of ethics in philosophy is noteworthy for succeeding not only logic but metaphysics as well. It may be inferred from this alteration that while Peirce was willing to call ethics a division of philosophy, he had not recognized any connection between logic and ethics. Specifically, he did not admit any dependence of logic on ethics – indeed, the converse is the case.

Publication in the *Century Dictionary* may have rendered a system perversely perennial, for the 1889 scheme reappears in the same manuscript – replete with *its* threefold enumeration.[30]

SCIENCE 3			
Mathematics 31			
Philosophy 32			
Logic 321			
Metaphysics 322			
Time 3221		Space 3222	
Special Science 33			
Psychics 331		Physics 332	
Nomological 3311		Nomological 3321	
Classificatory 3312		Classificatory 3322	
Descriptive 3313		Descriptive 3323	
Art or Applied Science 34			

(1135, [c. 1897])

9. *Classification of 1898*

The probationary inclusion of ethics under philosophy (at 1135, [c. 1897]) became an explicit rejection in 1898 on the grounds that it concerned the purpose of life, which is entirely psychical. It was therefore assigned to the special sciences and not to philosophy, which is concerned with the universal characters of experience. Peirce deemed that its search for a definition of the correct aim of life marked it as one of the theories of the arts (437.20, 1898). This reference to the classification of the sciences occurs in an omitted portion of "Detached

Ideas on Vitally Important Topics," published as the last item in the section on normative sciences in the *Collected Papers* (1.616–77, 1898).[31] It is evident that Peirce had not yet made any attempt to bring logic and ethics together under the umbrella of the normative sciences.

The occasion of this document is significant. Peirce had hoped to give a series of lectures on logic, but was asked not to discuss anything so abstract, and rather speak on something of more vital importance. Peirce, of course, regarded logic as of the utmost importance and he reluctantly (perhaps facetiously) addressed a subject more directly related to the concerns of daily life. The topic of that first lecture seems to have more affinity with casuistry than with the discipline that he eventually allocated to the mid-division of the normative sciences.

In this document, Peirce's primary reason for including ethics in philosophy, even tentatively, seems to have been to complete a triad. The more he examined the sciences, the more triads emerged. Perhaps it was inevitable that at some point he should approach the classification architectonically and seek them out where none had yet shown themselves, although he thought that he ought not to be persuaded by his predilection for the three categories. If the sciences were constrained to an architectonic, the classification would be unable to vindicate the categories. When Peirce set them aside, as he did in the following scheme, he was confronted with the problem of explaining why logic should precede metaphysics when neither had objects more abstract than the other.

MATHEMATICS
PHILOSOPHY
Logic
Metaphysics
SPECIAL SCIENCES

Psychics	Physics
Nomological	Nomological
Psychology	Dynamics
Classificatory	Classificatory
Linguistics	Chemistry
Anthropology	
Descriptive	Descriptive
History	Geology
	Astronomy

Geography

Hydrology

Meteorology

APPLIED SCIENCES OR ARTS

(Includes Ethics, Religion, Law, Cooking, etc.)

(437.18-22, 1898)

In this manuscript psychics preceded physics, and its connection with the divisions of philosophy was revived and explained: logic was more closely associated with psychics and metaphysics was more closely associated with physics. But without an explanation as to why the psychical sciences should precede the physical sciences this is unsatisfactory. Peirce's only independent explanation for the arrangement of the special sciences justified the reverse ordering.

This problem is taken up in Peirce's Logic Notebook. The first of two entries on the topic was occasioned by an enforced delay in his history of science, when Peirce filled in time by writing some notes for a logical treatise.

In an entry in French dated October 1898, Peirce maintained that all knowledge has two elements: one element is determined by the object; the other is a mode of thought. He thought this distinction prominent in the special sciences: physics is characterized as the science of things as such, and psychics as the science of things governed by the intellect. In mathematics the distinction is negligible, but some rudiments of an analogous division are found in philosophy. Logic, then, inquires into the theory of knowledge without distinguishing objects, while metaphysics inquires into the general character of objects. (This, of course, is not to say that logic confines itself to psychics, and metaphysics to physics.)

Psychology, Peirce continued, might discover that certain reasonings give rise to a feeling of gratification.[32] But, this does not concern the logician, whose interest in a piece of reasoning is to inquire into the relation of the truth value of the premises to the truth value of the conclusion. Peirce still claimed that a certain affinity holds between logic and the psychical sciences as well as between metaphysics and physics, for when we ask "in what, on the final analysis, does this truth consist?" we are confronted with the hypothesis that sufficient research would ultimately yield unanimous and steadfast agreement. Truth, then, consists in this ideal and supposed opinion, so that the logicians' aim is, of a psychological nature. Peirce noted one difference:

all things psychic are inherently imperfect, while truth is an ideal-
ization and, as such, is quite perfect. Metaphysics, meanwhile, inquires
into the characters of things apart from their significance to a mind
but with reference to physics (339.151r–6r, Oct. 1898).

Peirce has now made out a case for parallel divisions in philosophy
and in the special sciences; it remains to justify the precedence of
one division over the other. Here, Peirce argued for the primacy of
logic. For this argument to succeed, the ordering of the sciences in
terms of abstractness of objects (untenable if science is the activity
of a social group) must be abandoned. Without explanation, Peirce
shifted to ordering in terms of the generality of principles.

Only mathematics escapes a dependency on logic, for to Peirce at
this point, it provided the sole basis for logic. Without logic, errors
might remain undetected in metaphysics, which does not have the
constant check of experience that will sooner or later rectify errors
in the special sciences. Moreover, analysis suggests that genuine
metaphysical conceptions are a particular application of logical conceptions. Hence logic, invaluable to the special sciences, is utterly
indispensable to a sound metaphysics. But because a sound metaphysics
has been lacking, there was little evidence to support Peirce's contention
that physics is founded on metaphysics, and he thought that this dearth
impeded progress in physics. The dependence of psychology on logic
is more direct and Peirce believed that it too could profit by recognition
of this fact (339.156r–9r, Oct. 1898). The precedence of psychology
over physics he justified by the precedence of logic over metaphysics.

In the same year Peirce asserted that the connection between metaphysics and psychical sciences was the more direct one: the psychical
sciences were seriously impaired by the lamentable state of metaphysics
on which they depend for principles; while the effect on physics was
"almost as injurious" (6.2, 1898).

A subsequent entry in the Logic Notebook, entitled "The Place of
Logic among the Sciences," dated 7 April 1899, contains an argument
justifying the precedence of psychology over physics. (Unhappily, the
entry breaks off before any parallel is drawn with the divisions of
philosophy.) Two fundamental instincts, which assure the preservation
of a species, also provide the impetus for science forming two major
divisions: the instinct needed for food provides knowledge of things,
which leads to physics; while the instinct needed for reproduction
provides knowledge of persons, from which psychology is derived.
Psychology, Peirce wrote, is the more abstract science: its development

is earlier, and it lends more ideas to physics than it borrows (339.168r, April 1899). The psychical sciences would therefore be expected to precede physics in the classification of the sciences.

In the manuscript containing the 1898 classification Peirce inveighed against Plato for attributing the end and worth of philosophy to its moral influence. That mistake is countered, he suggested, by the equal but opposite error of calling the acquaintance with pure ideas the greatest good. It is instructive to note that this was not because the combination of these two erroneous propositions somehow provides the *summum bonum* of virtuous conduct for individuals (and especially for philosophers), but because they "express a correct view of the ultimate end of philosophy and of science in general" (437.26, 1898). The *summum bonum* of the scientist when he is engaged in scientific activity (and only then) is made more explicit in the 1899 review of Paul Leicester Ford's *The Many-Sided Franklin*. It is "to learn the ways of Nature and the reasonableness of things, and to be absorbed as a particle of the rolling wave of reasonableness."[33]

At this juncture in Peirce's thinking, ethics concerned the life-demands of day-to-day existence. Instinct surpassed reason as an adjudicator in most cases. He described the ultimate aim of an individual as "some definite duty that clearly lies before him and is well within his power as the special task of his life" (437.26, 1898). This may be construed in a variety of ways, but Peirce left no doubt as to its limitations. Vital importance, he said, is a quite inferior kind of importance (1.647, 1898).

The description of moral life and the analysis of ethical conceptions comprise two divisions of a "prolegomena to ethics" which Peirce found quite harmless (1429.1, 1900). The logical analysis of ethical conceptions might indeed be what he had in mind for the third division of philosophy in his classification. Such a discipline would appropriately follow logic. It was in order to improve upon Frank Thilly's attempt to classify endeavours of this sort that Peirce offered his own classification of *Rational Theories of the True End of Action* (1429.5[2], 1900).[34] In a fragment of this manuscript he wrote that there is no reason for the ultimate end to be limited to the individual or to society (1429 [fragment], 1900). In the published review of Thilly's *Introduction to Ethics* he favoured "a methodical ideal – like order, or rationality – neither specifically psychical nor physical, which somehow has a power of developing itself in thoughts and things generally." That which promotes or inhibits this development would qualify as good or evil respectively. This is item c of III. 3 in Peirce's classification of *Rational Theories*, and no subtlety of intellect is needed to identify the pragmatic method. The culmination of thought to which the community of investigators direct their inquiries is not itself a thought, but is the "perfect fruit of thought" and so is just "such a conception [which] refuses to be limited to any particular matter of realization."[35]

The aim of scientific activity is critical for pragmaticism.[36] With Peirce's growing recognition that the aim of any activity must involve ethics, the relation between ethics and logic became determinate.

At the close of 1900 Peirce continued to regard all motives for ethics as ulterior. Still, he did admit one non-ulterior motive: the reasonable itself is the motive ascribed to the sciences (8.140, Jan. 1901). This is item iii of C. III in a classification of aims roughly similar to that of *Rational Theories* (8.136 note 3, c. 1900). Peirce's reluctance to admit the aims of scientific reasoning as a purely ethical question found expression in another manuscript of about 1901 (7.201, c. 1901). In April 1901, however, Peirce acknowledged the importance of the question of aims and increased the divisions of philosophy to three: ethics, logic, and metaphysics. Although he stipulated that ethics can only have its beginnings in philosophy (872.21, April 1901), its advantages to logic are reiterated (872.28, 1901). By October 1901 Peirce forcefully confirmed his view that logic is founded on ethics (8.158, 24 Oct. 1901).

Another significant element of Peirce's philosophy then incorporated was "self-control." Its role in inference was probably recognized at an early date, and it featured prominently in Peirce's investigations into habit. His work with Joseph Jastrow, which resulted in the article "On Small Differences of Sensation," showed that even a sensory stimulus too tiny to impinge on consciousness could affect judgment (7.21–35, 1884), suggesting that unconscious inference could contribute to knowledge. Peirce reiterated the theory in his review of William James's *Principles of Psychology* (8.55–71, 1891). He maintained that unconscious inference is inference that is not recognized as such (8.67, 1891). In 1893 Peirce noted that unconscious mental processes cannot be controlled and hence cannot be criticized (7.444, 1893). The role of self-control as the essential link between ethics and logic remained hidden while he held ethics to be a practical discipline. Day-to-day problems should be pursued without self-criticism, Peirce asserted, although "actions which carry out our grander purposes" require critical reflection (7.448-9, 1893).

In 1896 Peirce admitted that self-control was a presupposition of morality. Yet at that time Peirce had a limited notion of ethics, which recognized only ulterior motives, and he thus found morality to be at odds with the experimental method. He surmised that morality would require adopting a method only if it led to the desired conclusion. People who think that reasoning presupposes self-control, in the same way as morality is thought to, convince themselves that their conduct is determined by reason; yet it is only after they discover the conclusion to which a specific method has led that they will accept the method. The scientific method would, of course, require unqualified acceptance (1.57, [c. 1898]; see also 6.3, 1898) involving a non-ulterior motive.

In the October 1898 French entry of the Logic Notebook, which leaves no room for ethics in the divisions of philosophy, Peirce maintained that if a mental process cannot be criticized or controlled it is not a subject for logic. A story of a dog and cyclist provided his illustration of uncontrolled reasoning. Peirce reported that once, while leading a horse along a country road, he was passed by a dog presumably in pursuit of its cyclist-owner. On reaching a fork in the road, he saw the dog pondering which route to take. Since the two roads reunited a short distance and the dog did not pass again, Peirce supposed it must have remained debating the issue for the ensuing hour and he surmised that the dog was waiting to see which road would be preferred by other cyclists. Such a limited consciousness, he concluded, would not permit controlled thought (339.161r-2r, Oct. 1898). The story was recalled two years later to urge the same point regarding the necessity of self-control, this time crediting the dog with reasoning.[36]

The notion of self-control led Peirce to the conclusion that logic is a branch of ethics. He reaffirmed that no mental process can assume the status of reasoning unless it is amenable to self-control; only then can it be regarded as worthy of praise or blame. But, he argued, if logic involves restraint on natural tendencies it is no different in that respect from other activities subject to moral control. Hence logic must be a branch of ethics (692.3-4, 1901).[37]

There are now two reasons for founding logic on ethics and both lend coherence to pragmaticism. Yet in spite of hints in manuscript 872, there appears to be no scheme recording the three divisions of philosophy. Another dangling thread has yet to be woven into the tapestry.

10. *Classifications between 1898 and 1902*

Not since the first scheme of manuscript 1345 [1896]; has any mention been made of phenomenology. It then comprised a major division that included both philosophy and the special sciences, as well as something called "episcopy."

The next encounter with phenomenology occurred under the name of "high philosophy" (7.526, n.d. [my estimate is c. 1899-1900]). High philosophy is more general than logic and metaphysics, but does not include those two disciplines:

> Mathematics
> High Philosophy
> Philosophy
> > Logic (philosophy of thought)
> > Metaphysics (philosophy of being)

Apparently high philosophy and phenomenology are one and the same. It makes no special observations: experience in high philosophy, "is the entire cognitive result of living, and illusion is, for its purposes, just as much experience as is real perception" (7.527, n.d.). Moreover, its business is to discover the fundamental elements of experience – here called the "kainopythagorean categories." The editor of this volume of the *Collected Papers* identifies these as the psychological versions of Peirce's categories, but since their discovery requires no special observations, they cannot be the product of investigations in the science of psychology. Nevertheless they are almost certainly the same categories that Peirce had formerly (misleadingly or mistakenly) referred to as "psychological categories." In three instances where they are regarded as psychological (1.364, c. 1890; 6.18 and .32, 1891; 1.303, c. 1894), phenomenology has not been brought into focus.

One other scheme has a place just prior to the 1902 scheme of the "Minute Logic" published in the *Collected Papers* (1.238-83). The divisions of philosophy first assume what will be their final shape:[38]

THEORETICAL SCIENCES
Sciences of Research

Mathematics
   Dichotomy
      Of Collections
          Enumberable
          Denumeral
          First Abnumerable
          Higher
      Of Continua
          Linear
          Superficial
          Solid
          Higher
Positive Science
   Cenoscopy
      The Categories
      Normative Science
         Esthetics
         Ethics
         Logic
      Metaphysics
   Idioscopy
      Psychognosy
         Psychology
         Ethnology
         History
      Physiognosy
         Physics
         Chemistry
         Biology
         Cosmography
Sciences of Review
   . . .

PRACTICAL SCIENCES
Sciences of Gratification
   . . .

Sciences of Utility
   . . .

(1340.[3–6], n.d.)

Under the special science (idioscopy), the psychical sciences are given first place, but this fragmentary manuscript is devoid of comment. The introduction of "Positive Science" precludes the divisions of the sciences of research from falling into three groups.

11. Classification of the "Minute Logic," c. 1902

With sundry threads woven more or less into place, Peirce felt sufficiently satisfied with the divisions of philosophy to draw up an elaborate classification which would form the opening chapter of a logical treatise. The problem that harassed him throughout is now vestigial and seems to have instigated at least one (strange) innovation. This was not his settled scheme, but the classification of the "Minute Logic" appears to have been viewed by him then as the culmination of his inductive investigations.

Virtually all of Peirce's inquiries into the characterization of a natural classification occurred around 1902, and in this document he was concerned to show that he had formulated a natural scheme. Thereafter, he continued to claim that his classification was a natural one, although he evidently felt no obligation to expound upon the topic at length. Peirce noted that the history of science was not a rewarding source. The more concrete sciences generally existed long before the theoretical sciences, which frequently emerged accidentally, so that nothing could be gained by referral to their historical beginnings. Comte professed to follow such a procedure in developing his scheme (427.85-7, c. 1902 omitted from 1.257-8; see chapter 2, section 1), which is possibly why he was not credited with furnishing the dominant idea governing Peirce's own classification then.[39] Peirce declared that a "science is defined by its problem; and its problem is clearly formulated on the basis of abstracter science" (1.227, c. 1902) and the ordering then proceeds according to the degree of abstractness. This arranges them in a linear series but, as Peirce pointed out in a draft version of the "Minute Logic," the lines of demarcation between the various sciences are yet to be drawn (426.2-3, 1902). How these divisions are to be characterized hinges on the investigations of the preceding sections of this chapter: the nature of science and the nature of classification.

Addressing this problem, Peirce stated: "in every intelligent natural classification any branch may be subdivided according to the different special determinations of the general ruling idea; and the resulting divisions of the branch are to be called its *classes*. Each class is distinguished by performing its part of the general purpose of the branch, or by carrying out the general idea in a special way" (1344.15, n.d.).

In the classification scheme of the "Minute Logic," Peirce affirmed that his classification preceded any allocation of divisions (1.238, c. 1902). This is apparent. But although the categories are evident in some divisions, they have not emerged everywhere in the scheme, and Peirce chose to omit all mention of them in this context.[40] Rough definitions of the several divisions follow, with the prefix "sub" denoting a modification of a division. Science is first divided into:

Branches – distinguished by fundamental purpose;
Classes – distinguished by mode of observation;
Orders – which form a hierarchy in accordance with their contribution of principles to other sciences;[41]
Families – which apply to the activities that qualify as sciences (1.238, c. 1902).[42]

THE SCIENCES

Branch 1. **Theoretical Sciences**
  Subbranch 1. Sciences of Discovery
    Class 1. Mathematics
        Order 1. Finite collections
        Order 2. Infinite collections
        Order 3. Continua
    Class 2. Philosophy (Cenoscopy)
      Subclass 1. Epistemy (Universal Philosophy)
      Order 1. Phenomenology
      Order 2. Normative Sciences
        Family 1. Esthetics
        Family 2. Ethics
        Family 3. Logic
      Order 3. Metaphysics
      Subclass 2. Theorics (Special Philosophy)
      Order 1.
        Family 1.
          Genus 1. Chronotheory (Science of Time)
          Genus 2. Topotheory (Geometry)
    Class 3. Special Sciences (Idioscopy)
      Subclass 1. Physiognosy

Order 1. Nomological Physics
  Suborder 1. Mechanics
  Suborder 2. Physics of Special Forces
Order 2. Classificatory Physics (Chemology)
  Suborder 1. Lifeless Chemology
  Suborder 2. Biology
Order 3. Descriptive Physics
  Suborder 1. Astronomy
  Suborder 2. Geognosy
Subclass 2. Psychognosy
  Order 1. Nomological Psychognosy
    Suborder 1. General Psychology
    Suborder 2. Special Psychology
  Order 2. Classificatory Psychognosy
    Suborder 1. Mental performances and products
    Suborder 2. Incarnations, or ensoulments of mind
  Order 3. Descriptive Psychognosy
    Suborder 1. Metrology
    Suborder 2. History
Subbranch 2, [Sciences of Review]
Branch 2. **Practical Science**

(1.238–83, c. 1902)[43]

This "Detailed Classification of the Sciences" is taken from chapter 2 of the "Minute Logic," which is manuscript 427, dated 20 February 1902. Manuscript 426 is an earlier draft dated 13 February 1902. Although Peirce insisted that all of the divisions could be "subdivided according to the different special determinations of the general ruling idea" (1344.15, n.d.), in subsequent classifications divisions accord with his categories but are not altogether coincidental with these.[44]

In the preceding chapter of the "Minute Logic" (2.1–118, manuscript 425), logic is characterized as normative (2.7 and 2.46, c. 1902), showing that it is a theoretical science and not an art or a practical science. This chapter also contains the previously described thirteen different methods of establishing logical truths that have contributed to the unsatisfactory state of logic. (Elsewhere [4.243, c. 1902] these are referred to as thirteen different views concerning the true aim of science, and investigation of aims is characterized as an ethical difficulty.) A subsequent passage of the same chapter states that normative sciences include another discipline, ethics, which is indispensable to logic and to the logician (2.82, c. 1902).[45] The moral integrity of the logician, however, has no direct connection with logic's dependence on ethics for principles; the application of ethics to logicians is the business of a practical science. While this may have had advantages for the theoretical science Peirce was discussing, it is not germane to its subject matter. No mention of aesthetics occurs in this chapter.

The families of the normative sciences are listed as logic, ethics, and aesthetics in the "Detailed Classification" (1.281, c. 1902). Yet in alternative pages of the same manuscript, Peirce asserted that the families, in decreasing order of abstraction, were: 1. Aesthetics, 2. Ethics, 3. Logic. This ordering was usually employed in later manuscripts, although at this juncture Peirce expressed doubt about the existence of a philosophy of aesthetics. His intention was to present a classification of the sciences as they are generally acknowledged to be, and thus he felt bound to include aesthetics (427.98^2 and $.122^2$, c. 1902).

In chapter 2, section 2 of the "Minute Logic," in which the relation between the normative sciences is discussed, the order is again reversed. Peirce declared that he did not have a clear idea of the relation of aesthetics to logic (2.197, c. 1902); nevertheless, he proceeded to present his initial views (2.199, c. 1902) as well as some more developed ideas of a theoretical ethics (2.198, c. 1902). Chapter 4 of the "Minute Logic" gives a fuller account (see 1.575–84, c. 1902); but Peirce again hesitated over the inclusion of aesthetics (1.575, c. 1902), and suggested that the relevant philosophical question for ethics makes it a pre-normative science (1.577, c. 1902).

It was the hedonist argument, Peirce wrote, that prevented him from accepting the dependence of logic on ethics, and that led him to the conclusion that ethics was an art. Later, when he steeped himself in the writings of the great ethical philosophers, he gradually became convinced of the importance of ethics to logic. As long as he omitted aesthetics from the philosophical sciences, he thought that he need not admit to hedonism. If he did include aesthetics, he would find himself defending the view that logic, as a special determination of ethics, must ultimately rest on aesthetic feeling;[46] but Peirce had impugned the attempts of others to found logic on psychology. The hedonist reasoning suggests that good and bad morals are, in the final analysis, a question of pleasure: what does not give satisfaction is not desired; and what is satisfaction but a feeling of pleasure? Therefore nothing but pleasure can be desired. It was not until 1903 that he declared the argument to be based on a "fundamental misconception" (5.111, 1903).

The other important element, the significance of self-control in the relation between ethics and logic, appears to have receded from view.[47]

It seems clear that in the "Minute Logic" the normative sciences are at a developmental stage. Hence, it would be unwise to accept any of these statements as representative of Peirce's final view.

The relation of the physical sciences to the psychical sciences and the relations among the divisions of philosophy may now be examined. The physical sciences are said to involve efficient causation and the psychical sciences final causation. Both physical and psychical are dependent on philosophy, with physics more dependent on metaphysics, and the psychical sciences more dependent on logic. As Peirce remarked, final causation is logical causation (1.249-50, c. 1902). Nothing was reported to follow from these affinities on this occasion.[48] The influences of the two sub-classes of the special sciences on one another was deemed insignificant, and not such as to involve principle-dependence. Peirce then believed that parallel subdivisions, neither having precedence over the other, were the most appropriate arrangement (1.252-5, c. 1902). Deciding which discipline should precede in the divisions of philosophy is complicated by the introduction of the normative sciences: with three divisions there could no longer be a strict parallel to the special sciences. Moreover, one of the tasks of philosophy is to examine causality and to determine its fundamental basis. This would be difficult if philosophy were to have two main divisions reflecting efficient and final cause. Nevertheless, Peirce believed that it did have two subclasses: one concerned with universal experience – this is Necessary Philosophy; and the other, called Theorics, concerned with special experience (1.273-9, c. 1902).

12. Classification of 1902 following the "Minute Logic"

One other scheme intervened between the "Minute Logic' and the one that would survive virtually unchanged in the remainder of Peirce's writings. The manuscript closes with the remark that a more detailed account of the theoretical sciences plus a minute classification of the practical sciences and a complete discussion have been ready for publication for some time. This can only refer to the classification of the "Minute Logic" (1339.13, [before 17 April 1902]).[49]

This classification is characterized by "three well-marked orders." Physics is placed ahead of psychics in light of the dependence of psychology on neurology, linguistics on acoustics, and archaeology on dynamics. But Peirce warned that any such dependence must be minimal and that parallel divisions would have been more appropriate. With this plan he turned once again to the alternative analogue – applying the nomological, classificatory, and descriptive divisions of the special sciences to philosophy.

SCIENCE

I. Theoretical
  I. Discovery
    1. Mathematics
    2. Philosophy
      i. Phenomenology (Nomological?)
      ii. Normative (Classificatory?)
        i. Esthetics
        ii. Ethics
        iii. Logic
      iii. Metaphysics (Descriptive?)
    3. Idioscopy

Physics	Psychics
1. Nomological	1. Nomological
i. Molar	Psychology
ii. Molecular	
iii. Etherial	
2. Classificatory	2. Classificatory (Ethnology)
i. Crystallography	i. Linguistics (Signs, etc.)
ii. Chemistry	ii. Psychical productions of races (Lore, Religion, etc.)
iii. Biology	iii. Arts (Pottery, Agriculture, etc.)
i. Anatomy	
ii. Physiology	
3. Descriptive	3. Descriptive
i. Geognosy	i. Archaeology
ii. Astronomy	ii. History (Biography)
	iii. Statistics

  II. Abstracts, Digests, etc.
II. Practical

(1339.5-12, [1902]

Although William James's California lecture of 1898 provided Peirce with an additional incentive to present a clear statement of pragmaticism, it is an exaggeration to say, as Murphey has, that his philosophy underwent a "sudden, almost spectacular, reformulation" largely in reaction to that lecture.[50]

Prior to James's lecture, Peirce had made several attempts to provide a classification of the sciences. The normative sciences emerged as a culmination of his investigations. Contrary to general belief, Peirce was not a novice in the field of ethics, but he provided ammunition to his detractors by confessing that his mastery of ethics was not comparable to his mastery of logic. Yet few, if any, of his contemporaries could have claimed such competency. He had studied ethics as a student under Dr Walker, and not without interest, although it was 1883 before he began to read in a "seriously thorough way" (5.111, 1903; s80.11, n.d.). This indicates that he had given at least ten years of study to the subject. Its role in his work and his reviews of ethical texts both published and unpublished (which include references to the works of many other moral philosophers) confirm this.

The introduction of phenomenology to Peirce's scheme was likewise not the haphazard effort that Murphey thought it to be (see note 29 above). When Peirce had recognized that the differentiating idea between mathematics, philosophy, and the special sciences was the mode of observation, he must have realized that the categories he had previously referred to as psychological were not strictly so-called, since their discovery required nothing more than careful attention to whatever anybody could observe (see 8.297, 1904).[51]

By the end of 1902, Peirce declared that the ordering of the normative sciences was in accordance with his categories (8.256, 25 Nov. 1902). He had come to realize that basing ethics, in the final analysis, on aesthetics was not to espouse hedonism. Among phenomena of pleasure and pain, he decided pain is the "control." The phenomenon of pain occurs in "certain states of mind, especially among states of mind in which Feeling has a large share, which we have an impulse to get rid of" (5.112, 1903). Because the impulse is strongest when feeling is preponderant, Peirce hypothesized that there is a feeling common to all such phenomena. He doubted that there could be a single quality of feeling common to all pain and another common to all pleasure, but maintained that even if there were, that feeling (those two feelings) would not be the principal element. The phenomenon of pain he called a "Struggle to give a state of mind its *quietus*" and the phenomenon of pleasure a "peculiar mode of consciousness allied to the consciousness of *making a generalization*, in which not Feeling, but rather Cognition is the principal constituent" (5.113, 1903).[52] This may be imperceptible in baser pleasures, but Peirce was concerned with aesthetic pleasure which he thought to be a kind of "intellectual sympathy" arising out of the recognition of the relations of qualities of feeling integrated into a unified whole. The relation of aesthetics to Peirce's categories will be taken up in the next chapter. Here it need only be noted that Peirce had come to believe that founding ethics on aesthetics did not commit him to hedonism.

In 1903 the parallel between logic and ethics, with regard to self-control, was also elaborated and the investigation of aims was ascribed to aesthetics (1.606, 1903; 5.108–11, 1903; 5.130, 1903; 451.5–8, 1903). Peirce had dispensed with the difficulty of determining the hierarchy of philosophy's divisions arising from the fact that all alike have experience available to everyone as their object of observation. The objects being classified were deemed sciences and considered to be the activities of groups of living persons; and ordering was accomplished in accordance with principle-dependence.[53] Hence by 1903 most of Peirce's problems with his scheme had been resolved.

4. THE PERENNIAL VERSION

The lectures on pragmatism delivered at Cambridge and the Lowell lectures of 1903 provided opportunities for Peirce to augment and consolidate his views. As a supplement to the Lowell lectures, a pamphlet entitled *A Syllabus of Certain Topics of Logic*[54] was distributed. This contained a classification scheme which, in its major divisions, was substantially that with which Peirce prefaced virtually all of his subsequent writings in logic. He thought it "sufficiently satisfactory" as late as 1911 (675.9–12). The scheme is reproduced as "An Outline Classification of the Sciences" (1.180–202, 1903), and Peirce acknowledged his debt to Comte's principle, noting that most of the divisions are "trichotomic." Even without pursuing the third method for obtaining a *natural* classification directly, the categories emerged as coincident with the various special determinations of the central idea governing the divisions.

1. Principle-Dependence

The best classification, according to Peirce, "is a diagram usefully expressive of significant interrelations of the objects classified" (328.20, c. 1905). He stated that any two sciences could be related in three different ways.

The first, the relationship of *material content* of the sciences, may itself occur in one of three ways: by Inclusion, when one is part of the other; by Intersection, when one part is held in common while each has another part entirely distinct from the other; and by Exclusion, when no part is held in common. Of greater moment is a second relationship of *dynamical action* wherein one science animates the other by a "compulsive quality of action," for example, by requiring it to answer a problem. This generally is how the practical sciences influence the theoretical sciences. The third relationship, of *rational government*, is more uniform and more significant for a natural classification.[55] Here, one science gives the other principles (7.52 [1906]; 601(s).9, [1906]).

Peirce had no illusions that any one scheme could capture all of the relations of dependence between two sciences. Understood as the concrete activity of social groups, he found sciences "just as real as the collection of cells that constitutes a man's body. Not so well compacted dynamically, they are perhaps more so rationally" (601.33, [1906]). He therefore proposed to limit his scheme to a representation of the third type of relationship, that of principle-dependence.

The second relation of dynamical activity was represented incidentally, since the science that receives principles may reciprocate by supplying problems; but while there can be only one originating source of principles, any one of a number of sciences might provide a problem that activates the same solution by the science supplying principles. Hence there is no strict order in the representation of the dynamical relation.

It would be mere coincidence for a regularity of the first mode of relation (that of material content) to be represented in the classification. Peirce considered this mode of relationship to be of minimal significance.[56]

The ordering of the sciences into a hierarchy is considered a logically admirable procedure. It is always necessary to assume the truth of something before the truth of another thing can be demonstrated. But if the assumed truth is then proved by appeal to the truth of the second, the whole strucure crumbles. The vicious circle is avoided by arranging the sciences in a vertical series, such that of any two sciences, one appeals to the other for principles and not the converse; or both receive principles from some third science which does not itself depend on either. Accordingly the sciences may be arranged into a "ladder" or set of ladders.

For a number of reasons Peirce felt that two sciences could not be mutually dependent with regard to principles. If two scientists were constantly consulting one another, they would soon become so intimately involved with each other's investigations that they would not actually be pursuing different sciences. One science could not depend on the other, in this case, because of the close association of the scientists. The reason here depends on language – on what is to be *called* the same or a different science (693a.32-6, [1904]). A second and substantive reason for Peirce's claim has to do with the nature of scientific studies. Each science, he thought, has the propensity to increase the number of objects within its scope, not through any arbitrary selection, but by the very "nature of things": whenever a false path is recognized by its dearth of significant results, it is promptly deserted. The justification for a science to employ a principle from another science without submitting it to examination is simply that the latter science numbers among its objects those objects investigated by the former science. (The objects a science studies are "those of which its conclusions hold good"; 693a.58-60, [1904].) Hence, a science could lend a principle to another only by including all of the objects of the broader science within its province. Of course it is possible that, following a revolution of the sciences, the dependence relation might undergo a reversal such that the science that had once supplied principles to another is placed in the position of receiving a principle from that very science instead. But this can only occur if the initial dependence is renounced. Peirce cited the example of dynamics, which was once used to explain the action of special forces including electricity; when electricity came to explain mass, the earlier explanation of electricity in terms of dynamics had to be abandoned (693a.48-62, 693b.346-68, [1904]).

Peirce did not deny that reciprocal consultation may occur with peripheral problems. A medical researcher might consult a plastics expert for a suitable container to hold a vaccine for lung cancer, and the plastics researcher might take the opportunity to consult the medical researcher about the effects of inhaling plastics' fumes. Neither problem has to do with the essential subject of their respective inquiries (693a.36-40, [1904]). Nor did he deny that in the infancy of science, individuals may cull principles from several other sciences simply by drawing upon their own studies in other disciplines (693a.40-6, [1904]).

Peirce also recognized the importance of the mutual dependence in which testimony in one science may reinforce testimony from another. No "vicious circle of reasoning" is involved, because such testimony has value only if the two sciences are logically independent of one another (693a.48, [1904]). When they are logically dependent, the testimonies of the two sciences have no firm foundation but "like two lying witnesses in court, sustain each other's credit" (1334.33, 1905).

Since a researcher into positive fact is bound to assume that certain principles are already established by a logically independent investigation, it must be assumed (provisionally) that there is a science antecedent to all the rest (426.1-2, 1902). Peirce maintained that, with the single exception of mathematics, every science employs without question a principle discovered by some other science. The latter science may call upon the narrower one for data, problems, suggestions, and fields of application.

Providing new facts is the most common sort of help given to one science by another. These are treated as direct observations by the receiving science and melded with a host of other facts to provide the basis for a generalization. When this is the case, the supplier of fact must be the narrower science. As noted above, any science furnishing data is just one of the contributors to the generalization. Hence, it is unlikely to be indispensable to the generalizing science (although it might be necessary for a particular advance in the specific circumstances). There can be no unique ordering in terms of data-dependence. Once the generalization is completed, the receiving science can provide the principles with which to interpret the observed fact (693b.374-6, [1904]). In practice, a particular problem cannot generally be attacked until some previous problem is more or less solved; and any solution virtually clears the way for the answer to another quite definite problem (601.10[1], [1906]).

In one manuscript, the foregoing principle is given the Greek name *batêris* (a mounting ladder) (1338.5, [c. 1905-6]). This captures the idea that the "classification of sciences is a ladder-like scheme where each rung is itself a ladder of rungs, so that the whole is more like a succession of waves each of which carries other waves, and so on, until we should come to single investigations" (328.20, c. 1905). The principle is to be applied to co-ordinate groups as well as to individual sciences, and also to those having divisions with close internal relations (673.45, c. 1911). A stereoscopic diagram is needed to convey Peirce's three-dimensional scheme.

2. Firsts, Seconds, and Thirds

A number of interpreters have understood Peirce to be less than confident about his three universal categories on the grounds that he frequently referred to his investigations into a second order of categories. Indeed, Peirce professed to have expended considerable effort in their pursuit without developing anything that would satisfy him (for example, at 1.525, 1903; 1.284, 1905; 8.213, c. 1905).[57] Yet it is a mistake to think that this second series (and Peirce did not rule out still other series) was ever intended to supplant his univesal categories.

Phenomenology, or phaneroscopy, is the science that investigates and describes the phaneron, by which Peirce meant the collective total of all that is ever present to the mind in any sense whatever, irrespective of whether or not there is any corresponding reality. An examination of the indecomposable elements of the phaneron (that is, those which through direct inspection seem to be irreducible and also those which logical analysis shows to be irreducible [cf. 908.5, n.d.]) led Peirce to conclude that there are at least two quite different, though not unrelated, orders of categories (1.288, [c. 1906]).

First, there are the *particular* categories. These are sometimes referred to as "material" categories, or as categories "consisting of phases of evolution" (5.38, 1903), and register qualitative distinctions between the various elements of thought (1338.26, [c. 1905–6]). They "form a series, or set of series, only one of each series being present, or at least predominant, in any one phenomenon" (5.43, 1903). They permit classification of things in accord with their matter; for example, wooden things, plastic things, leather things, etc. (8.213, c. 1905). The categories of Hegel's *Encyclopaedia* belong to this order. Peirce was quite sure that they were wrong. Even while he remained dissatisfied with his own efforts, he believed them an improvement on Hegel's (5.38, 1903; 1.284, 1905; cf. L463, July 1905).

Second, there are the *universal* categories represented by Hegel's three grades of thinking (Peirce was careful to deny any direct influence from that quarter [5.38, 1903]). All of the universal categories are evinced in every phenomenon, although one might predominate in one aspect of a phenomenon. This series permits classification of the structure of the elements in thought and consciousness: their "differences of quantitative complexity" (1338.26, [c. 1905–6]), which Peirce believed most important for almost all intents and purposes (8.213, c. 1905; 5.469, c. 1907; 908.5, n.d.). For purposes of natural classification, distinctions of form take precedence over distinctions of matter. Who, Peirce asked, would consider linking alcohol to methyl ether or separating alcohol from alcoholates? And who would catalogue Raphael's paintings by their dominant tinge instead of by the nature of their composition? A decisive reason for the superiority of formal distinctions in any natural and rational classification, Peirce claimed, is "that Form is something that the mind can assimilate and comprehend, while Matter is always foreign to it, a recognizable but incomprehensible something." The whole purpose of natural classification is to render phenomena comprehensible (499(s).[20–1], [1907]).

The universal categories that emerge from Peirce's investigations in phenomenology, which he found no reason to doubt (1338.26, [c.1905–6]), are the ideas of firstness, secondness, and thirdness. He once made the immodest claim that the triad ($\curlywedge$) is "an emblem of fertility in comparison with which the holy phallus of religion's youth is a poor stick indeed" (4.310, c. 1902). Professor Max Fisch demonstrated that,

ideally, Peirce thought, the categories of the longer list should stand in some determinable relation to those of the shorter list. He tried various ways of generating the longer out of the shorter . . .

In the end, Peirce concluded that the longer list was incompletable. It was not derivable from the shorter in any *a priori* fashion. One had to wait on experience and on the progress of the sciences ... The best we could hope for was that as new categories were added to the long list, or took the place of old ones, they would yield to analysis in terms of the short list.[58]

The three categories are found in every department of thought and it seems likely that Peirce first encountered them in his logical studies. Even so, their phenomenological description is rationally prior (as will be seen in the next chapter). The elements are not to be found already separated in experience; hence the *a priori* investigation into the indecomposable elements anticipated in the phaneron is antecedent to phenomenological studies (1.294–9, c. 1905).[59] Through logical demonstration Peirce showed that three indecomposable elements may be expected in the phaneron, and that no fourth is possible. This is vindicated by the phaneron itself.[60]

Firstness. The idea of firstness is whatever is before the mind that is such as it is positively and regardless of anything else. Feeling that possesses a positive character yet is devoid of all relation and therefore lacking all vividness (for vividness involves excitation) is not really feeling any more but simply a sense of quality (8.267, 1903). Contemplating something in such a way as to focus attention on the whole, while completely ignoring the parts results in an approximation. It is close enough to see that, for the instant, there is nothing in the consciousness but a quality of feeling (908.16, n.d.); but it is not possible to experience pure uncontaminated firstness.

A quality of feeling is not an abstraction, because abstraction involves something being true of some other thing. Neither is it individual, for individuality involves contrast. Its firstness lies solely in the *"quantitative* form of self-sufficiency" (1338.31-2, [c. 1905-6]). A first could be simultaneously complete and simple only if it is indefinite as to generality. "It is vague in the sense of being unanalysed, and as being unidentifiable is indefinite in logical form." Furthermore, "its essential characters beyond its logical form, that is, its logically material characters, are, positively, that it has or rather is, a certain positive character absolutely peculiar to itself, and negatively that it is devoid of existence" (339.251r, 1905; see also 284.Add 10, c. 1905). It is the "embryo of being" (478.31, 1903).

Secondness. Secondness is whateever is, such as it is, second to some first regardless of any sort of third or medium, and in particular regardless of any law (5.66, 1903). Genuine secondness can be found in the phenomenon; it is an experience (not a quality, nor a conception, which are firsts and thirds). Our conception of it, which is a general (as all concepts are), might mislead us into overlooking "the *here*ness and *now*ness which is its essence" (8.266, 1903).

The idea of secondness is at its most characteristic in the idea of opposition or of struggle. "Effort is a phenomenon which only arises when one feeling abuts upon another in time, and which then always arises" (908.19, n.d.). It is clearly evinced in the shock of reaction between ego and non-ego. Through "contentment" and "habituation" we contrive to insulate ourselves against the edges of brute fact (908.19, n.d.) that rudely assert themselves when one expects a certain thing and another eventuates. In that moment, Peirce maintained, a double consciousness is experienced – the ego, which is the anticipated idea incisively terminated, and the non-ego, which is the startling appearance of the unlooked-for happening (5.53, 1903). The logical form of secondness is definiteness, individuality; its logical matter is existence

(284. Add 10, c. 1905; 339.252r, 1905).

Thirdness. The idea of thirdness is whatever is "such as it is by virtue
of being Third, or Medium, between a Second and its First" (307.1,
1903). The phaneron is observed to be intelligible: it is subject to
law, which means that it can be represented (8.268, 1903). Predictions
can be based on these laws to which "actual events still in the womb
of the future will conform to a marked extent, if not perfectly" (478.33,
1903). "Representation" was Peirce's earliest characterization of thirdness (1.555, 1867), but he decided that this did not convey sufficient
generality, and revised it to "mediation" (4.3, 1898; 1.530, 1903).
Thirdness, he said, predominates in the phenomenon whenever mediation is dominant; still it "reaches its fullness in Representation" (5.104,
1903).

The logical form of thirdness is "generality" (that is, distributive
generality); its logical material character is rationality (284.Add 10,
c. 1905; 339.252r, 1905).

Consider the relation between the three categories in their logically
material characters: for firstness it is positive possibility; for secondness,
it is existence. A quality is related to matter accidentally. The very
relation of inherence imparts existence, but the quality itself does not
change; it still is positive possibility even when it is not embodied.
If, however, matter is devoid of qualities, it ceases to exist even as
a possibility. It is constituted by its relation to qualities so that, if
it is left without any qualities, a second is nothing at all. That which
determines the second is a third. The logically material character of
a third is rationality. Consider law, for example: law never can be
embodied except by determining a habit. Thus, habit as determining
agent is a third, but as determined, it is a second. The more thoroughly
genuine third, Peirce suggested, is representation (1.536, 1903).

While the ideas of secondness and thirdness are themselves basic
ideas, they are complex. Thus pure secondness cannot be subdivided
because the very idea of subdivision involves thirdness, albeit a thirdness
that can be thought of as a complex of secondness (307.5, 1903).

These references to genuine thirdness and pure secondness indicate
that we must sometimes encounter the categories in forms that are
not genuine and may not be pure. The less than genuine versions
of the categories are divisible into degenerate forms. On one occasion,
Peirce wrote that "degenerate" means "merely formal." There is no
degeneracy in firsts, for the idea in its perception is basic. Degeneracy

does occur in seconds. It is to be found in purely dyadic relations, which remain intact even when the correlate is destroyed (for example, similarity). Peirce also claimed that,

in perception there is a sense of reaction without striving, which we think of as belonging to the outward thing. It is, as we may say, a *degenerate* form of Secondness. The idea of Secondness seems here to be unnecessarily imported into the phenomenon, which might have been regarded as a mere dream, or rather as the quality of our being, without being materially different, except in the absence of the element of Secondness.[61]   (478.29, 1903)

Although these seconds are degenerate, they are nevertheless pure. Evidently there are impure seconds also, which have the distinctive character of being "imputed" and are constituted by the representation of the relate and correlate. In the idea of the bad, the *opposition* between good and bad is constituted by *its* relation to some conditional purpose (1338.34-5, [c. 1905-6]).

The third category has two degenerate forms because it involves the ideas of both firstness and secondness. Therefore, thirdness has degrees of degeneracy. A representamen, for example, has "symbol" as its genuine form. "Index" is its first degenerate form, and "icon" its second. The first degeneracy again divides into a relatively degenerate form and a more genuine form, and this more genuine form can also be characterized in that way, so that there may be an unlimited number of relatively degenerate forms of thirdness (307.9-10, 1903).

Peirce thought that investigation into degenerate forms might be a way to generate the series of particular categories from his universal categories (see 1.528, 1903). When he abandoned that project, his pursuit of the degenerate forms of categories was more or less limited to the efforts in 1903.[62] The degenerate forms do not appear to be involved in the application of the categories to the classification of the sciences. Instead, the universal categories are used as an instrument of analysis on each level of the scheme.

Peirce chose to call his categories "firstness," "secondness," and "thirdness" partly in order to dissociate them from any rigid pre-conceptions which might attach to alternatives. He did not permit them to be amorphous or vague, but he deliberately allowed them considerable flexibility. Thus they can serve as excellent analytical tools without themselves being distorted and without requiring that the subjects under investigation emerge from the analytical process sub-jugated by the architectonic. Hence their application on different levels of the classification scheme should not be expected always to occur in precisely the same way.[63]

3. *Analysis of Divisions in the Perennial Classification*

The role of the categories as the differentiating device is reserved until the classification of the sciences in order of principle-dependence approaches completion. The divisions that emerge should coincide with the categories.[64] It remains to analyse those divisions by means of the categories.

Science is understood in terms of the activities of those who pursue it. At this broad level it can be related to other pursuits. Peirce thought people might fit into one of three groups. First: those who seek enjoyment; these are the most numerous. Second: those who lead lives of action and who aim at achieving results; included are the makers of civilization, the builders of industry, and the wielders of political power. Third: those whose lives are directed to developing ideas and truth, the scientists.

A classification of the sciences is not concerned with the first two groups: the whole scientific enterprise falls within the third category. Science, regarded as the activity of those in search of truth, falls into the category of mind. If this is ignored, the allocation of the theoretical sciences to the first of the three divisions in the classification would be incomprehensible in terms of the categories (although appropriate in terms of principle-dependence).

The determination of each division requires that the division as a whole (in this case "science") be analysed in the light of the differentiating idea. Accordingly, *Science* divides into three grand divisions, each distinguished by its different *motives*. Indeed, Peirce felt that the term "science" underwent slight shifts in meaning when applied to each, although not so drastically as to affect the definition of science. Concerning firstness, for example, it might be asked, what motive could animate a science in itself without reference to anything else? Which aspect of the categories will be involved in each special determination is not always obvious and different analysts might arrive at different conclusions (which is another reason for allowing the divisions to emerge). Considerable familiarity with the categories and with their application is needed if they are to be employed successfully. Peirce himself experimented with various approaches and the outline here is culled from his more perspicuous efforts.[65] The ultimate appeal must be to those for whom the classification was intended – the scientists themselves.

The group of sciences usually called theoretical falls into the first division; but Peirce thought that the term "theoretical" was not exclusively the prerogative of those activities and that it did not capture the essence of the differentiating idea (the motive that animates these sciences). Thus it was not his preferred term.

3.1 *Heuretic sciences* (that is, the sciences of discovery) seek only to learn new truth; they are concerned with discovery for its own sake.

3.2 *Sciences of review* seek to make the works of discovery comprehensible in the broadest sense. They order the results of the heuretic sciences, submit them to critical examination from a wider perspective than is possible for the specialist to perform, and then supplement them where necessary. The results are digested into handbooks, such as Auguste Comte's *Cours de philosophie positive* (1830–42) and Herbert Spencer's *A System of Synthetic Philosophy* (1862–93).

3.3 *Practical sciences* seek to satisfy human desires. They take the systematic statement of discovery, supplement it where necessary, and make it available for application to areas in which it is expected to have some utility.

Sciences that appear on the heuretic level are likely to recur in the sciences of review, and again in the practical sciences. They will be closely related in many ways; were the hierarchy to be a single linear series, these important connections would be obscured. Peirce thought in diagrams and his constructs were often three-dimensional. A three-dimensional lattice arrangement can depict the direct connection between sciences on one level and corresponding sciences on another level.

Indeed, the sciences of review did not receive much attention from Peirce. Although he formulated a very considerable classification of the practical sciences, he regarded it as one of his failures (602.16, 1903–8).[66]

An examination of the heuretic sciences requires an idea that will govern the special determinations of the sciences that seek to discover truth for its own sake. Every discovery has its origin in an observation, and it is just that character, Peirce contended, that explains the particular breakdown of the sciences into specialties, although those divisions are often obliterated and the sciences are now more clearly distinguished by social group. Still, observation is the foundation on which the sciences are erected. The differentiating idea at this level appears to be concerned with the relation of the sciences to phenomena, either in terms of kinds of phenomena observed, or in terms of the kinds of assertions made as a result of reasoning on those observations; that is, the sort of orientation each heuretic science takes towards truth.

3.1.1 *Mathematics*. Observations in this case are of the creations of the imagination (usually diagrams and most likely mental diagrams in the form of lines or an array of letters) that instance hypotheses. Mathematics studies what may be true and what cannot be true of those hypotheses without inquiring whether or not the described circumstances occur. As a result it makes no appeal to any asserted premises at all, and is therefore able to occupy the foundation rung of the ladder of the sciences with impunity.

3.1.2 *Philosophy* or Cenoscopy. Observations are of the phenomena common to all. Utilizing the familiar experience acknowledged by everyone, it inquires into positive universal truth using principles discoverd in mathematics.

3.1.3 *Special sciences* or Idioscopy. Observations are of previously unknown phenomena. By means of special training, special instruments, or special circumstances, they inquire into individual experiential events and infer truth that is usually only plausible but nonetheless worth testing. In doing so they assume the truth of propositions that are outside the scope of their own investigations. Thus they appeal to mathematics and philosophy for principles, in particular to methodeutic (the branch of logic that investigates the general principles on which scientific studies should be founded), and to metaphysics (that which examines the foundations of the special sciences).

The differentiating idea of mathematics concerns the general nature of the hypotheses it creates. First they are distinguished by the multitude of elements hypothesized, then they are subdivided in terms of the relations between those elements.

3.1.1.1 *Finite collections* concern the simplest conceivable system distinguishing only two values.

3.1.1.1.1 *Pure deductive logic*.

3.1.1.1.2 *General theory of finite collections*.

3.1.1.2 *Infinite collections* concern discrete systems.

3.1.1.2.1 *Arithmetic* inquires into collections having the least infinite multitude.

3.1.1.2.2 *Calculus* inquires into collections having higher multitude.

3.1.1.3 *Continua* (topical geometry).

The divisions of philosophy examine the phenomenon of ordinary experience in terms of its mode of being.

3.1.2.1 *Phenomenology* studies the phaneron as it immediately presents itself. It provides the observational groundwork for the rest of philosophy, endeavouring to determine the universal indecomposable elements in whatever appears before the mind.

3.1.2.2 *Normative sciences* study the phenomenon insofar as we can act upon it and it upon us, and endeavour to determine the conditions required for an object to be fine irrespective of whether any specific objects possess that fineness.

3.1.2.3 *Metaphysics*, using principles of logic, inquires into what is real (and not figment) as far as can be ascertained from ordinary experience.

Normative sciences divide according to different objects criticized and subdivide according to the different aspects of investigation.[67]

3.1.2.2.1 *Aesthetics* inquires into the deliberate formation of habits of feeling that are consistent with the aesthetic ideal.

3.1.2.2.1.1 Physiology investigates the *summum bonum* and discovers the physiology of phenomena in their firstness.

3.1.2.2.1.2 Classification inquires into the conditions of conformity to the ideal.

3.1.2.2.1.3 Methodology studies the principles governing the production of the aesthetic object.

3.1.2.2.2 *Ethics* inquires into the theory of the formation of habits of action that are consistent with the deliberately adopted aim.

3.1.2.2.2.1 Physiology discovers the ethical ideal and the physiology of conduct.

3.1.2.2.2.2 Classification inquires into the conditions of conformity to the ethical ideal.

3.1.2.2.2.3 Methodology inquires into the principles for actualizing the ethical ideal.

3.1.2.2.3 *Logic* studies the deliberate formation of habits of thought that are consistent with the logical end.

3.1.2.2.3.1 Speculative grammar inquires into the logical end and analyses reasonings into ultimate components.

3.1.2.2.3.2 Critic studies the kinds and degrees of trust that are appropriate to different ways of reasoning.

3.1.2.2.3.3 Methodeutic studies ways of pursuing different kinds of inquiry.

Metaphysics is differentiated by the various relations in the different kinds of phenomena discovered to be real.

3.1.2.3.1 *Ontology* discovers the kinds of phenomena in the psychophysical universe and endeavours to determine their nature.

3.1.2.3.2 *Physical metaphysics* studies the dynamical relations in the essential descriptions of phenomena in the universe.

3.1.2.3.3 *Religious metaphysics* investigates the universe in relation to human spiritual interests.

The special sciences are initially split into two parallel wings depending on the nature of the objects investigated. On the one hand there are the physical sciences, which study the material nature of phenomena, and on the other hand there are the psychical sciences, which study the mind of humans and other intelligences, together with its products. Peirce seems to have concluded that the psychical sciences do depend on the physical sciences but that this dependence does not involve an appeal for principles. Accordingly, these sciences range side by side and are differentiated by their mode of investigation, by different kinds of training, and by the opportunities required.

3.1.3.1 *Nomological* division studies the ubiquitous phenomena of the psychical and physical universes, ascertains their general laws, and measures the quantities involved.

3.1.3.2 *Classificatory* division describes and classifies the various kinds among the objects studied and endeavours to explain them by means of the general laws.

3.1.3.3 *Descriptive* and *explanatory* division studies and minutely describes individual objects and events which it subsequently seeks to explain using the findings of the nomological and classificatory sciences.[68]

4. The Perennial Classification – Summary

3 **SCIENCE**
  3.1 **HEURETIC SCIENCES**
     3.1.1 **Mathematics**

3.1.1.1 Finite collections

    3.1.1.1.1 Pure deductive logic

    3.1.1.1.2 General theory of finite collections

3.1.1.2 Infinite collections

    3.1.1.2.1 Arithmetic

    3.1.1.2.2 Calculus

3.1.1.3 Continua

3.1.2 Philosophy

3.1.2.1 Phenomenology

3.1.2.2 Normative sciences

    3.1.2.2.1 Esthetics

        3.1.2.2.1.1 Physiology

        3.1.2.2.1.2 Classification

        3.1.2.2.1.3 Methodology

    3.1.2.2.2 Ethics

        3.1.2.2.2.1 Physiology

        3.1.2.2.2.2 Classification

        3.1.2.2.2.3 Methodology

    3.1.2.2.3 Logic

        3.1.2.2.3.1 Speculative grammar

        3.1.2.2.3.2 Critic

        3.1.2.2.3.3 Methodeutic

3.1.2.3 Metaphysics

    3.1.2.3.1 Ontology

    3.1.2.3.2 Physical metaphysics

    3.1.2.3.3 Religious metaphysics

3.1.3 Special sciences

	Physics	Psychics
3.1.3.1	Nomological sciences	Nomological sciences
3.1.3.2	Classificatory sciences	Classificatory sciences
3.1.3.3	Explanatory sciences	Explanatory sciences

3.2 SCIENCES OF REVIEW

3.3 PRACTICAL SCIENCES

The diagrams included here attempt to capture Peirce's stereoscopic image. He left a verbal description only, but it is known that he thought in three-dimensional diagrams and that he participated in the early development of lattices. Figures 3 and 4 reflect the ladder conception, while figure 5 expands on the wave suggestion conveyed in Peirce's statement that the "classification of sciences is a ladder-like scheme where each rung is itself a ladder of rungs, so that the whole is more like a succession of waves each of which carries other waves, and so on, until we should come to single investigations" (328.20, c. 1905).

In one of his youthful explorations into a classification of sciences, Peirce provided a snail-like diagram to illustrate the idea that "knowledge proceeds in irregular spirals from one of the three divisions to another" (357.28, 1866). Although he did not refer to this image in his later discussions, it suggests figure 6, which may be the most perspicuous of these illustrations.

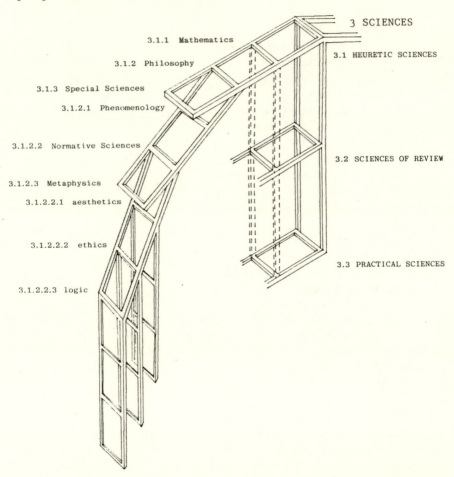

Figure 3 shows ladders attached to the normative sciences rung, which in turn is attached to the philosophy rung on the heuretic sciences ladder.

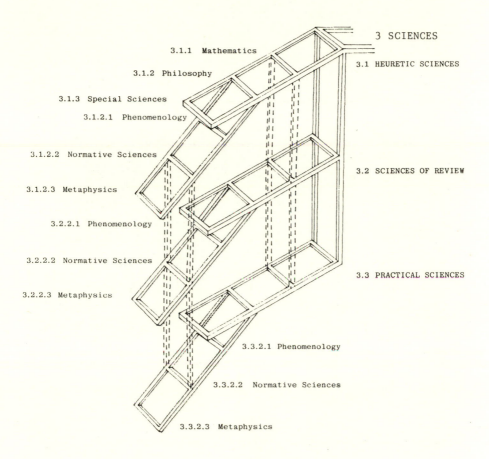

3 SCIENCES

3.1 HEURETIC SCIENCES

3.1.1 Mathematics

3.1.2 Philosophy

3.1.3 Special Sciences

3.1.2.1 Phenomenology

3.1.2.2 Normative Sciences

3.2 SCIENCES OF REVIEW

3.1.2.3 Metaphysics

3.2.2.1 Phenomenology

3.2.2.2 Normative Sciences

3.3 PRACTICAL SCIENCES

3.2.2.3 Metaphysics

3.3.2.1 Phenomenology

3.3.2.2 Normative Sciences

3.3.2.3 Metaphysics

Figure 4 shows the relations between corresponding divisions of philosophy on the three major levels of the sciences. It is difficult to convey the three-dimensional array on a two-dimensional surface, and an attempt at actual construction might be like trying to realize an Escher drawing.

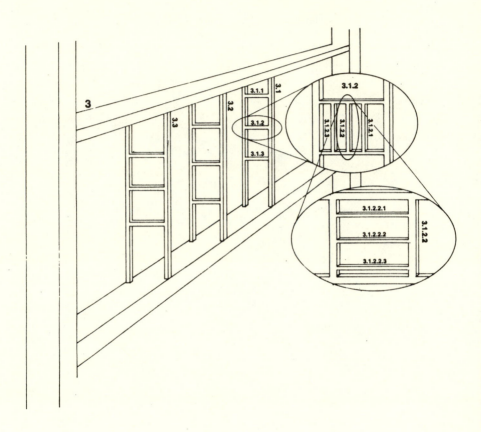

Figure 5 shows the sciences and divisions of philosophy. Each rung is telescoped into a ladder of rungs just as a wave can be magnified to reveal the smaller waves that comprise it, and those waves magnified in their turn, and so on.

3 SCIENCES

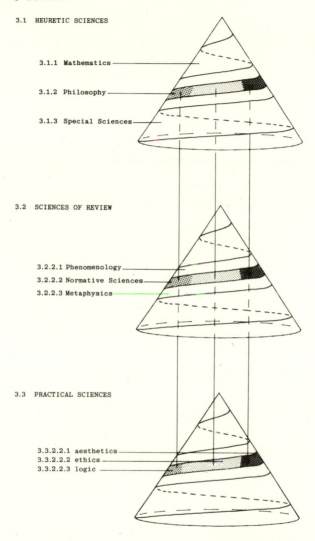

3.1 HEURETIC SCIENCES

3.1.1 Mathematics

3.1.2 Philosophy

3.1.3 Special Sciences

3.2 SCIENCES OF REVIEW

3.2.2.1 Phenomenology
3.2.2.2 Normative Sciences
3.2.2.3 Metaphysics

3.3 PRACTICAL SCIENCES

3.3.2.2.1 aesthetics
3.3.2.2.2 ethics
3.3.2.2.3 logic

Figure 6 shows the direct connections between corresponding sciences on each of the major levels of the sciences (represented by separate cones). The spiralling ribbons convey the principle-dependence relation while the three retractable vertical threads convey the categorial connections linking the corresponding science on each cone. The categorial connections must be imagined as retractable because their location is entirely dependent on where the specific sciences occur on the cones. Since it is a dynamic construct, the locations may be expected to shift.

V

Logic in Its Third Grade of Clearness

It is now possible to view logic within the context of the classification. Here the normative sciences obtain their principles from the two preceding sciences, and logic further depends on aesthetics and ethics. To understand what Peirce meant by logic, these sciences and their relations to one another need to be examined along with their relations to logic. His meaning can be clarified further if the relationship of subsequent sciences to logic is examined: they provide the data and problems for logic while depending on it (either directly or indirectly) for principles.

Although Peirce analysed the normative sciences in terms of categories, it would be misleading to regard aesthetics as a first, ethics as a second, and logic as a third *per se*. Many writers have attempted to do so, thereby attributing to Peirce the view that aesthetics studies feeling, ethics studies action, and logic studies thought. On the contrary, all three normative sciences must be seen as seconds of philosophy. This means that aesthetics, ethics, and logic are *all* sciences (thirds – 3) pursuing knowledge for its own sake (firsts – 3.1) from experience available to everyone (seconds – 3.1.2) inasmuch as we can act upon it and it upon us (seconds – 3.1.2.2).

1. PRE-NORMATIVE SCIENCES

Peirce's classification scheme shows mathematics to be the science that depends on no other. Yet how can *any* theoretical science be pursued without first studying the science of reasoning? Indeed, how can the science of logic be studied without resting that investigation on principles that logic itself discovers? Does this present the dilemma that logic can only be pursued through correct reasoning while correct reasoning can only be possible after a sound theory of logic has been developed? Peirce denied this. He insisted that people have a natural logic that enables them to pursue normal activities as well as mathematics and the three other sciences that take no principles from logic; it even allows them to make initial advances into the science of logic (1.417, c. 1896). This rudimentary theory has traditionally been referred to as *logica utens* or "logic in possession" (692.5, 1901) in contradistinction to *logica docens* which refers to the results of the scientific inquiry.

Reasoning of any sort, Peirce has said, involves self-control so that even inference through one's *logica utens* must be compared with norms. A given piece of reasoning is approved because it is a kind usually free from error. Yet if reasonings are subjected to criticism, those which pass the scrutiny will be approved, meaning that *those* reasonings cannot be doubted. Why, then, should a science of reasoning be embarked upon if these reasonings are perfectly satisfactory?

Peirce saw no inconsistency in regarding *logica utens* as less than perfect while continuing to uphold it until an adequate science is developed. This is because:

thought in its infancy usually attacks complicated problems, because the thought is excessively vague, and in that state of vagueness the problems cannot be analyzed with the vague sort of reasoning that is brought to bear upon them. What in that stage seems to be indubitable is indubitable for such thought. Later the former excessively vague concepts become replaced by somewhat more precise ones. When that happens, the old state of mind is, for the most part, buried in oblivion. It is thus impossible to place the vague concept and the preciser concept, side by side before the mind, or to compare them. The same words are used, and the new concept is identified with the old one. But now the same sentence of speech that formerly seemed indubitable (and in its state of vagueness when attacked only by vague thought, probably really was so ...) now expresses a different and more precise thought which is far from indubitable. For it is only in so far as a proposition or an inference is vague ... that it can be quite indubitable. (290.21^2–3^2, 1905).

Although it generally functions correctly within its limited capabilities, humans' existing *logica utens* is not completely reliable. It is not only vague, but on some points positively erroneous. Worse, it is insufficient. Hence it should be replaced by a sound theory as soon as possible (596.19, c. 1902).

(The number in parenthesis, which follows the division of the classification under discussion, indicates the position of that science and its analysis in terms of the categories as it occurs in the perennial classification.)

The heuretic sciences (3.1) (or sciences of discovery) form the first major division of the sciences. Their task is to inquire after new truth for its own sake, and at their head is mathematics. Mathematics can develop its own reasoning from a *logica utens*, without appeal to a science of logic.[1]

1. Mathematics (3.1.1)

The term "mathematics," Peirce noted, can be traced to an ancient Greek expression meaning "what belongs to lessons." This suggests that mathematics commonly antedated reading as the first step in instruction (685.3, 1913).

Peirce had long been satisfied with his father's definition of mathematics as "the science that draws necessary conclusions" when he decided to emend it to "the science of exact conclusions concerning merely hypothetical states of things" (608.2-3, [1905-6?]) and again as "the science of the necessary and definite results that would flow from the truth of propositions as to whose actual truth the group of mathematicians, as such, professes neither responsibility nor interest" (601.21^1-2^1, [1906]).

Of course, a necessary conclusion can only be justified if the premises are hypothetical and require no actual state of things; nothing substantive is added to Benjamin Peirce's definition. His son merely underlined the distinction between mathematics and the positive sciences that vindicates mathematics as the first science in the classification scheme: it is founded on no asserted premises and requires no experimental support beyond the creations of the imagination. If mathematicians assume nothing unconditionally, on what do they rest their assertions? What assurance do they have that their imagination and "generalizing intellect" will not lead them astray? Peirce called these "question-begging questions" of no moment to mathematicians. On the one hand, *qua* mathematician, they are unaware of the faculties of imagination and intellect. On the other hand, these faculties do not lead them astray. Occasionally they will blunder as a result of inattention, but such errors are infrequent and immediately rectified and thus need not pertain to their studies. Mathematical demonstrations have theoretical infallibility; if they have been submitted to adequate mathematical criticism they cannot genuinely be doubted. When doubt does not and cannot arise, mathematicians have no need to investigate the validity of those reasonings, for they are more evident than any theory about them can be (693b. 288–300, [1904]). Of course, inability to doubt at a given juncture should not mean cessation of all future criticism.

A mathematician's only interest in a theoretical step is that it should be extremely convenient. If it eliminates complications without sacrificing security, he or she is satisfied. And whether or not it can be omitted is of no consequence. Accordingly the mathematician's demonstrations may have steps that are not logically necessary (4.614, 1908).

Although the security of such demonstrations requires no observed fact, Peirce held that observation should play a key role. As a heuretic science, mathematics is engaged in discovery. Discovery occurs through observation of a geometrical diagram or an array of algebraic symbols representing the formal elements of the described universe to the extent that there are regularities. Not all regularities need be represented, Peirce noted. Still, "the complete mathematical form of any state of things, real or fictitious, represents every ingredient of that state of things except the qualities of feeling connected with it. It represents whatever importance or significance those qualities may have; but the qualities themselves it does not represent" (5.550, 1906). Even when the mathematical form is incomplete, the relations between the parts of the representation not expressed in the original hyptheses are made accessible to observation in the image, which unites all of the premises into a single copulative proposition.

Yet as long as hypotheses are expressed and nothing else is imagined, few consequences can be observed. To discover relationships, the mathematicians must set their image in motion according to the general rules included in their postulates (693b.336–44, [1904]). Various procedures may be employed. One way to introduce new terms is by means of abstractions; for example, by taking collectively a term that was formerly understood distributively. (The procedure is complicated if relative terms are involved and non-relative logics would be misleading in such cases [s97.210–11, n.d.].)[2] Changing the image may require some ingenuity, whatever the procedure; but the source of ingenuity is of no concern to the mathematician, nor to the logician, who is interested only in controlled thought. The process of suggesting a certain operation which might enable the mathematician to observe a hidden relation is a study for the psychologist.

Peirce viewed the mathematician's reasoning as a dialogue between past and future selves; but he considered these two selves to converse in different languages (693b.302, [1904]). Because mathematics is indifferent to whether or not the premisses express imagined or observed fact, all such reasonings are necessary. Mathematics is the only purely hypothetical science, and thus all necessary reasoning is mathematical. So-called non-mathematical necessary reasonings are usually so simple that the conclusion is immediately apparent and its mathematical nature elusive (466.4-5, 1903). The necessary consequences of a hypothesis might not be worked out only if nothing new is foreseen and no one bothers, or else when the hypothesis is so vague that no one can fathom it (601.22^1-23^1, [1906]).

Anything necessary must be definite and the mathematician must have precise statements in order to educe necessary consequences. (The usefulness of approximation devices, Peirce maintained, is largely confined to applied mathematics.) As a result, the mathematician must use abstract statements; only thus can general propositions – all mathematical propositions – be expressed precisely. The mathematician needs the language of abstractions for generalizations. Unfortunately it is impossible to determine consequences in general terms. This may not be entirely obvious in most syllogistic reasonings, in which a conclusion is so immediate as not to allow direct observation of the process. Yet in more complicated problems it is quite evident that the mathematician resorts to a language of images. The image is taken to instance an indefinite but nonetheless individual object (693b. 306-24, [1904]). Every step in mathematical reasoning consists in the application of a rule to an evident instance of it, so that the conclusions are uniformly universal. When abstractly stated and generalized they can be applied to every diagram constructed according to the same precept. Mathematicians need two languages then: the abstract expression and the image – and that is all they need.

Insofar as the relation to logic is concerned, it may be granted that pure mathematicians who appeal to no more adequate assurance of mathematical theorems than their own reasonings can still suppose that they have need of logic; for example, when disagreement arises over what consequences follow from given hypotheses. But logic is not necessary here, because such difficulties are almost certainly resolvable without recourse to the science of reasoning, by merely subjecting the hypotheses to a more careful examination: a task for mathematicians (1.247, c. 1902). A different kind of difficulty occurs when the mathematician is presented with a problem in which the hypotheses are confused at the outset. The logician may well be needed to elucidate the problem but, as was noted earlier (see chapter 3 note 24), in this situation the logician is required to resolve a problem involving the *application* of mathematics and not relating to pure mathematics directly. Moreover, the logician resolves such difficulties by reducing them to questions of mathematics. Mathematical ideas need be analysed only so far as to allow consequences to be deduced (4.243-9, c. 1902; 7.525, n.d.).

The logician's interest in mathematical reasoning is limited to describing it (2.192, c. 1902); the same sort of reasoning can be applied to experience with equal security (7.524, n.d.). The mathematician never makes a categorical assertion, but the logician makes a positive assertion about the world. Deduction, Peirce believed, is coextensive with necessary inference: formal logic is mathematics in that it is restricted to pure hypotheses. The results of necessary reasoning apply to the world only insofar as reasoning's hypotheses are true of the world, and *that* cannot be shown by mathematical reasoning.

Logic, of course, is not limited to deductive inference. Induction even more obviously appeals to facts and its validity receives no assurance from mathematics. Yet while retroduction and induction are not reducible to deductive reasoning, Peirce thought that the rationale of those reasonings must be deductive; that what ultimately jutifies the validity of all reasoning is also what sustains the validity of mathematical reasoning (312.47[1], 1903).

Philosophy, or *cenoscopy* (3.1.2),[3] is the second of the heuretic sciences. It encompasses all the positive sciences that depend on familiar experience. Peirce carefully distinguished it from synthetic philosophy, which collates and organizes the discoveries of various special sciences that cannot be established by any particular one. This other discipline was pursued by Bacon, Comte, Spencer, and Whewell and belongs at the head of the sciences of review (283.12-14, 1905).

The cenoscopic study with which Peirce was concerned gets its principles from mathematics, but is distinguished from it in the following ways: it is concerned with discovering real truth; and experience provides it with premises, not merely suggestions. It is also distinguished from the special sciences: it is not limited to the reality of actual existence but includes the reality of potential being; and its premisses are not special facts that require special instruments or skills to discover, but are based on the universal experience accessible to all.

The task of philosophy is to develop an understanding of the "*omne* of being and of non-being and of its principal parts" (339.268r, 1905; see also 283.23, 1905). It has three branches: first, phenomenology makes a general study of the elements from which concepts are constructed; second, the normative sciences study "the general way in which the mind, if it is to act deliberately and under self-control must respond to the blows of experience" (339.268r, 1905); third, metaphysics unites those two studies to develop a theory of reality.

2. Phenomenology (3.1.2.1)

As the first of the positive sciences, phenomenology cannot seek principles from any other positive science. It is the heuretic science that studies the universal phenomenon in its firstness, as it immediately presents itself (5.122, 1903; 311.2, 1903).

Phenomenology studies the contents of the "phaneron" which comprise the collective total of all that is present to any mind in any way or in any sense whatever, ignoring its cognitive value, its truth, and whether or not it corresponds to anything real. Peirce referred to "any mind" because he thought that any particular consciousness is substantially any other; "in any way whatever" allows the inclusion of memory and habitual cognition, and does not "limit the reference to an instantaneous state of consciousness" (908.4, n.d.). In this way it can encompass all that is experienced and even what conceivably could be experienced (5.37, 1903).

By directly observing the phaneron and by generalizing those observations, the phenomenologist sorts its ubiquitous elements into several broad classes, describing their features and revealing the quite disparate characters that can be identified (although not isolated) from the confusion of experience (1.286, c. 1904).

Because of the difficulties in determining the material components of the phaneron, and because of the complete neglect of the dynamic elements that have been put forward as mere possibility, phenomenology remains a single study at present. Hence it is limited to a study of the Cenopythagorean categories which, according to Peirce, comprise the highest class of categories.[4] The phenomenologist's task is to identify the short list of formal categories and to show that there can be no others. That done, the principal subdivisions of the categories (by which Peirce presumably meant their degenerate forms) can be listed (1.286, c. 1904).

Phenomenology, Peirce claimed, is not an easy undertaking. The indecomposable elements of the phaneron are not arrayed for the investigators. Three different faculties are needed for them to pursue their studies effectively: first, they need the artist's ability to see what is before them without the modifications and interpretations experience has taught; second, they require a careful discrimination that recognizes the feature under study through all its guises; finally, they must have a generalizing ability in order to grasp the very core of the studied feature, freed from inessential trappings (1.280, c. 1902; 5.42, 1903; 1.287, c. 1904).

If phenomenology is to have a sound foundation, the task of observation must be preceded by a preliminary study requiring exact reasoning. Mathematical logic can ascertain what it is possible for observation to reveal and so reduce the number of surprises observation might produce (5.40, 1903; 602.12-13, 1903-8; 908.7-8, n.d.); such an *a priori* investigation eliminates a number of alternatives at the outset. Peirce's studies in the logic of relatives demonstrated to him that any formal divisions in the phaneron must resemble chemical combination in having a strict valency; thus medads, monads, dyads, triads, tetrads, and so forth might be expected. In this context a medad is an indecomposable element logically distinct from all others: an instantaneous mental flash devoid of all effect which, according to Peirce, is one candidate that can be eliminated in advance. A monad has only the characters that are complete in it without reference to anything else, and so on (1.292, 1905; 5.469, c. 1907). Peirce's mathematical investigation demonstrated that there are three irreducible categories and that no fourth is possible (see 4.309, c. 1902; 908.7-12, n.d.).

Observation of the phaneron confirms this opinion by showing that there are three classes of characters that correspond to the categories of formal logic. (Peirce's phenomenological account of the three formal categories was examined in the preceding chapter.) It is clear that, on Peirce's view, a phenomenology that ignores pure mathematics will be a puerile work unfit to fill the nomological division of philosophy on which the normative sciences are to be grounded. But although Peirce emphasized that phenomenology needs to employ deductive logic, he was equally insistent that it should make no appeal to the

positive science of logic (8.297, 1904). Phenomenology "describes the
essentially different elements which seem to present themselves in what
seems" (2.197, c. 1902). In so doing it makes no categorical assertions
about its observation of the phaneron other than "that there are certain
seemings" (2.197, c. 1902). The phenomenologist makes no attempt
to determine that the objects investigated correspond to anything real,
nor that any physiological facts support the phenomenological categories, and no hypothetical explanation is attempted (1.287, c. 1904).
Consequently, a *logica utens* is adequate.[5]

As a codicil to this discussion, it should be noted that on at least
one occasion Peirce equated phenomenology with "pragmaticistic
ideology" (1338.22 [c. 1905–6]).

2.   NORMATIVE SCIENCES (3.1.2.2)

In one of his more definitive statements Peirce characterized the task
of the normative sciences as finding out "how Feeling, Conduct, and
Thought, ought to be controlled supposing them to be subject *in a
measure*, and only in a measure, to self control, exercised by means
of self-criticism, and the purposive formation of habit, as common
sense tells us they are in a measure controllable" (655.24, 1910).

To clarify this statement, the position of the normative sciences in
the classification scheme should first be examined. They form the second
division of philosophy and, accordingly, examine familiar phenomena
in their secondness; that is, inasmuch as we can act upon phenomena
and phenomena can act upon us (311.2, 1903; 339.268r, 1905). The
concern of the normative sciences is not with mere organic interaction,
for their normative character requires that the relevant actions be free
(856.8[1], [1911]); their secondness is not simply the dualism evident
in distinguishing good from bad and true from false. At times Peirce
merely cautioned that the importance of these distinctions should not
be exaggerated, but his more consistent view recognized that such hard
duality belongs to the practical sciences that correspond to and are
informed by the normative sciences. They are heuretic sciences, albeit
of practical activities.[6] Yet the distinction between the approved and
the disapproved does not constitute the dualistic character of the
normative sciences. Peirce did not think that this seemingly obvious
explanation could withstand investigation. In the first place, preferences
have varying degrees; and in the second place, an equally marked
dualism occurs even where the question of approval or disapproval

does not arise, as in ego and non-ego (283.41^4-2^4, 1905). More importantly, disapproval is not a pure second, according to Peirce, but is imputed. The opposition between the approved and the disapproved, the good and the bad, is constituted by the relation to a conditional purpose (1338.34-5, [c. 1905-6]). In this context, a purpose is "the idea of a possible general regarded as desirable together with a sense of being determined in one's habitual nature" (283.76, 1905). Dualism is not dominant in such an idea, for clearly it involves the category of thirdness. If the task of the normative sciences is to study the laws relating phenomena to ends, where is the secondness?

Secondness is characterized by struggle, by the sense of effort encountering resistance. The quintessence of self-control is inhibition, which involves effort opposed by resistance. For Peirce, "all direction toward an end or good supposes selfcontrol; and thus the normative sciences are thoroughly infused with duality" (283.84, 1905). Finding ways for a deliberately adopted purpose to be realized constitutes the fundamental dualism that unites the normative sciences.

There can be no proper distinction between the approved and the disapproved until a science has determined what is excellent and what conditions must obtain for an object to possess that excellence. Theoretical science does not have favourites, so it does not declare for one member of a dichotomy (836.[4], n.d.). None of the normative sciences are concerned with actual occurrences in the world, beyond assuming that whatever phenomenology has determined to be present to the mind is so. It is not surprising, then, that they refrain from making distinctions. Individual facts are only considered insofar as they are a constant element in the phenomena (8.239, 1904).

The guidance obtained from phenomenology is augmented by mathematical reasoning. The first of the normative sciences can appeal to no other science for principles.

1. Aesthetics (3.1.2.2.1)

Aside from an early introduction to Whately's *Elements of Logic*, Peirce's initial encounter with philosophy was through aesthetics. In 1855, throughout the entire year, he examined various works on the subject and concentrated particularly on Schiller's *Aesthetische Briefe*, which had profoundly impressed him. Thereafter Peirce neglected the study completely, attributing his disinterest to the "feeble" nature of the writings (2.197, c. 1902; 5.129, 1903; 310.4, 1903; 683.17, [1913]; s80.11, n.d.).[7]

Peirce disclaimed any artistic talent of his own (683.18, [1913]), yet he was not without aesthetic discrimination. His father had assiduously encouraged sensuous and aesthetic discrimination in its broadest aspect, in particular a delicate refinement of palate. In characteristic excess expressing this refinement, the younger Peirce devoted two months and considerable money to the acquisition of a near-professional discernment of red Médoc wines (619.5, 1909; see also 682.48^2, [c. 1913]).

Neither artistic sensibility nor aesthetic appreciation is necessary to the scientific study of aesthetics, still less to the determination of its subject. Yet Peirce investigated the science early in his life and was never indifferent to the subject matter, although no contemporary work inclined him to study further, even after he had recognized its considerable importance to logic. Presumably, then, he did not feel confident that this particular science could be viewed in terms of the activities of those who pursue it.[8] This being so, Peirce's discussion of aesthetics must have received at least some of its impetus from other sources. In fact, at least three more or less conflicting elements received Peirce's allegiance at various times.

In accordance with his declared procedure (5.146, 1903; 311.11–16, 1903), Peirce presented innumerable disconnected discussions as well as some in which he attempted to draw his disparate views into coherent and consistent statements. The result is that his accounts of aesthetics are permeated with anomalies and sometimes with bizarre assertions. This continues until 1910 when his last major difficulty was resolved.

On the one hand, Peirce developed an increasingly clear idea of the sort of science aesthetics must be if it is to harmonize with his architectonic develpment; and, on the other hand, he was encumbered by several convictions that prevented a coherent and unequivocal account. Chronological sorting of Peirce's ideas is of only partial value here because in examining aesthetics from one of his positions Peirce did not always divest himself of his other ideas.[9] It was not until 1910 that Peirce reversed his opinion on one significant preconception, and thus he did not give a thoroughgoing unified presentation. To reconstruct that position, we require only a certain amount of selectivity facilitated by hindsight; we merely have to disqualify the assertions that stem from the rejected views.

I propose first to identify the elements of Peirce's thought that underlie the confusion; second, to examine the various different positions Peirce adopted as a consequence of one or more of those elements; third, to indicate Peirce's resolution; and, finally, to reconstruct the coherent view that emerges from the residual.

The earlier examination of Peirce's development of the classification of the sciences has shown that his view of ordering the normative sciences generally, and aesthetics in particular, was very much in the formative stage until 1902. It will be more useful to seek out Peirce's position from subsequent writings. No dearth of material results from this limitation, notwithstanding commentators' fondness for remarking on the paucity of writings on the subject.

One critical element that influenced Peirce's thought in this area concerns the position occupied by aesthetics within the classification scheme. It suggests a number of characters aesthetics might be expected to have: it is a positive theoretical science, of course; and since it succeeds phenomenology, the discoveries of that science, with some help from mathematics, will provide the fundamental principles for aesthetics. It remains to be determined precisely what those principles are. Because it belongs to the second division of philosophy, aesthetics will possess a fundamental dualism in common with all the normative sciences. As the first of the normative sciences it will reflect the category of firstness in some distinctive manner. One of Peirce's difficulties was to decide in what that firstness consists. Ultimately he decided that aesthetics contributes principles to ethics and logic.

The second element that influenced Peirce's examination of aesthetics was his conviction with regard to the problem of evil. Peirce had accepted the solution of the elder Henry James, in *Substance and Shadow*, that God approves of evil as such, not because it is the only way to achieve his purposes (which would be inconsistent for an omnipotent being) but because he finds evil admirable *per se*; evil is something that mortals should struggle against and (impossible as it may be) should endeavour to understand as laudable in itself (5.402 note 3, 1905; 8.263, 1905; 330.4-5, n.d.). God's perspective might discern that everything is good (283.43[4], 1905); but from the lesser pinnacles to which humans may aspire, comprehension of such an ultimate good must remain inaccessible (6.479, 1908; cf. 1334.20-1, 1905). Indeed, to presume to define God's purpose could be interpreted as sacrilege (8.263, 1905). This has implications for the status of the good and bad, of the fine and vulgar. The relation of pleasure and pain to good and evil is also at issue.

The third influence on Peirce derived from his pragmaticism. Here the relevant feature is that it seeks an end. The popularized versions of the theory of pragmatism had action as the ultimate end. Peirce reported that he had "entertained a suspicion that such was the character of pragmaticism and ... almost abandoned the principle, on that account" (284.4, c. 1905; see also 8.256, 1902; 329.16 and .20, c. 1904; 5.433, 1905). His reaction to that misconception was an inordinately severe (subsequently tempered) assessment of his early articles and a brief flirtation with a fourth grade of clearness (later recognized as merely a more adequate understanding of the third grade of clearness).[10] Peirce's new understanding of pragmaticism makes the *summum bonum* consist in a process of evolution in which the existent increasingly embodies those generals that are recognized as reasonable (329.20, c. 1904; 5.433, 1905; 284.4, c. 1905; 5.402 note 3, 1905). Such a conception has at least an impress of thirdness, and its precise relation to aesthetics was of considerable moment to Peirce.

Peirce generally allocated the task of discovering the *summum bonum* to the first of the normative sciences. His quandaries of 1902 (for example at 1.575-7, c. 1902; 2.197, c. 1902) were caused by his early uncertainties. But even when his views appeared to be established, uncertainty was expressed once more: aesthetics is reduced to a branch of ethics on the grounds that there can be no criticism of an idea in itself (1334. Add 36, 1905). The lines of demarcation between the sciences are not important, Peirce explained (1.574, 1905; 283.35[4], 1905), but to the ordering of the sciences according to his categories, they do indeed have significance. In yet another manuscript (902.R9.7, 1910) Peirce observed that when one of two divisions is further bifurcated, it is often found that the resulting three divisions are of the same rank. If ethics is divided in this way, ethics and aesthetics might be accorded equal status in due course. It remains to be seen if criticism of an idea in itself *is* an appropriate characterization of aesthetics.

What implications do the three preconceptions have for the investigation of the *summum bonum*? The effects dictated by architectonic will be examined first.

Phenomenology has shown that there are three indecomposable elements in the phaneron, which suggests that an adequate ultimate end needs to integrate all three categories in a way that permits their distinctive characters to be expressed. Discussions of the *summum bonum* appropriate to pragmaticism have taken account of the categories in this way. The same consideration may have influenced the suggestion that "an object, to be esthetically good, must have a multitude of parts so related to one another as to impart a positive simple immediate quality to their totality; and whatever does this is, in so far, esthetically good, no matter what the particular quality of the total may be" (5.132, 1903). Phenomenological findings also may have inspired the statement that the aesthetic quality is "the total unanalyzable impression of a reasonableness that has expressed itself in a creation. It is a pure Feeling but a feeling that is the Impress of a Reasonableness that Creates. It is the Firstness that truly belongs to a Thirdness in its achievement of Secondness" (310.9, 1903). It becomes a little easier to understand why Peirce tried to characterize aesthetic quality in this manner, when it is realized that he was caught between two possible ways in which the ultimate end for aesthetics could be characterized by firstness. On the one hand, it might refer to what is fine in general in itself and without any other reason (1.191, 1903; 1.611, 1903; 5.130, 1903; 288.23-5, 1905). (This opinion would cohere with the fundamental dualism, characterizing the normative sciences, of an aesthetics that discovers laws relating feeling to that end.) On the other hand, the firstness of the ultimate end might be that quality which is fine in its immediate presence (2.199, c. 1902; 1334.36, 1905). It was probably in attempting to relate the findings of phenomenology to the second alternative that Peirce produced the two obscure passages quoted.

Indeed, a number of difficulties arise with the second alternative. If the *summum bonum* is a quality of feeling, Peirce would have maintained that logic is founded on feeling. Obviously, whatever quality of feeling constituted the *summum bonum* could not be such as to admit of excess. Hence no particular quality of feeling will do, for any given feeling may cease to satisfy after a time although the quality of the feeling remains the same. Peirce admitted that pleasure is the only possible state that is perfectly self-satisfied, but he found the "unrestrained gratification of a desire" abhorrent. "It would be the doctrine that all the higher modes of consciousness with which we are acquainted in ourselves, such as love and reason, are good only so far as they subserve the lowest of all modes of consciousness" (1.614, 1903). Moreover, the adoption of pleasure as the *summum bonum* ignores the findings of phenomenology. By making the aesthetic pleasure a sort of "intellectual sympathy" (5.113, 1903) Peirce contrived to make it more acceptable.

In another recourse Peirce attempted to reconcile the present position with the pragmatic ideal: he refused to grant that the aesthetic ideal must be a static result. By admitting process, Peirce was no longer limited to a self-satisfied ideal. He could adopt an end that would always anticipate an improvement in its results. Such is the growth of reason: "The essence of Reason," Peirce maintained, "is such that its being never can have been completely perfected. It always must be in a state of incipiency, of growth" (1.615, 1903). Yet with this solution he rejected the second alternative and embraced the first, for the *summum bonum* is no longer a quality of feeling.

Another difficulty arises if the aesthetic ideal is the immediately present quality: there can be no criticism since simple qualities are neither good nor bad, they merely are. Peirce approached this dilemma in a variety of ways. On one occasion he allowed that as long as an aim is consistently pursued it cannot be criticized (5.132-3, 1903). If carried through to ethics this would grant the egoist an ethically coherent position.[11] In another approach Peirce argued that it is only because of humans' limited sympathies (478.41, 1903) or because they introduce moral considerations, imagining themselves acting in accordance with the moral ideas or regarding them as unsuitable for some purpose (5.127, 1903; 310.5-7, 1903) that they make discriminations. The aesthetic ideal, he thought, should be admired deliberately in itself wherever it leads (5.36, 1903). In yet another approach, Peirce granted that pleasantness and unpleasantness of qualities are feelings but insisted that they are secondary feelings. "The question whether a feeling is pleasant or the reverse is the question whether it attracts or repels; so that pleasantness and unpleasantness are, immediately, characters of the action which the feeling excites" (283.35[1]-6[1], 1905). Accordingly, it is possible to distinguish between the attractive and the repulsive. Effort and resistance must be involved, and in this context Peirce appears to have thought that herein lies the dualism of aesthetics. Still, the same sort of dualism is unlikely to characterize ethics and logic, and the requisite secondness must have its parallel in all the normative sciences.

Finally, the second alternative was largely responsible for Peirce's quandries over the selection of an appropriate term with which to express the relevant quality. "Beauty" was considered altogether unsatisfactory, and "fine" was thought a poor stand-in; the French *beauté* or *beau* were a little more appropriate, according to Peirce, but only the Greek *kalos* or even *agamai* expressed the requisite generality and included the unbeautiful within their scope (2.199, c. 1902; 310.5, 1903; 1334.39, 1905).

Many of the difficulties described also were generated by Peirce's conviction that the solution to the problem of evil is that found in *Substance and Shadow*: that evil is perfection in God's eyes. If this is so, the aesthetic ideal needs to include the unbeautiful; thus the preconception contributed to Peirce's terminological difficulties. Since everything is good on this view, there *is* no discrimination between the fine and the vulgar. But people cannot see that everything is good unless they possess the vision of God (283.43[4], 1905), which they don't. Thus, this view makes the *summum bonum* beyond their comprehension. Peirce tried to provide more insight by maintaining that aesthetic good and evil are pleasure and pain as viewed from the vantage of the "fully developed superman." Then, with his view that pleasure and pain are secondary feelings symptomatic of the attractive and the repulsive, he made an unwarranted leap to the assertion that the good is what appears attractive to the "sufficiently matured agent" (5.552, 1905). Even so, this brings us no nearer to the ultimate end.

From this point of view, the *summum bonum* cannot be limited to the human mind (5.128, 1903). Nor is there reason to think that any ultimate end for humanity is endorsed by a celestial mind (5.119, 1903; 5.536, c. 1905). In these circumstances, Peirce thought, people should try to understand that the occurrence of evil is good: "Man comes to his normal development only through the socalled *evil passions*, which are evil, only in the sense that they ought to be controlled, and are *good* as the only possible agency for giving man his full development" (330.[4], n.d.). By the operation of self-control we may develop a *summum bonum* which will enable us to participate in God's creation to the extent that He permits (5.402, note 3, 1905). This is assuming "that in the long process of creation God achieves his own being" (313.20, 1903)[12] which is, it seems, the aesthetic ideal. Self-control is to be employed to combat evil although it is not clear how evil is to be identified (unless it is equated with pain). If we succeed we would be "fulfilling our appropriate offices in the work of creation. Or to come down to the practical, every man sees some task cut out for him. Let him do it," Peirce enjoined, "and feel that he is doing what God made him in order that he should do" (8.138 note 4, 1905). Unabashed by the implication that all people ought to admire just what they will admire, Peirce confirmed that those who suffer as a consequence can take comfort by telling themselves that "the secret design of God will be perfected through their agency" (6.479, 1908). The difficulty in discovering an ultimate end for which humans may aim (given the assumptions here) would seem to be insuperable.

The foregoing is in strong contrast to the pragmaticist's position. To begin with, pragmaticism concerns intellectual concepts and a concept can only enter the mind as a general term or symbol. Symbols are derived from human conventions so that they "cannot transcend conceivable human occasions" (288.143, 1905; see also 5.553, 1905). Although Peirce was willing to extend pragmaticism to extra-terrestrial minds, they must be minds that operate with symbols. As for God, a disembodied spirit is not likely to have a consciousness (6.489, c. 1910). Hence, "we cannot so much as frame any notion of what the phrase 'the performance of God's mind' *means*" (6.508, c. 1906).

Therefore the *summum bonum* must be acceptable to the human mind and must concern itself with human purposes. Yet the end for humans need not satisfy the desires of any particular individual. In this context, "human" means "belonging to the communion of mankind" (8.186, c. 1903).

Peirce stressed that careful deliberation without any ulterior reason should determine the appropriate end. He saw neither selfishness nor Epicureanism in individuals seeking an end which would best satisfy themselves since they cannot be moved by an impulse other than their own. People are free, capable of reasoning, and possessed of an apparently endless capacity to exert self-control in determining their actions. Only time interferes with deliberations prior to action. It would be wise then to spend time in deciding this supreme question (649.19–21, 1910). Peirce used several devices to explain the full meaning of the project.

In one of these, a fairy grants the reader a dream that will in fact last a fraction of a second, but will appear to be just as vast and as complex as desired. It will be entirely dissociated from any previous or subsequent experience. No detail will be remembered and no subsequent effects will occur. Only a "perfectly unanalyzable impression of its totality" will remain (310.7, 1903).[13] Would one choose a dream of a delightful sensation, or pure bliss? Peirce thought not:

If it were me, I should say "Not a bit! On the contrary, it must be a dream of extreme variety and must seem to embrace an eventful history extending through millions of years. It shall be a drama in which numberless living caprices shall jostle and work themselves out in larger and stronger harmonies and antagonisms, and ultimately execute intelligent reasonablenesses of existence more and more intellectually stupendous and bring forth new designs still more admirable and prolific." And if the fairy should ask me what the *denouement* should be, I should reply, "Let my intelligence in the dream develope powers infinitely beyond what I can now conceive and let me at last find that boundless reason utterly helpless to comprehend the glories of the thoughts that are to become materialized in the future,[14] and that will be *denouement* enough for me. I may then return to the total unanalyzed impression of it."   (310.8-9, 1903; see also 675.15¹-16¹, [c. 1911])

Another device involves the reader's consideration of two possible ends. One of these has seemed pre-eminently satisfactory for fifty-nine years but in the sixtieth year, when intellect and capacity for enjoyment are failing (although logic and memory remain sound), a thorough and impartial review shows the aim to have been an empty mockery which has thwarted any pursuit of genuine value. With the other possible aim the reverse is the case: for fifty-nine years it has been the source of frustration and misery, until in the sixtieth year it turns out to be thoroughly satisfying only because of an increased understanding of what is satisfactory; the ability to evaluate reasons has not altered, so the change in the sixtieth year must be due to some factors receiving value that they had not been given formerly.

Peirce thought that the latter end is to be preferred even if one's demise coincides with the discovery. The point is to find the end that no amount of further deliberation would alter: the *summum bonum* is what one would conclude after thoroughgoing consideration. Hence, how one actually felt about it for the greater part of one's life is not relevant (649.22-4, 1910; cf. 5.375 note 2, 1903).

Both devices suggest that the completely satisfactory aim will be one that evolves and comes to its full meaning only in the distant future. Accordingly, the pragmaticist makes the *summum bonum* consist "in a process of evolution whereby the existent comes more and more to embody a certain class of generals which in the course of the development show themselves to be reasonable" (329.20, c. 1904; see also 5.3, 1901; 5.433, 1905).

Such an ideal succeeds in incorporating all three of the Peircean categories. This is even more clearly evinced in another manuscript that calls the *summum bonum* "the continual increase of the embod-

iment of the idea-potentiality" (283.103, 1905). Ideas are transmitted
in the mind from one point in time to another by means of thoughts,
which is to say, by imaginary signs. But the *ideas* are not actually
thoughts; they are "some potentiality, some form, which maybe
embodied in external or in internal signs" (283.102, 1905). The
contribution of action to that process should not be overlooked.
According to Peirce, "signs which should be merely parts of an endless
viaduct for the transmission of idea-potentiality, without any convey-
ance of it into anything but symbols, namely, into action or habit
of action, would not be signs at all, since they would not, little or
much, fulfill the function of signs; and further, that without embodiment in something else than symbols, the principles of logic show
there never could be the least growth in idea-potentiality" (283.103-
4, 1905; see also 284.4, c. 1905). In potentiality there is firstness; in
embodiment there is secondness; and in idea there is thirdness. Consequently, the "growth of concrete reasonableness" provides an ideal
to encompass all three elements in the phaneron. Self-control in the
acquisition of habits is the method by which the pragmatic ideal is
to be attained.

In quite different ways, growth through self-control is common to
both the pragmatic approach and that linked to *Substance and Shadow*.
Is a synthesis of these two views possible?

As early as 1903 Peirce remarked on a flaw in *Substance and Shadow*:
"it represents the desire of God to confer independence upon that
which is most opposite to Himself to be a special peculiarity of God.
But God has no whimsies nor pet weaknesses: it is on the contrary
the essential nature of Purpose that it cannot be directed toward itself
but developes itself in Creating" (478.19^1-20^1, 1903). This allowed Peirce
to accommodate the pragmatic evolutionary ideal: "Our ideas of the
infinite are necessarily extremely vague and become contradictory the
moment we attempt to make them precise. But still they are not utterly
unmeaning, though they can only be interpreted in our religious
adoration and the consequent effects upon conduct" (8.262, 1905). That,
Peirce maintained, is pragmatism.

Since the *summum bonum* for pragmaticism is of an evolutionary
nature, the denouement of which may be approached asymptotically
but might never be reached, the suggestion has some credibility.
Furthermore, people evidently have some affinity to God or to nature
for they have been able to discover laws that enable them to predict
with fair success. It would seem, then, that the end for human beings

ultimately could coincide with the end for the divine being (5.119, 1903; 8.211–12, c. 1905). Still, this is not an adequate resolution of the difficulties arising out of the *Substance and Shadow* solution for the problem of evil. That God should delight in evil remains an enigma impeding any attempt by people to posit a viable end for themselves that cannot be construed as a blasphemous endeavour to define God's purposes. Consequently, Peirce rested with the unsatisfactory resolution in which human beings create an ideal that is not fully theirs (8.263, 1905; 5.402 note 3, 1905; 6.479–80, 1908).[15] Fortunately, this was not his last word on the subject. In 1910 Peirce re-examined the relationship of pleasure and pain to the problem of evil.

The discovery of anaesthetics posed a dilemma to those who believed in an omnipotent, omniscient, and benevolent God – creator of an intelligible universe – for it now seemed evident that the universe could have been created and could have accomplished its ends without pain. Yet humans are so constituted that they cannot consider pain other than an evil (649.32, 1910). Peirce noted that many reacted by rejecting anaesthetics on the grounds that God had explicitly stated that women should suffer in childbirth and so, by analogy, all pain should be endured.[16]

The only recourse, Peirce maintained, is to conclude that pain is not *per se* evil. After all, how does pain constitute an evil? Is it the quality of feeling itself, or is it because it is a feeling we are impelled to avoid? The masochist has an impulse to seek pain, and some people are even known to rejoice in the pain inflicted on a limb that has been instrumental in committing an offense. Thus the desire to avoid pain does not make pain an evil. On the other hand, the widespread use of anaesthetics has rendered people less accustomed to pain and thus its occurrence is more intensely repugnant than formerly. Moreover, pleasure and pain, Peirce thought, are signs of satisfactions and wants; they function well when used intelligently, but it would be a mistake to confuse them with the wants they signal. They are very susceptible to change and "do not, *in themselves*, carry any sound *Reason* for acting one way, influential as they are in the purely Brutal mode, but are only *rational* motives as being veridical signs of real needs" (649.29, 1910). Peirce concluded that pain is not, as such, evil:

Pain *per se* is nothing but a Feeling or class of pure Feelings, and as such involves no relativity, duality, or plurality whatever. It is nothing more than what it seems to be and it seems to be nothing but a Quality *sui generis*.

But the ideas of Good and Evil have essentially reference to [an][17] indefinite End *for* which they are Good and Evil. Thus they only apply to things in their relations to ends.   (649.37-8, 1910)

If pain *per se* is not evil, Peirce's former conclusion – that God's willingness to permit pain (which we necessarily regard as evil) can only mean that God loves evil – no longer holds. The existence of pain, taken by itself, proves nothing about the problem of evil.

No reference to *Substance and Shadow* occurs here, but Peirce forcefully reaffirmed this opinion later (683.26, [1913]). Moreover, the following footnote occurs in a succeeding manuscript: "Three books from the study of which I have profitted [sic] concerning morality and otherwise are Henry James the First's 'Substance and Shadow,' 'The Secret of Sw[ed]enborg,' and 'Spiritual Creation'. The fact that I have been unable to agree with much, not to say *most*, of the author's opinions while not quite confident of my own has, no doubt, increased their utility to me. Much that they contain enlightened me greatly" (675.16 note, [c. 1911]). Finally Peirce had renounced the *Substance and Shadow* solution to the problem of evil; he no longer needed to posit an end known only to an inscrutable deity.

One more difficulty needs to be resolved before a coherent account of the science of aesthetics is possible: is the *summum bonum* to be an immediate feeling or an ideal deliberately adopted for its own sake and without any ulterior reason? We have seen the conundrums Peirce confronted when he accepted the former. Yet if the pragmaticist's answer to the latter is accepted, which now seems warranted, in what sense is this end appropriate to a science that enables people to discriminate among creations of the imagination and feelings generally? If Peirce was correct in maintaining that the normative sciences discover laws that relate ends to feeling in the case of aesthetics, to action in ethics, and to thought in logic, the task of aesthetics cannot be confined to the discovery of the *summum bonum* posited by pragmaticism.

The answer to this difficulty is concealed in an alternative sequence to a manuscript, but the manuscript is of considerable importance to this topic. Here Peirce maintained that "there must be a theory of the *beau*, the Fine, the ideally admirable. Beauty, or what is admirable in sensuous presentation, is degraded from its rightful dignity if it be not recognized as a special case of the ideally fine in general" (283.35^4-6^4, 1905). This insight allowed Peirce to incorporate into aesthetics both the pragmatic ideal and a special determination of that ideal appropriate to the discrimination of feeling.

A criticism that might be directed against such a procedure is that the ideally admirable in general, because of its evolutionary character, might be more appropriately pursued by a science prior to aesthetics. Within Peirce's classification scheme it would need to be a division of phenomenology.[18] Alternatively, it might be subsumed under a more general study that encompasses both phenomenology and the proposed study. Three reasons for moving it to the first division of philosophy are that there is no element of secondness involved in its investigation,[19] that it provides the essential principle to all three normative sciences, and that it receives its data from all three. However, if investigation of the *summum bonum* is a task confined to the first division of aesthetics, those reasons are not very cogent.

The discipline as it remains when purged of the rejected aspects can now be reassessed. The following account was never presented by Peirce in quite this way; but given more time, he would certainly have reformulated his account in some such manner: it is all to be found in his writings.

The classification of the sciences provides the framework into which a coherent science must fit. Aesthetics is a positive theoretical science in which a phenomenon is examined in the light of our ability to interact with it. Herein lies the fundamental dualism shared with all of the normative sciences. As the first of the normative sciences, it examines the phenomenon in its firstness. Further, aesthetics subdivides into a physiological, a classificatory, and a methodological department.

Physiology (3.1.2.2.1.1). Assuming that the general ideal is a study for aesthetics, its investigation will be the very first task for that science. The findings of phenomenology will provide the fundamental principles; and Peirce's own studies in that field indicate that the general ideal must take account of the three indecomposable elements of the phaneron. The distinctive firstness of the ideal is that it should satisfy in itself and without reference to any ulterior reason.

Could unalloyed bliss or the unrestrained gratification of desire be such an ideal? Bliss fulfils the last requirement, but as a state of pure feeling it gives no expression to the second and third categories. Peirce maintained that only an ideal that is continually evolving would comply with both requirements. The creation of the universe is just such an end but is not one that human beings might pursue directly,

and the normative sciences are concerned with the phaneron insofar
as we can act upon it and not just as it can act upon us. The pragmatic
ideal of the "continual increase of the embodiment of the idea
potentiality" acknowledges that the phaneron does force itself upon
people; and Peirce has noted that the human mind must have some
affinity with nature so that there is reason to hope that the pragmatic
ideal, which *is* pursuable by humans, might eventually coincide with
the final creation. Peirce declared that if

it be conceivable that the secret should be disclosed to human intelligence,
it will be something that thought can compass. Now thought is of the nature
of a sign. In that case, then, if we can find out the right method of thinking
and can follow it out – the right method of transforming signs – then truth
can be nothing more nor less than the last result to which the following
out of this method would ultimately carry us.   (5.553, 1905)

Moreover, the pragmatic ideal gives expression to all three categories.

In positing the pragmatic ideal, Peirce trespassed into the field of
the aestheticist, which he reluctantly felt obliged to do because so
little of account had been done there. Peirce's findings, both there and
in phenomenology, are important to an understanding of what he
meant by logic.

In addition to investigating the general ideal, then, the first division
of aesthetics involves the study of the special determination of it that
applies to phenomena in their firstness. Whether this will require an
examination of the physiology of the immediately contemplated
(1334.36, 1905), of creations of the imagination (478.34^1, 1903), of
possible forms (478.41, 1903), or of all three will no doubt depend
on how the specific ideal is understood.

Classfication (3.1.2.2.1.2). The classificatory division investigates the
conditions of conformity to the ideal and is where dualism is most
pronounced (478.41, 1903).

Methodology (3.1.2.2.1.3). The methodological division studies the
principles that govern the production of the aesthetic object; that is,
the immediate feeling, the creations of the imagination, and/or the
possible forms. The aesthetic ideal is fostered, according to Peirce,
through the cultivation of habits of feeling. Peirce used the term "habit"
in a broader sense than that currently employed. He invoked Aristotle's

usage referring to any enduring state in which, under circumstances of a certain kind, the subject would be more or less sure to act in a definite way – it is a real "would-be" (673.14–15, c. 1911; see chapter 4, note 13). It is common knowledge that quite extensive self-control can be exerted over habits so that a perfected method of this control might facilitate their alteration. The deliberate acquisition of habits of feeling that have "grown up under the influence of a course of self-criticisms and of hetero-criticisms; and the theory of the deliberate formation of such habits of feeling" (1.574, 1905) comprise the task of the third division of aesthetics.

That study is an important propaedeutic for both moral and logical self-control and is crucial for the pragmatic ideal. But it is not just the methodological branch that has such significance. Because each of the normative sciences concerns a particular aspect of the general ideal, each will continually rectify and add content to the others, and in doing so augment understanding of the general ideal. On the practical level, the intellectual purport of a symbol can be subjected to constant re-evaluation by the interplay of an application of aesthetics, ethics, and logic.

It is evident that at this heuretic level the normative science of aesthetics, as Peirce saw it, confines itself to an investigation into those principles to which the discipline as it is generally conceived must appeal.

2. Ethics (3.1.2.2.2)

Peirce's acquaintance with the literature of ethics was fairly extensive and he frequently claimed that, of the three normative sciences, ethics was the most advanced. Yet the science that Peirce had in mind for the second division of the normative sciences may not have been ethics as it is traditionally understood (see 288.23, 1905). Like aesthetics, the investigations of this science as Peirce conceived it are on a very general level indeed. Ethics as pursued on the heuretic level is not concerned with principles of justice and still less with the justice of any specific law; neither is it concerned with the value of various types of conduct, nor with specific moral issues, all of which are appropriate to a parallel inquiry within the practical sciences. A science that aims at systematizing the conclusions of the practical science under general principles, using principles from the heuretic science, undoubtedly has its place in the sciences of review. Neither of those sciences will be able to proceed on a sound basis without appeal to the principles discovered by logic (the scientific method for example), and this they may properly do since they succeed logic in the classification scheme.

Much of the opposition to Peirce's ordering of the normative sciences stems from a failure to distinguish the three levels on which their subject matter might be investigated. Indeed, the relations between those disciplines are difficult to identify if the classification is not considered in its entirety. The relation of the first level study to preceding sciences will be examined first.

In Peirce's scheme, the science under discussion is a positive theoretical inquiry. A well-grounded ethics will need to recognize its basic dependence on aesthetics for principles, supplemented by appeal to mathematics and phenomenology and to no other science. It might be contended that ethics will also need to appeal to logic for principles. Peirce addressed himself to this objection, pointing out that although logic is concerned with necessary reasoning in some respects, the science that investigates its formal treatment and its practice is mathematics. Logic primarily studies probable reasonings, and ethics, like all the normative sciences, is concerned only with what ought to be and not with what actually is. Thus it has no need of logic (693a.132-4, [1904]).

But logic has need of ethics. Once Peirce had satisfied himself that ethics provides important principles to the science of logic, he reiterated that relationship of principle-dependence without further equivocation.[20]

The principles of formal logic in combination with a *logica utens* are thought to be adequate for this heuretic study. As for phenomenology, it is the category of secondness to which ethics makes its greatest appeal.

Because it occupies the mid-position of the normative sciences, ethics is doubly embued with secondness. In addition to the secondness common to all three normative sciences (that of relating phenomena to us in accordance with ends) ethics must include secondness in a particular manner of its own. The firstness of aesthetics is a function of the kind of phenomena that concern it. Hence the secondness of ethics should be a function of the kind of phenomena peculiar to it, namely, action. The task of ethics, Peirce wrote, is to study the general conditions required to make the deliberately adopted aim existent. The general aim, of course, is the principle supplied by aesthetics. The ethical study undoubtedly depends on what aim is accepted. Yet whatever that is, its realization will require the agency of self-control.

Thus ethics is, in effect, the theory of the self-control of conduct (478.35¹-6¹, 1903; 602.8, 1903-8; 288.25, 1905; cf. 693a.86, [1904]). Ethics makes its own observations and studies the theory of the deliberate formation of habits of *action* consistent with the ethical ideal, just as aesthetics studies the theory of the deliberate formation of habits of *feeling* consistent with the aesthetic ideal.

Physiology (3.1.2.2.2.1). The ethical ideal should be a special determination of the general aim found out by aesthetics. The general aim is not defined in terms of what is thought fine by any particular individual, but in what would be thought fine by anyone given sufficient time to contemplate it. Accordingly, it is defined with reference to the ubiquitous elements of experience revealed by phenomenology. In defining *its* end, ethics limits the general aim to what is attainable, for what one ought to do is circumscribed by one's abilities and one's opportunities, whereas the limits of the fine extend much further. It makes sense to declare a sunrise beautiful and a headache agonizing because no action is involved and such judgments are within the domain of aesthetics. Yet it would be idle to declare the sun's rising in a particular way as morally good, or the head's aching as morally bad. Analysis will reveal the absurdity of such judgments (600.5, [c. 1902]); 5.109, 1903; 329.12, c. 1904). It seems reasonable, then, to criticize actions (the province of ethics) only insofar as judgment may affect the relevant conduct. Accordingly, Peirce recommended the principle that *what is beyond control is beyond criticism* (598.7, [c. 1902]). It is common knowledge that people have some measure of control over their own future actions and sometimes over the future actions of others. This is the province of ethical criticism and the ethical aim must recognize those limitations: criticism is thereby limited to oneself and to those one can control; past actions are only to be criticized with a view to the future (288.163, 1905).[21] But what cannot be controlled at present, Peirce cautioned, may be controllable at another time. Circumspection is required. Moreover, at any given time limited information might obscure the need for control. Consider the recent myopia with reference to pollution; or the fear and repugnance of certain animals that led to their indiscriminate slaughter until belated recognition of their contribution to ecology and the variety in nature (an aesthetic diminution) changed attitudes and actions (cf. 437.26-7, 1898). Such examples of behaviour underline the significance of an evolutionary ideal for it is "the development of the ideal, which really creates and resolves the problems of ethics" (4.243, c. 1902). According to Peirce,

> in order that the aim should be immutable under all circumstances, without which it will not be an ultimate aim, it is requisite that it should accord with a free development of the agent's own esthetic quality. At the same time it is requisite that it should not ultimately tend to be disturbed by the reactions upon the agent of that outward world which is supposed in the very idea of action. It is plain that these two conditions can be fulfilled at once only if it happens that the esthetic quality toward which the agent's free development tends and that of the ultimate action of experience upon him are parts of one esthetic total.   (5.136, 1903)

It is the metaphysician who must inquire into the question of whether or not this is the case. Meanwhile it is apparent that the pragmatic ideal will fulfil these requirements (see 313.12, 1903). In any event, the investigation of the physiology of conduct and of the ultimate aim attainable is the business of the first division of ethics.

Classification (3.1.2.2.2.2). Determining the conditions of conformity to the ethical ideal is the task of the classification division, which is permeated with duality. It may also be termed the theory of the conditions of right action. The most important condition is that the action be voluntary. Peirce was in general agreement with the view that volition is an essential ingredient, though he favoured the expressions "action" and "brute will" because they exclude reference to a purpose. At the moment that the operation of self-control is implemented, there is no power over actions and certainly none over past actions. (Review of past actions is useful, of course, in the creation of habits, but that is the province of the methodological division.) The predominant elements of self-control are "giving a command to" and "obedient fulfilment by" a future self. Experience of the imagination, Peirce thought, is quite as effective as outward experience. If reference to the forming of habits (which imports thirdness) is ignored, the lecture of oneself upon another future self involves a consciousness of two selves or two attitudes of mind: in exerting effort to counter resistance one acts upon oneself (650.28–34, 1910).

Methodology (3.1.2.2.2.3). Finally, the methodological division studies the principles that render the ethical ideal existent. This primarily involves an examination of the operation of self-control and is so intimately connected with the creation of habits of feeling that it is very difficult to determine where the methodological division of aesthetics ends and that of ethics begins.

It is important to recognize that by "self-control" Peirce did not mean a spontaneous, automatic self-control which has its origin in the action itself; rather he meant control by the "self" issuing from the person who determines the action (letter to F.C. Russell, L387, 1908; 6.454, 1908). Peirce also used the term "self-control" with respect to a given action. Rigorous self-control of one specific passion is of no import to an unrelated action except as indicative of one who regularly reviews his or her conduct and so is prone to form habits consistent with a deliberately adopted aim (614.6[1], 1908).

Peirce regarded the complexity of self-control as the characteristic that distinguishes the rational being from other creatures (5.419, 1905; 650.33, 1910). While animals do exert self-control, humans are able to exercise control on many more levels (5.533, c. 1905; 831.11–13, n.d.). Without self-control only the normal course of events is possible; with it, people can resist their natural impulses, enabling their behaviour to approximate the deliberately adopted end (4.540, 1906; 770.7–8, n.d.). Thus Peirce thought that a person's activity is free in the sense that the human machine is equipped with such control (601.26, [1906]; 8.320, n.d.). For this reason he thought that the rules of morality are not binding: "a man that is bound is a slave, and a man who thinks he is bound *is* bound . . . But a normal young man judiciously brought up will have been led to meditate upon the beauty of certain kinds of conduct, and will desire to give his own that character" (675.17[1]–18[1], [c. 1911]). People will recognize the need to curb their wanton impulses by exercising rigorous self-government. When that government is steadfast a person is indeed bound, but "only by his own free and reasonable act, which is world-wide apart from being bound by nature. It is a free government" (675.18[1], [c. 1911]). Insofar as self-control is inhibitory it is, according to Peirce, not unlike an automatic governor attached to an engine. Excess action may be curbed by an automatic governor of the governor; but in a machine, each additional device is further complication that cannot be constantly replicated without soon creating serious problems of its own. The human brain, in contrast, seems able to exert self-government indefinitely, limited only by the time available before the action must be performed. "Man's machinery is provided with an automatic governor upon each and every governor to regulate it by a consideration otherwise not provided for" (649.20, 1910; see also 673.6–7, c. 1911). Genuine self-control, then, requires something more than self-government and Peirce considered that a machine possessed of self-control would need to be endowed with consciousness (283.98–9, 1905).

No doubt there is a sense in which self-control is in direct proportion to the impulse controlled. Regarded thus, temperance in eating and drinking and sexual continence would be the greatest virtues and far superior to intellectual virtues. They are given more value, Peirce concluded, because such assets as beauty, intellect, and artistic genius do not result from a person's own efforts. However, the degree of self-control exerted is not sufficient by itself to constitute a virtue as supreme. Its value must be seen in relation to the ultimate aim. Peirce recognized this (see 5.535, c. 1905) for he claimed that the highest virtues have to do with a person's sociality. This coheres with his pragmatic aim. Science, he believed, is a social discipline in which the individual's achievement is of significance insofar as it contributes to the end attainable only by a distant posterity (499(s). [fragment], [1907]).

On several occasions Peirce wrote that the principles that should govern a free self-control are directed towards the regular self-criticism of conduct in order to acquire good habits. The acquisition of habits is itself governed by the principle that when a certain character of a reaction to a specific kind of stimulus once occurs, a similar character is more likely to recur when any subsequent stimulus of that kind is encountered than if it had not characterized the first reaction. This assumes that fatigue is not a factor (5.538, c. 1902).

Humans are entirely oblivious to some of their inhibitions and there are cases in which self-control is purely instinctive. But the self-control that concerns ethics is acquired by training. By reviewing past behaviour and rationally deliberating future actions it is possible to train oneself and in effect to exercise control over self-control. To do this, it is necessary to compare one's conduct with a standard – a moral rule. The rule (perhaps arbitrary) might itself be subjected to criticism through appeal to a principle, thus permitting control of control of control. Ultimately, the principle can be controlled by reference to the general ideal studied in aesthetics (5.533, c. 1905; 288.29–31, 1905; 8.320, n.d.).

Having affirmed that no appeal to special scientific knowledge is needed, Peirce elaborated on the actual process of purposely forming a habit in order to exercise self-control. While habits are most obviously reinforced by practice, they may be formed almost as effectively by repetition in the imagination. This is especially so when the imagined process is vivid; and it is possible to make it vivid by considering the consequences of all the possible actions and by reflecting on all eventualities. The vividness might be further intensified by concentrating on the feelings generally attendant upon the relevant actions, and by focusing on the complicated segments. Forming a resolve in accordance with one's deliberately approved end requires effort of a different kind: it is effected by vigorous self-command. Repeated commands in conjunction with a vivid imagination of the act concludes the process. At this juncture one may dismiss one's resolve from the mind, Peirce maintained, because whenever the appropriate cue is received, performance in accordance with one's deliberations will occur almost unconsciously. Of course regular reinforcement in practice or imagination is usually needed to confirm the habit. Indeed, if at the time of self-criticism the desired habit has already been established, its implementation will be all the more facile. The very habit of forming habits is conducive to behaviour that invokes feelings of satisfaction and is approved on reflection (5.538, c. 1902; 614.5^1-6^1, 1908; 675.18^1-21^1, [c. 1911]).

The formation of habits comprises the thirdness of the methodological division, and all three divisions, of course, are not exceptions to the principle-dependence that governs the entire classification scheme. Logic is the focal point for Peirce's ordering of the sciences.

3. Logic (3.1.2.2.3)

Peirce was greatly dissatisfied with the state of logic and his views made it impossible for him to fill out the content of that science through an examination of the activities of those who pursued it.[22] Logic, then, will be examined here in terms of its relations to the other sciences, once more starting with the relation to preceding sciences.

If it were impossible to reason unless the theory of reasoning had been studied previously, none of the preceding sciences could advance one step, and logic itself would be confronted with a serious dilemma. Peirce's arguments averting that particular predicament have already been stated together with his conclusion that none of the foregoing sciences are inhibited by the absence of a prior science of logic.

The distinctions that Peirce drew between mathematics and logic have been explored; it remains to examine logic's dependence on mathematics. In common with all sciences, logic appeals to a branch of mathematics, that is, to formal logic. The logician finds that pure deductive logic can be applied to the world with as much security as when it is applied to mathematical hypotheses: as a normative science logic is not concerned with any specific state of affairs but with how to proceed in order to attain the truth. It must assume something as true, but aside from certain definite assumptions, its method will be acceptable as always leading to the truth only if it allows the state of things to be just what it happens to be. The proof of this procedure lies in showing that, given the truth of those definite assumptions, that procedure will be the surest way to the truth whatever else might be the case. This is reasoning from pure hypotheses, which is a study of mathematics (693a.102–6, [1904]). Thus in the final analysis it may be said that "the logician reasons about objects that are not even real" (693b.286, [1904]). The logician, indeed, does not have to decide whether or not there is a reality, even while recognizing that there are objects much like real things. He or she discovers the habits of inference that lead to knowledge, including positive knowledge (supposing there is a reality), and to such semblance of knowledge as phenomena permit (supposing there is no perfect reality) (2.64, c. 1902). Accordingly, the logician represents things as real, leaving the metaphysician to determine whether they are real or not. Thus, although the logician must consult the mathematician to ascertain the truth so fundamental to logic, logical hypotheses remain distinct from mathematical in that they express real possibilities.[23]

In addition, the theory of reasoning has an interest in the methods of mathematics. Devices such as abstraction are needed to disclose relations not expressed in the premises (4.370, c. 1903).

Finally, mathematical reasoning is of interest for the different modes of logical inference. Mathematical deduction has direct reference to imaginary objects or to arbitrary hypotheses and in this respect it differs from the logical inference of the normative sciences. Deduction in logic is but an application of mathematical deduction to experience. Induction and retroduction are decidedly not reducible to deduction, nor is any one reducible to the other, yet Peirce believed that the "rationale" of these inferences must be deductive and that the value of such reasonings is ultimately a question of the accuracy of deduction (312.47[1], 1903; 751.4, n.d.). Peirce called the division of mathematics relevant to the logician "Dyadics." Since the most serious problems encountered by the theory of probabilities are logical, the doctrine of chances is another mathematical study relevant to the logician (693b.278-80, [1904]).

Logic has need of phenomenology in several important respects. Not the least of these is the peculiar sort of thought developed for the difficult task of examining the phaneron – the ability to disentangle total confusion (1.280, c. 1902; 2.197, c. 1902). In common with the other normative sciences, logic assumes that the characteristics that phenomenology has shown to be always present to the mind, are so (8.239, 1904). The successful pursuit of speculative grammar particularly requires direct appeal to phenomenology (1338.40, [c. 1905-6]). As soon as he commences his studies, Peirce claimed that the logician discovers that he does not know the meaning of the terms he must use. Until he can arrive at satisfactory definitions his pursuit is mere guesswork. The findings of phenomenology are of fundamental value in overcoming this difficulty. Peirce observed that when the logician "can show what goes to the constitution of truth in terms of those universal elements which the phenomenologist has shown to be primary, he has done all that in the nature of things is possible" (693a.120-2, [1904]). In Peirce's own investigations, the three categories become the template for all logical analyses (see, for example, 478.164-5, 1903).[24]

Normative logic asks which theories and conceptions *ought* to be accepted. The question can only receive an answer in relation to an end, and discovering the end of thought is one of the first tasks of logic. As with ethics, it is a special determination of the general aim investigated by aesthetics. And because of the evolutionary nature of that aim, the modifications resulting from aesthetics' specific aim have indirect implications for logic's particular end. Indirectly also aesthetics influences logic through ethics.

From one point of view, Peirce stated, the principal subject of logic is reasoning. Reasoning is thinking, which is a kind of action. Thus logic is a particular application of the more general theory of action but with its own special peculiarities. Reasoning or rational inference is invariably attended with the belief that it is a particular instance of a more general type of inference.[25] Needless to say, such inference is not just any kind of thought. There are mental processes logically analogous to inference except that they are unconscious and therefore not amenable to control (5.108, 1903). But normative sciences essentially include interaction with the phaneron and not mere reaction to it. Thus the normative character of logic implies that reasoning is a free act and not simply an impulsive response to stimulus. According to Peirce, the essential difference between inference and other mental operations is that it is conscious, deliberate, and self-controlled. Control need not actually be employed; it is enough that the mind recognizes the possibility of such endorsement (939.3-4, [1905]). But if a conclusion is not rejected in the very act of declaring against it, that operation is not reasoning (5.108, 1903).

To grant that reasoning is self-controlled is to give credence to the claim that logic depends on ethical theory. Peirce thought that a review of the whole operation of self-control was needed, as logical self-control is but a species of ethical self-control. What links logical and ethical self-criticism is their mutual reliance on certain properties found in human nature at an early age. Consequently, the application of this control is already habitual and viewed as simple common sense. An abstract formulation of the principles involved tends to be ignored by philosophers (673.14-15, c. 1911) although in either discipline the process may be quite complex. In the case of logical control the "essential features are review, critical comparison with previous decisions or with ideals, rehearsal in the imagination of future conduct on various possible occasions, and the formation [or] modification thereby of habits or dispositions of the occult something behind consciousness" (939.4-5, [1905]).

From ethics, logic adopts the principle that whatever is uncontrolled is beyond criticism. Hence whatever we cannot help believing we cannot be responsible for and so cannot be blamed for, even though what we cannot conceive today may be conceivable tomorrow. If what is not doubted is beyond dispute, it must be whole-heartedly accepted as true. Pretending to doubt is futile, according to Peirce; it is important to adopt a method such that we will be able to doubt what we cannot doubt now (598.5-7, [c. 1902]; 8.191, c. 1904; 329.12, c. 1904; 5.419, 1905; 326.10, n.d.). "Credibilism"[26] and fallibilism, which comprise critical common-sensism, are seminal to this. Credibilism is the affirmation that some propositions are free from geniune doubt; these concern beliefs beyond our control. Fallibilism is the denial that any proposition can be completely immune to doubt; it is the rationale to pursuing a method that has a self-corrective tendency.

Aesthetics is needed at this point for, inasmuch as logic is the theory of deliberate thinking, thought is controlled to conform to a purpose. Thus right reasoning is reasoning that converges upon an ultimate aim: "thought, controlled by a rational experimental logic, tends to the fixation of certain opinions, ... the nature of which will be the same in the end, however the perversity of thought of whole generations may cause the postponement of the ultimate fixation" (5.430, 1905). Obviously, Peirce had in mind the scientific method that underlies pragmaticism. Nothing but future conduct can be so regulated and, indeed, Peirce believed that the final interpretant (cognition of a mind) consists in the way every mind *would* act, which is to say that it consists in a truth that might be formulated in a conditional proposition. No amount of actual occurrences in any mind, nor yet in any multitude of minds, can exhaust such a proposition (8.315, 1909).

The significance of ethics to logic in Peirce's own philosophy is evident. He was convinced that a "logic which does not recognize its relations to Ethics must be fatally unsound in its Methodeutic, if not in its Critic" (478.42, 1903).

Peirce used the term "logic" to refer to a variety of studies. Even within the context of the normative sciences the term is used ambiguously for, besides the dissociation of formal logic from the normative study, Peirce admitted to having used the term to refer to both the general normative theory and a specific branch of it. Originally he used the term to designate the narrower study of critical logic, but later he came to think that those persons who investigate how reasonings ought to be criticized are best able to inquire into the general laws of signs (1.444, c. 1896; 675.24, [c. 1911]). Peirce thought that the science should encompass not just symbols but all kinds of signs or representations, taking account of such things as a musical concerto or an instrument, a resolution or a painting, an archaeological expedition or a politician (449.60-1, 1903; 602.7-8, 1903-8; 4.9, 1905). The study of these other kinds of signs might stimulate suggestions for the more specific inquiry for, after all, if poetry is genuine it must also aim at a truth of sorts (although not the truth expressed in propositions, presumably it could be translated into a proposition). Moreover, Peirce suggested, lessons obtained from figurative ideas might provide more rigorous logical analyses (634.15-18, 1909; see also 5.571, 1901). Logic in this general sense is more appropriately termed "semiotic."

Normative semiotic, then, is the science that occupies the third division of the normative sciences. In the first place it is a theoretical science: the logician tries to bracket all knowledge except that known to everyone who reasons. It is not required that a precisely defined body of knowledge be delineated. The meaning of language is assumed to be known, although it may not be analysed, nor may all of its elements be recognized distinctly (449.54-5, 1903). By observing the characters of the known signs and with the aid of abstraction, an account is obtained of what the characters of signs used by experimental minds *must be*. As it is based on observation as well as on diagrammatic (mathematical) thought, logic is a positive science. It nevertheless differs markedly from the special sciences, not only because it lacks special objects of observation, but also because it seeks what ought to be rather than what is (3.428, 1896; 2.227, c. 1897). Because it is the third normative science, logic is a member of the second division of philosophy, and is characterized by the dualism of the normative sciences – that of relating phenomena to people in accordance with ends. It can be expected to have a special character of thirdness: in the normative sciences previously discussed the distinctive characteristic was a function of the kind of phenomena that concerns it. In the case of logic the distinctive characteristic is thought.

From its position in the classification of the sciences, then the business of logic must be to study the deliberate formation of habits of *thought* consistent with the logical end. That end will be a special determination of the general ideal investigated in aesthetics. For Peirce, the general ideal for pragmaticism was expressed as "the growth of concrete reasonableness" or "the continual embodiment of idea potentiality." This suggests that the particular end for the science of thought is reasonableness (or idea potentiality). Hence, the task of logic is to cultivate reason and bring it more nearly into conformity with reasonableness, which phenomenology has discerned as the third element of experience. Whether or not there is such reasonableness in the universe is not for logic to determine; any assurance vouchsafed by metaphysics has to be founded on logic. Thinking *about it* will not alter the real object, on Peirce's view, since that is what he meant by "real:" the real is precisely that which is independent of any particular individual's thought about it.

In the final anaylsis, what guarantees that the conclusion of any reasoning is true? Peirce pointed out that such assurance must be unreasoned, thus it can only have the character of faith. But unless it is assumed that the universe is characterized by a reasonableness on which the ultimately destined opinion might converge, there is no possibility of knowledge. If it should turn out to be destined to a limited fulfilment there would, at least, be an approximate reality. Equipped with that hypothesis and with the familiar facts of everyday experience, the logician may determine rules for reasoning that have mathematical definiteness (5.160, 1903; 634.8-9, 1909; 655.27, 1910; 735.4[1], n.d.).

Speculative grammar (3.1.2.2.3.1). For the first division of normative logic, Peirce adopted Duns Scotus's term "speculative grammar" which examines the physiology of signs of all kinds (2.83, c. 1902; 449.59-60, 1903). It inquires into their nature and meaning and so determines the general conditions to which they must conform to be signs; it analyses reasonings into their essential elements and exhibits their manner of composition unconstrained by the structure of the language in which they were originally expressed (1.444, c. 1896; 3.430, 1896; 2.206, 1901; 2.93, c. 1902; 1.191, 1903; 602.6, 1903-8).[27]

Analyses structured by Peirce's categories are found throughout his discussions of speculative grammar, for example, in the fundamental division of signs or representamens into icons, indices, and symbols. An icon is characterized by firstness in that it represents its object by its resemblance; an index belongs to the category of secondness in that its representative character consists in its dynamic relation to its object; and the thirdness of a symbol lies in the fact that what constitutes it as a sign is precisely that it will be used and understood as such.

As early as 1867 Peirce had spelled out the divisions of inference in accordance with his categories. In subsequent writings prior to 1900 he confused retroduction with induction and vacillated over the ordering. However, he eventually reaffirmed his original opinion, which he still maintained in 1910 (312.43[1]-7[1], 1903; 8.227-34, c. 1910).[28] Thus retroduction "or the suggestion of an explanatory theory, is inference through an Icon, and is thus connected with Firstness; Induction or trying how things will act, is inference through an Index, and is thus connected with Secondness; Deduction, or recognition of the relations of general ideas, is inference through a Symbol, and is thus connected with Thirdness" (312.44[1], 1903).[29]

In addition to the obvious reasons for escaping the strictures of a given language, arguments do not cede smoothly to analysis because there are no essential divisions in the expressions of natural languages. Even where parts are evident, the place of severance is usually obscure. Consequently, one of the first tasks of analysis is to frame a symbolic system representing a completely regular and exceptionless grammatical syntax that exhibits all the logical relations of a proposition so that minute analysis is made possible (452.11, 1903). Of course, the mathematician evolves systems of perfectly regular notation, but these are designed to make reasoning (principally about quantity) extremely convenient. The logician, in contrast, primarily aims at a symbolic system that precludes the interchange of "any" with "some one or other" and allows a minute analysis. Peirce's system of existential graphs comprises his specific contribution to this endeavour (856.8–9, [1911]).[30]

Critic (3.1.2.2.3.2). Critic is the second and classificatory branch of logic. Equipped with the analyses of speculative grammar, critic takes the constituent parts of arguments and inquires into the conditions to which symbols and other signs must conform if they are to approximate the reasonableness hypothesized of the universe; it ascertains the conditions necessary for stability in the beliefs expressed by the assertions. It studies the "perceptible relations between possible facts" and sheds light on the nature of the confidence that ought to be accorded the various kinds of reasonings. Thus the acceptance of truth of one set of facts may warrant accepting the truth of others (3.430, 1896; 2.205, 1901; 2.93, c. 1902; 1.191, 1903; 602.5, 1903–8; 675.7, [c. 1911]; 677.1, [c. 1911]; 735.1[1], n.d.).[31] The conclusions of the three distinct kinds of reasoning do offer different measures of assurance.

Retroduction is the most hazardous of inferences relying as it does on an affinity between the human mind and the laws of nature. It is the form of reasoning that occurs when a striking peculiarity is encountered. A suggestion that goes beyond the original data is made which, should it be confirmed, would explain the peculiar phenomenon. Because the hypothesis is quite divorced from the data, it can only be posited as an interrogation and it must be tested, confirmed, and refined by induction. The justification of a retroductive inference is that it might lead to important discoveries that no more secure reasoning could provide. Peirce maintained that it is the only means of acquiring new experiential knowledge and exerting rational control over future conduct. Neither deduction nor induction can augment the data of perception (692.23–7, 1901; 2.270, 1903; 856.3–4, [1911]; 682.42–4, [c. 1913]).

Induction is the experimental testing of a theory depending on real, not merely on imaginary experiments. It endorses knowledge already known, but only to a degree of probability. Yet perseverance in the same mode of reasoning, Peirce claimed, will reduce error indefinitely and converge on certainty. Hence the justification of an inductive inference is that "if the Prediction does not tend in the long run to be verified in any approximately determinate proportion of cases, experiment must, in the long run, ascertain this; while if the Prediction will, in the long run, be verified in any determinate, or approximately determinate, proportion of cases, experiment must in the long run, approximately ascertain what that proportion is" (2.269, 1903; see also 313.14, 1903; 856.3, [1911]).

Deduction is the most secure of all inferences. Still, it can only be applied directly to imaginary states of affairs or to arbitrary hypotheses. Such reasoning is "valid if and only if the state of things represented in its conclusion would be realized in every supposable consittution of the universe in which the premises should be true" (313.13, 1903; see also 3.641, 1901; 4.611, 1908; s97.208, n.d.). If a description of the psychological process involved in the imagined diagram is needed to illustrate the basis of deductive inference, the logician can refer to the psychologist. The logician, indeed, has no business in justifying the conclusions of deductive inference. Assurance in logic comes through mathematical reasoning, and the mathematician's warrant is that nothing could be more evident. Application to the world is trusted only if the arbitrary hypothesis is true of the world – something that can't be settled by deduction (s97.209, n.d.).

To the extent that reasoning is to predict facts, Peirce thought that the variation in the kinds and degrees of confidence justified in the different modes of reasoning might be generalized by saying that "an argument is sound if it necessarily must predict facts in the measure in which it promises to do so" (313.15, 1903).

Methodeutic (3.1.2.2.3.3). Methodeutic, the third branch of logic, is founded primarily on critic. It studies the general conditions of the relation of symbols and other signs to their interpretants. The thirdness distinctive of methodeutic is that triadic relation (1.559, 1867; 4.116, 1893; 2.93, c. 1902; 1.191, 1903; 793.13 [fragment], n.d.). The basic function of a sign is to make the relations efficient, not by instigating individual actions (because the final logical interpretant must be general), but by creating a habit which, when deliberately formed through analysis of the experiences that animate it, eventually issues in a general principle or law (8.332, 1904; 5.491, c. 1907; 322.10–11, [c. 1907]). The function of self-control, in accordance with the logical ideal, underlies that process. The general study of methodeutic must encompass an examination of the general conditions for exhibiting

the relations found in certain other relations. Thus it studies the order
or procedure appropriate to any inquiry (2.105-6, c. 1902; 452.6-7,
1903; 602.6, 1903-8; 606.17, [1905-6?]; 640.6, 1909).

Methods based on experience, without this theoretical study, are
bound to mislead whenever they are wrongly applied because they
can neither correct themselves nor signal their inappropriateness. *With
the theory we are not at the mercy of our method.* The deliberate
approval of it is tempered by our readiness to re-examine it and subject
it to constant criticism. Its only shortcoming is that there can be no
final criticism that is not itself liable to criticism. Confidence in the
method lies in the disposition to pursue criticism and inquiry further,
for if a problem is solvable, incessant criticism must eventually lead
to its solution (831.10-12, n.d.). Sound reasoning, then, adopts methods
that aim at the truth attainable when sufficient generations of investigators have deliberately pursued it. Absolute truth or an indefinite
approximation to it must ensue if the methods are persisted in, because
the assumption is that the truth will be attained at length (606.19,
[1905-6?]). Such is the character of that exemplary product of methodeutic, the scientific method. Applying that method to the meaning
of words yields the following maxim: "Consider what effects that *might
conceivably* have practical bearings, - especially in modifying habits
or as implying capacities, - you conceive the object of your conception
to have. Then your (interpretational) conception of these effects is the
whole (meaning of) your conception of the object" (322.11-12, [c.
1907]).[32] The pragmatic maxim, then, really is a rule of methodeutic.[33]
It is but a special application of the method of the special sciences
(320.23, [c. 1907]; 322.14, [c. 1907]; see also 8.191, c. 1904).

Although the experimental method is well known, its significance
to Peirce's philosophy warrants a closer look at the general method
and the methods of inference involved, particularly as it concerns the
not so well-known retroductive inference.

In the theoretical sciences, discovery begins with some kind of
surprising occurrence. Hence all such discoveries may well be regarded
as accidental. Galileo claimed that his discoveries were made with
the aid of common sense and with *il lume naturale*. This *lume naturale*
- this insight - is of the nature of instinct, according to Peirce (660.14,
1910). Nonetheless, Peirce recognized that humans have some sort of
divination, however imperfect, that enables their guesses to be right
with a much greater frequency than could be attained by chance. Since
human minds have evolved under the laws of nature, it is not altogether

unlikely that human mental processes should have some affinity with the laws of nature.

Retroduction involves the invention, selection, and entertainment of hypotheses. Accordingly, it begins with the formulation of one or more testable hypotheses that explain the surprising occurrence. If those hypotheses are the result of insight, retroduction would seem to lack the essential feature of all reasonings, namely, that they be self-controlled and not a mere instinctive performance of the organism. But self-control can only inhibit action or, at best, stimulate it; it cannot originate it. Consequently, the actual creative act of forming a suggestion is not controllable (5.194, 1903).[34] Yet to say that humans have a natural tendency sufficient to make countless scientists over many centuries guess correctly is not to say that the first guess hazarded by any individual has a greater probability of being right than wrong (692.30, 1901). It is, after all, usually the trained observer who is surprised, and thus his or her guesses will not be altogether baseless. The components of the hypothesis are already present in the scientist's mind. It is bringing the previously unrelated and seemingly disparate elements into a unified whole that constitutes the iconic insight (5.181, 1903). On encountering surprise, then, the scientist views it in the context of his or her systematized experience and devises a theory to explain the facts in a way that is consistent with the existing body of knowledge. Of course, the more extensive that knowledge is, the more costly will be the adjustment to the existing ordered experience. It may be necessary, Peirce held, to pursue entirely new lines of thought. Further, one should not stay with an isolated surprising experience, but should compare it with surprises that seem related, perhaps borrowing from other fields of research, particularly where the form of surprise is similar (778.5-6, [c. 1909]).

A good guess requires great genius. Short of that, it may safely be expected that whatever guess is first taken up on probation will be one of a long line to be tested and abandoned. Yet the part of retroduction that involves selecting the hypothesis is amenable to quite definite guidelines, and Peirce offered a number of suggestions: the principle governing the choice of hypotheses is economy – economy of such things as money, time, and thought. Rather than attack an entire theory at once, economy dictates that a hypothesis should be reduced to its smallest logical elements and no step should be taken until the preceding one has been experimentally tested.[35] If there are sound reasons for thinking that a particular hypothesis is correct, it will be the economical one to test; but usually one should be wary of one's preconceived ideas. Often the least likely hypotheses should be chosen simply because they can be readily dismissed. A contender for early selection is one which "bisects the probabilities" (778.6, [c. 1909]; 7.220-1, 1901; 691.96-7, .117-18, and .121 [fragments], 1901). Peirce ordered such factors as likelihood, naturalness, simplicity, breadth, cheapness, and smallness into a system of maxims that can be methodically applied by every retroductive inference.[36]

Once a hypothesis has been selected, the next task is to map out the necessary and probable consequences that can be submitted to experiment. This is deductive inference. *Deduction* is coextensive with necessary inference, which is limited to an ideal state of things. The hypothesis provides the ideal state here, so there is no difficulty concerning the deduction of necessary experimental consequences. But what of the probable consequences? Deductive reasoning guarantees that the conclusion is as certain as the premiss, but it makes no claim about the certainty of the premiss. Thus probable deductions are those claiming only that whatever probability is true of the premiss is necessarily true of the conclusion.

When deduction has drawn a set of "predictions" from the hypothesis, the third stage of testing those predictions is by experiment. This is *induction*. The deduction should have provided the researcher with a fair sample of experiments, none of which should be surmisable other than through the hypothesis. Economy (again) dictates the order in which predictions should be examined. That which is least likely to be verified should be chosen because that one experiment could refute the hypothesis positively. Upon comparing the prediction with the results obtained, the experimenter may find that the hypothesis has been confirmed or that some modification of it is indicated, or else that it needs to be abandoned. When one prediction after another gets verified, it is granted standing among scientific results (7.206, 1901).

It must not be thought that the scientific method is the only methodological study. The proper procedure for the doctrine of chances, for example, is another important topic that may also be investigated usefully.

With methodeutic, the discussion of logic as normative semiotic is brought to its completion and the groundwork is prepared for a sound metaphysics.

3. POST-NORMATIVE SCIENCES

1. Metaphysics (3.1.2.3)

Metaphysics is the third and completing division of philosophy, the department of the heuretic sciences that investigates phenomena common to all. While phenomenology studies the phenomenon in its firstness, sorting out the ubiquitous elements from which concepts are constructed, normative science studies the phenomenon in its secondness and culminates in an inquiry into how the mind must respond to the impact of the phenomenon when the *summum bonum* is deliberately pursued. Metaphysics mediates between these two divisions by studying the phenomenon in its thirdness (339.268r, 1905), as it really is. Metaphysics, then, inquires into the general features of reality and into whatever has individual reality (437.20, 1898; 655.23-4, 1910). "Reality," Peirce believed, "consists in regularity. Real regularity is active law. Active law is efficient reasonableness, or in other words is truly reasonable reasonableness. Reasonable reasonableness is Thirdness as Thirdness" (5.121, 1903).

Peirce was emphatic about the necessity of approaching metaphysics with a fully developed, rigorous science of logic. He cited Aristotelian and Kantian systems as precedents for this approach (although Peirce was of the opinion that Kant's metaphysics, in particular, suffered precisely because the logic on which it was based was less than adequate). He gave two reasons for his conviction. The first and most obvious was the folly of immersing oneself in metaphysics without any assurance of the nature and validity of the reasoning to be used. The second and more significant reason is that many of the metaphysical conceptions are logical conceptions applied to reality, so that their explication must proceed through logical investigation (283.34-5, 1905). Thus, before it is possible to answer questions such as whether substances, qualities, relations, laws, causation, and so on, are real,[37] a prior inquiry is needed, – one which assumes that what no one doubts is true. By analysing these common beliefs, their objectivity or lack of it is made apparent. And with these answers in hand, resolution of the metaphysical problems is immediately forthcoming (1.16, 1903).

If this is correct, a study of the logic of relations, of finite and infinite multitudes, of continuity, and of abstractions (in the sense in which a collection is an abstraction) is indispensable (310.1-2, 1903).[38] Indeed, if the propositions of metaphysics are not to be a meaningless series of words defined by other words, without ever attaining a real conception, it first must be recognized that metaphysics is an observational science. This is often overlooked, as the observations of metaphysics rest on familiar experience. But once it is conceded, the applicability of the scientific method is evident. Its scrupulous implementation will forestall practices in which preconceived ideas dictate conclusions disregarding common sense, as was the fashion, Peirce thought, in most previous systems (6.5, 1898; 322.15bis, [c. 1907]).

With the pragmatic method, then, the most difficult questions of metaphysics will be unravelled. It will become clear that most unanswered questions must merely await certain definite experience or information that will be attained if the investigation is pursued long enough (322.15–16, [c. 1907]).

The relation of logic to metaphysics is a question requiring a study of its own. The few remarks made here are intended merely to hint at the direction of Peirce's thinking and to indicate the broader relations.[39]

At this point in the classification scheme, it comes as no surprise to find that metaphysics has three divisions.

Ontology (3.1.2.3.1). Ontology, the first of these, inquires into the nature and kinds of reality. It does this by determining the essential relations of the kinds of phenomena experienced in the psycho-physical universe that ought to enter into the very descriptions of the phenomena (602.2, 1903–8). Thus metaphysics is grounded in those categories identified by phenomenology and validated by logic (1338.39–40, [c. 1905–6]).

In attempting to define "reality," the logical priority of the science of logic is manifest. Every sentence ever pronounced assumes that there is such a thing as truth, and thus the assumption must be one that no one genuinely doubts. The essential character of the truth is that the universe that it represents is independent of how it is represented. This is not to say that it is independent of mind, or of the general, or of thirdness (for representation *is* thirdness), but that it is independent of how any individual or any generation of individuals represent it (313.18, 1903). If every true proposition declares something concerning an independent reality, truth must represent the real as it really is. Hence the abstract definition of truth amounts to an abstract definition of the real (655.30, 1910). Reality, then, is that which is such as it is independently of how anyone thinks of it. Consider what the pragmatic maxim does to an understanding of truth and falsity:

> The rule is explicit: we are to ask what will be the conceivable practical effects of error. It maybe [sic] that we shall come across a fact which manifestly refutes it; but whether quite this happens or not, according to our maxim, either error means nothing at all, or else under some conceivable conditions it would inevitably lead to some definite result. Under what conditions, and to what result? To the result of refutation and recantation, supposing genuine inquiry were to be carried far enough. That is the plain lesson of pragmatism: error is that which sufficient inquiry would refute. Consequently, truth is that belief to which sufficient inquiry would inevitably lead. But truth is the assertion that subjects have the attributes that they in reality have. Hence, the pragmatistic doctrine must be that the immediate object of that conception of things in which minds would ultimately concur, if inquiry were to be pushed far enough, is the very reality itself. (322.20-1, [c. 1907])

As soon as the question of what is reality is settled, other ontological questions, such as whether or not necessity and contingency are real modes of being, or whether or not the laws of nature are real, jostle for attention (5.496, c. 1907). Peirce thought that his system readily answers these with the aid of the pragmatic method and the three categories.

Physical Metaphysics (3.1.2.3.2). Physical metaphysics forms the second branch of metaphysics. It studies the dynamic relations found in the kinds of phenomena of the universe that ought to feature in their ultimate descriptions (602.2, 1903-8) and it studies the process whereby phenomena are evolved (311.2, 1903). Such investigations comprise the foundations of the physical sciences (693a. 88, [1904]). It has three divisions: cosmology, the doctrine of time and space, and the doctrine of matter (1.192, 1903; 693a.72, [1904]).[40]

Psychical or Religious Metaphysics (3.1.2.3.3). Psychical or religious metaphysics is the third and completing branch of metaphysics. It inquires into the rational relations among the ubiquitous elements involved in the essential descriptions of the phenomena, and into the necessity of the phenomena becoming just what they do become (602.2, 1903-8). This branch thus studies reality as it concerns the spiritual aspirations of humans (693a.88, [1904]). It divides into metaphysical theology, the theory of freedom, and the doctrine of another life (1.192, 1903; 693a.72, [1904]).

Metaphysics makes constant appeal to the special sciences for data, but it derives no principles from that source. Yet not one of the special sciences can proceed properly without the aid of metaphysical principles (1336.12, [1892]).

2. The Special Sciences or Idioscopy (3.1.3)

The special sciences form the third and last department of the heuretic sciences. They observe previously unknown phenomena using special means and training. Such special investigations presuppose entire batteries of truth which, prior to scientific inquiry, can be vaguely characterized as the spectrum of instinctive or inherited beliefs reinforced by the day-to-day experiences familiar to all. In its original guise that unscientific legacy is much more reliable than any discovery brought to light by the special sciences, if only because it has been taken for granted in such investigations. And although the indefiniteness of that "knowledge" is no drawback to its sway in daily experience, it is an inadequate basis for scientific theory until it has been subjected to criticism (299.2–3, c. 1905). The scientific study of ordinary experience is, of course, the business of philosophy.

Insofar as logic is concerned, Peirce was of the opinion that the criticism that had been forthcoming had produced very dubious results (see chapter 3, section 5). Some logicians had even attempted to found it on one of the special sciences. If logic appealed to any of the special sciences for principles, it would call into question the universal validity of the resultant logical theory. In fact, Peirce thought that no scientific investigation could pretend to be a rigorous undertaking if it advanced one step without first determining the appropriate method to be pursued. But before the proper method could be selected, it was necessary to consider the method of selection. Peirce thought that the search must continue "until we reach (as we probably may) a point at which the results of all further questioning along that endless line can be evidently foreseen, and its limiting upshot ascertained" (299.3, c. 1905). It is after the more rigorous and general principles of methodeutic have been worked out that a survey of the various methods leading science to the truth is needed, in order to ascertain inductively the method that best satisfies both speed and economy (693a.212–14, [1904]).[41]

The special sciences do not simply employ logical reasoning, but actually seek principles from the theory of logic. Generally, more proximate sciences have more direct and intimate dependence, while those further separated in the classification scheme receive logical principles mediated by a preceding special science. But this is not always the case. The classificatory sciences have to consult logic when appraising their own classifications, and descriptive sciences, such as history and geology, occasionally appeal directly to the "theory of evidence" (2.121, c. 1902).

Logic is not the only department of philosophy to which the special sciences must appeal. The more abstract questions go beyond the province of special sciences and require the general conceptions of metaphysics. Hence, whenever those sciences are pursued without regard to metaphysics they are allowed to rest on unidentified and thus on unexamined theories (7.579, c. 1867; 2.121, c. 1902; 311.5, 1903).

Mathematics is the other important source for principles. Physics depends on calculus for its very existence and, even if other sciences do not depend on mathematics quite so directly, they do receive mathematical principles indirectly through physics if they are pursued with scientific rigour (328.21–2, c. 1905).

The task of the special scientist is to discover phenomena not previously known, to subject those phenomena to criticism, and to devise truths that are generally merely plausible (655.18, 1910). Accordingly, it is necessary to acquire unusual experiences by means of specially contrived observations. This requires special training and a special body of information providing the context within which the new observation is to be contrasted and interpreted. The necessity for different natural talents, different training, and different surroundings, tends to splinter the sciences – particularly when they are still in their infancy (299.6–7, c. 1905). Apart from that, Peirce thought it unwise for individuals to devote themselves to more than one science because of the time, energy, and thought necessary to arrive at new discoveries. The very reason that those discoveries escaped detection in the past is that no one was in a situation to ascertain them (601.19[1]–20[1], [1906]), perhaps lacking the necessary technology and instrumentation. As might be expected, the solution to any problem allows passage to the solution of a specific other problem (601.10[1], [1906]).

The special sciences form two divisions according to the nature of the objects investigated. Physics studies the material universe, confining itself to phenomena as they occur, independently of how anyone thinks about them. The psychical sciences investigate the products of finite minds, of humans and other intelligences; they are limited, therefore, to phenomena as they are dependent on how people think and feel. Peirce appears to have concluded that the psychical sciences depend on physics, but as that dependence is not of the required kind they form two parallel wings (1334.24-5, 1905; 1338.8, [c. 1905-6]; 615.20, 1908; 655.18, 1910). These two major divisions present a dissonance in the trichotomic symmetry exhibited elsewhere in the classification scheme. At one point, however, Peirce suggested that in time a third division may emerge to observe "the workings of ideas like Truth, Humanity, etc." (693a, 86, [1904]).[42]

Analogous triadic divisions occur in each wing and these do follow the pattern of principle-dependence. Differentiation is by mode of investigation, that is, by the different training and environment required. Peirce suggested further subdivisions that are more or less similar to each of the six cenoscopic divisions.

Nomological Sciences (3.1.2.1). The nomological division first examines the ubiquitous elements that pervade the universe under investigation. The physical universe is examined in the light of metaphysics and mathematics in order to formulate general laws and to measure constants. Its major divisions are dynamics, physics of special forces, and physics of the constitution of matter. In Peirce's system, the psychic universe draws principles from metaphysics, logic, and phenomenology, and studies the laws of association and of fatigue as well as any other universal mental phenomena. Under nomological psychics, then, there is general psychology, general sociology, and general economics. Peirce was of the opinion that both nomological wings aspire to converge on metaphysics.

Classificatory Sciences (3.1.3.2). Following the sciences of laws are the sciences of kinds, which comprise the second, classificatory division of the special sciences. These sciences endeavour to order phenomena and to study the resulting classes of facts. The universal laws of nature that were discovered by the nomological sciences are needed to explain why the statistical properties of a class are such as they are. Not infrequently, the classificatory scientist ascribes the status of a law to the regularities he or she has discovered. Although these sciences are constantly extending their discoveries and converging on the nomological sciences, these so-called laws (for example, Mendeleev's law) are different from those discovered in nomology. For one thing, their methods of discovery differ. The nomological laws are discovered through retroduction, while the regularities of the classificatory sciences are found by sorting through the confusion of facts. Peirce ascribed chemistry, crystallography, and biology to the classificatory sciences of physics; and he allocated special psychology, linguistics, and ethnology to psychics.

Explanatory Sciences (3.1.3.3). In Peirce's scheme, the special sciences of the descriptive or explanatory division inquire into individual events and single objects. They describe them in detail and explain their pecularities in terms of the principles of the nomological and classificatory sciences. Analysis of the phenomena is furthered by theories that are much simpler than the facts being explained. In political economy, for example, Peirce thought that the rational procedure is to consider people as streamlined role players rather than as complex members of human society, which they really are. In this way it is possible to obtain models that can be altered by inputs of varying complexity. But because such theories are simpler than the facts they purport to explain, it is essential to treat radical results with considerable circumspection. On the other hand, any refutations of the theories that depend on such extreme consequences should also be viewed with suspicion. The explanatory sciences of physics include astronomy and geognosy (geography and geology). Those of psychics endeavour to describe and explain individual manifestations of minds, either in artifacts or in actions. Included are history, biography, and criticism of arts and literature (7.84-5 and .96, 1901; 1.187-201, 1903; 693a.72-6 and 693b.422-32, [1904]; 1334.25-6, 1905; 1338.9-14, [c. 1905-6]; 601.14^1-20^1, [1906]; 655.18-22, 1910; 675.11, [c. 1911]).[43]

The principles made available by the classifactory sciences, enable the explanatory sciences to understand the facts gathered; astronomy and geognosy, for example, borrow principles from chemistry and crystallography. At the same time, both the physical and the psychical wings of the explanatory sciences afford considerable data to the classificatory sciences. Furthermore, they tend to coalesce with the classifactory sciences.

The explanatory sciences complete the divisions of the special sciences, which round out the heuretic sciences.

· *3. The Sciences of Review (3.2)*

The heuretic sciences aim at the discovery of truth in complete disregard of the practical consequences. The sciences of review, however, are concerned to make those discoveries accessible to other disciplines, be they educational, philosophical, practical, or recreational. Their aim, then, is to assemble the mathematical deductions, the philosophical analyses, and the discoveries of the special sciences so that their findings can be readily grasped and manipulated for any application whatever, either in action or (more likely) in cognition. The very narrowness of their respective specializations prevents the heuretic scientists from subjecting their own discoveries to any comprehensive criticism. It is left to the systematic scientists to generalize and criticize those fragmented discoveries, as well as to collect, arrange, and digest them into handbooks. Consequently, their studies of the preceding sciences (supplemented by investigations peculiar to their own pursuits) are of the same high calibre. An essential task of the sciences of review is to develop a classification of the sciences and to explain what characterizes the various classes, using principles found out by logic. Ultimately these scientists produce such general surveys as Comte's *Cours de philosophie positive* (1830-42) and Spencer's *System of Synthetic Philosophy* (1862-93) (1.182, 1903; 693a.78, [1904]; 605.6-7, [1905-6]; 1338.3-4, [c. 1905-6]; 601.26[1], [1906]; 326.20, n.d.). Peirce made no attempt to fill out his classification scheme with any enumeration of the sciences of review, but it seems likely that every one of the heuretic sciences would have had its systematic counterpart.

4. The Practical Sciences (3.3)

The task of the third major division of the sciences is to discover truth for some defined human need, although the researchers themselves may not be involved in the practical application of their investigations. Peirce noted that this group of sciences attracts significantly more scholars than the previous groups. While these disciplines primarily involve reasonings and related operations, an enormous number of facts not previously assembled, must be collected also. These facts concern either the want that is waiting to be satisfied or the physical means to its implementation. Although they are bound to make their own observations and amass their own data, the practical scientists are quite dependent on the discoveries of the heuretic sciences; but those diffuse findings are of little use to them until the sciences of review have provided them with systematic studies of the discoveries in the appropriate fields. The need to appeal to the sciences of review bears out the rational precedence of those sciences (693a.78-80, [1904]; 601.27^1-30^1, [1906]; 655.17, 1910). Peirce claimed to have devoted considerable effort to classifying the practical sciences, but he regarded the attempt as a failure (602.16, 1903-8).[44]

These three groups – the heuretic sciences, the sciences of review, and the practical sciences – comprise the whole of science.

In the hierarchy of principle-dependence, sciences usually (though by no means always) obtain principles directly from the more nearly contiguous sciences. Yet it now seems clear that each of the three major groups of sciences contain sciences with more or less similar subject matter. Ethics, for example, probably has its parallel in the sciences of review, and there certainly is a practical science of morals (cf. 5.125, 1903; 693a.122-6, [1904]; 605.5-6, [1905-6]). In addition to the direct appeal to immediately prior sciences, there is a direct appeal to the corresponding science in the group of preceding sciences. This in no way compromises the hierarchical ordering.

Peirce seems to think that the tendency for sciences to merge into those immediately preceding is characteristic of the entire system. The modification just noted, however, may also be operative in this respect. At all events, the practical sciences are attempting to become more systematic and the sciences of review are converging on the heuretic sciences. All of the special sciences tend to become nomological and these tend to merge with metaphysics. Metaphysics, in its turn, is moving towards logic, and logic is converging on mathematics (437.26-8, 1898; 693a.88-90, 693b.424-8, [1904]; 601.15, [1906]). On what will mathematics converge?

An answer is found in a digression in "Detached Ideas on Vitally Important Topics," in which Peirce turned to matters more significant than mere vital importance. Remarking that it is not uncommon for researchers pursuing quite unrelated studies to arrive at hypotheses with the same form, Peirce went on to say:

All this crowd of creators of forms for which the real world affords no parallel

... are, as we now begin to discern, gradually uncovering one great cosmos of forms, a world of potential being ... [T]he typical pure mathematician is a sort of Platonist. Only, he is [a] Platonist who corrects the Heraclitan error that the eternal is not continuous. The eternal is for him a world, a cosmos, in which the universe of actual existence is nothing but an arbitrary locus. The end that pure mathematics is pursuing is to discover that real potential world. (1.646, 1898)[45]

It is, after all, natural for a science to begin with gross distinctions of quality and, as it progresses, to advance towards the more minute distinctions of quantity (see 706.27, 1909).

The multi-directional interaction between the sciences in terms of principle- and data-dependence indicates an evolutionary development, which, if true, would seem to vindicate the pragmatic ideal (or something very like it) as the only adequate *summum bonum*.

Peirce intended his scheme to be a natural classification of the sciences, of which there can be only one. If he was correct in this, his scheme should indicate the relations of a particular science to other sciences; and in doing so, it should exhibit the real connections and major facts regarding the various sciences insofar as they are responsive to scientific inquiry (1334.9–10, 1905). Further, it should disclose the varying degrees of confidence appropriate to each science. Peirce was careful not to claim that the absence of a scheme would prevent discoveries being made sooner or later. Yet it is not simply a convenience. He believed that it actuated progress. The systematic pursuit of antecedent sciences should accelerate problems toward their ultimate solution (448.47–8, 1903; 8.297, 1904; 601.17[1], [1906]) and this was expected to have a positive effect on the economy of time, money, and energy (4.242, c. 1902).

I have suggested that setting forth a science so as to exhibit its relations to other sciences amounts to indicating the pragmatic meaning of that science. I have further suggested that one of Peirce's reasons for developing a classification of the sciences was to elucidate what was meant (or at least what he meant) by the science of logic. A composite diagram representing the relations of logic to other sciences (as Peirce saw them) and illustrating the more marked conceivable effects has now been presented. A fuller assessment of logic in its third grade of clearness requires a more detailed examination of the relation between the sciences, for it is characteristic of classification schemes that they exhibit only the simpler relations. This simplicity is generally regarded as a positive attribute, as in this instance, because it does provide the basis for an inquiry into finer relations. Presumably the scientist pursuing normative semiotic would be best equipped for such an undertaking.

The principles that Peirce identified as underpinning normative semiotic are not the only possible relevant principles that could ensue from the sciences of ethics and aesthetics. Peirce did not claim to be an expert in those sciences, and it is primarily because so little had been done at the heuretic level that he felt it necessary to pursue those inquiries himself. If anyone had convinced him that the principles he discovered in those two disciplines were mistaken or inadequate he would have re-examined and either abandoned or modified a logic that was thus shown to have an uncertain foundation. In fact, his earlier belief – that pragmatism presupposed an aesthetic principle – which he considered to be false, had brought him to the brink of renouncing pragmatism. His rejection of action as the *summum bonum* did lead him to the reformulation of his doctrine.

Another reason for Peirce's developing a classification of the sciences was his expectation that it would vindicate his three universal categories. This has not been demonstrated. That the categories provide a formal differentiating principle is a step towards their confirmation, but is not enough. It needs to be shown that, over an extended period of time, the classification has practical advantages to practising scientists. The misconceptions surrounding the scheme, have worked against its acceptance.

VI

Implications for Pragmaticism

Throughout the preceding investigation I have suggested that the developments indicated have implications for pragmaticism. Peirce expressed the opinion that an examination of the classification of the sciences is a useful preliminary to understanding that doctrine (327.5, n.d.). It is now clear that this is because the classification conveys, in a most explicit way, the pragmatic meaning of the maxim itself. The pragmatic principle is a special application of the scientific method and is a result of the investigations of methodeutic. Thus the conceivable effects of the pragmatic principle itself can be ascertained by viewing it in the context of the classification.

Since the scientific method involves all three modes of inference, the pragmatic principle will be augmented by any improvements resulting from analyses in critic and from investigations into self-control pursued in ethics. But the pragmatic maxim is purpose-oriented and appeals to the general ideal found out by aesthetics. This in turn is refined by the dynamic interaction of the specific ends in each of the normative sciences. Presumably there will emerge a more perfect understanding of what constitutes that reasonableness or idea-potentiality that is the *summum bonum* for pragmaticism. The content of the maxim will evolve to enrich the principle. Any illumination cast on logic by relating it to other sciences may also reflect on methodeutic and thus also on pragmaticism.

The classification of the sciences indicates logic's connections with the immediately surrounding sciences as well as with those normative sciences studied in the sciences of review and the practical sciences. The logician, of course, would want to study those connections in greater depth, monitoring refinements as they occur.

Although the previous chapter focused on the pragmatic meaning of logic, the classification displays the conceivable effects of each science in a complex lattice so that the pragmatic meaning of any given science can be ascertained.

This chapter will attempt to marshal the classification's more specific bearing on pragmaticism.

1. PRELUDE TO THE MATURE DOCTRINE

Although Peirce's 1878 pronouncement of the pragmatic maxim clearly aligned meaning with concepts and not with action, he did think that a cursory reading of it might lead to that kind of misapprehension. Indeed, he had all but yielded to such an interpretation himself at one point and came close to forsaking pragmatism altogether for that very reason (329.16, c. 1904; 284.3-4, c. 1905). Peirce thought that it was folly to make action – in itself and irrespective of the thought it enacts – the ultimate end of life or of thought, because action itself supposes an end (5.3, 1901). He thought that his account of the hardness of an unexamined or unexperienced diamond had been most conducive to that error. In his early article, "How to Make Our Ideas Clear," Peirce maintained that calling a diamond hard or soft was merely a matter of how speech is used. Yet the question for the pragmatic maxim was not what *did* occur, but what action would be appropriate if investigation were pursued sufficiently far. Disavowing his early account, Peirce maintained that the principle should not be taken in such an individualistic way. The pragmatic end, he said, was the "development of embodied ideas" and could not be attained by single events because individual action is a means rather than the end (5.402 note 2, 1893). In "How to Make Our Ideas Clear" Peirce said that the purpose of thinking is to establish a belief, a habit of thought. To consider the hardness of the diamond as simply a verbal question was to regard a habit as being made up of actual events. This, he later maintained, amounts to representing a general "as constituted by the existence of individuals of a given kind instead of by the unvariable non existence of individuals of the opposite kind" (289.11-12, [c. 1905]). Moreover, by attending only to what actually takes place, potentiality is reduced to actuality; what *would be* is resolved into what *will be*. Peirce needed to modify his view of possibility for, as long as he did not acknowledge the reality of the unactualized possibility of the diamond's hardness, action would seem the be-all and end-all of meaning.

At an early date Peirce maintained that generals were real. Real necessities were also soon accepted, and real possibilities might have been expected to succeed them forthwith; but in the 1878 paper Peirce vacillated (288.129, 1905; cf. 5.527, c. 1905). He was late in adopting a decisive position. By 1897 the logic of relations had convinced him that the Philonian (or material) conditional could not interpret every conditional proposition. Recognition of its inadequacy, Peirce ventured to say, was "one of the most important points of pragmatism as to which I have been compelled to reverse my former opinion" (292.51, [c. 1906]). An additional interpretation of the conditional proposition was needed, he believed, to give formal recognition to objective possibility. The possibilities that are neither actual nor existent are, nevertheless, not figments. According to Peirce, "they are such as they are whether you and I think them to be so, or not. The *future* does not exist. But it is really true that *if* I find the air in my study stuffy, I *can* open the window" (939.21, [1905]). For purposes of logic, of course, the reality of real possibilities is of the nature of representations. Their mode of being is for metaphysics to determine (735.13^2, n.d.). Acknowledging the reality of unactualized possibility has far-reaching implications. Not only does it unequivocally resolve the diamond dilemma, but it shows that the meaning of a concept lies in future possible instances (see appendix 4), and provides the link needed to make pragmaticism an intelligible theory (288.129, 1905).

Those who interpreted pragmatism as making action the *summum bonum* were not limited to opponents of the theory. Peirce credited William James[1] with extending the doctrine in that direction (5.3, 1901). Some of these interpretations were the more insidious because they originated with zealous proponents of pragmatism. It is not clear if Peirce had one of these in mind, but he evidently thought it necessary to insist that the pragmatic maxim is not just a handy device to be used as long as it was found "serviceable," and also to deny that the maxim is a "convenient fiction" (8.191, c. 1904; 328.6, c. 1905).

2. PRAGMATICISM: PEIRCE'S SPECIAL THEORY

In order to dissociate his doctrine from popularized interpretations, Peirce chose the name "pragmaticism" to indicate a special version of the more general theory. He thought that all pragmatists should agree to the meaning of a concept extending beyond what is contained in the thought itself (908.2-4, n.d.). Thus to ignore the relations involved in the thought would be as idiotic as to refer to people being parents in themselves, without reference to their offspring. A thought refers to an object (either real or fictitious) but is also assumed to be interpretable and must be related to an interpretant. The pragmaticist of Peirce's stripe makes the additional claim that "if the ultimate interpretation of a thought relates to anything but a determination of conditional conduct" (908.4, n.d.), it cannot be of an intellectual nature and therefore is not strictly a concept. Pragmaticists are concerned only with the intellectual portion of meaning and disregard the experience of brute force even though it is an important aspect of the practical. In maintaining that exertive force is not the same as a concept, they deny that what import it has is enough to make practical reality into an idea (8.195, c. 1904).

Peirce usually tempered his criticism of fellow pragmatists by selecting from their doctrine what he could accept with minimal modification. But more than once he cited James and Schiller as maintaining that an endless series cannot be completed and cannot properly be conceived (599.31^1, [c. 1902]; 6.179, c. 1911); yet, for Peirce, the concept of infinite series is a theoretical requirement for pragmaticism (see appendix 3 below). Other related shortcomings are noted in a less guarded statement in which Peirce wrote parenthetically that they made pragmatism "imply 'the will to believe,' the mutability of truth, the soundness of Zeno's refutation of motion, and pluralism generally" (675.Add 8 [13-14], [c. 1911]; see also 318.77^3, c. 1907; 655.27-8, 1910 [deleted passage]). If such was indeed his opinion it is little wonder that he endeavoured to divorce his doctrine from those interpretations. Neither is it surprising that he expended considerable effort in attempting to establish pragmaticism on a sound basis.

One way of accomplishing this would be to present a proof of pragmaticism, but although Peirce pursued many arguments through various avenues, he seems not to have presented a definitive proof. It is Peirce's claim, vindicated by his writings, that the argument for pragmaticism "is one of these large arguments having many points of support, upon no one of which it rests very heavily, which require large volumes for their full presentation and large intelligence for their full appreciation, and are far more likely to be underestimated, or even entirely missed, than to be overestimated" (283.67^4-8^4, 1905).

Nonetheless Peirce left no doubt that a proof of some kind is to the purpose. He denied that the principle is merely a device of expediency and he was no less adamant in denying that it is self-evident. To assume that it is, Peirce argued, is in conflict with the principle itself:

For this principle would reduce the questions of philosophy to questions of practical life, which is a matter of experience. There is no sense or meaning in saying that you know anything as a practical truth as selfevident. For to say it is selfevident is to say that nothing contrary to it can be imagined; and to say that you know a thing as a practical truth is to say that you know a rule of conduct with reference to it. Now it is nonsense to talk of a rule of conduct where only one mode of conduct can be imagined. Therefore, if so fruitful a principle is true, then, according to this very principle itself it is a great experiential truth, a generalization of all the facts of life.

(328.5, c. 1905).

Accordingly, even those persuaded of the truth of pragmaticism are, it seems, bound to grant that it is subject to proof. And if it is a "generalization of all the facts of life" it is no doubt a retroductive inference, which is subject to inductive support. That being so, it never could be accepted with apodictic certainty, for confidence in it *cannot* be expected to exceed a high degree of probability.

Peirce also tried to establish pragmaticism in contradistinction to pragmatism by showing that the ultimate end cannot be action but must be an idea. He contended that when the pragmatist claims that meaning resides in the way a symbol might lead people to act, a description of the action that is directed toward some purpose is intended, and not any sort of mechanical movement that might result; for what makes the effect of one possible action more satisfactory than another is its closer conformity to an intention. An intention is a thought; and what makes one intention more satisfactory than another is *its* closer conformity to an ultimate purpose. Thus it is solely the idea that confers value on an actual occurence (328.6, c. 1905). Of course, when Peirce denied that action was the end of thought he was confronted with the corollary that the pragmatic principle is purpose-oriented. That precipitated the need to inquire into an ultimate purpose that could satisfy a course of action that might be pursued deliberately for an indefinite period (5.135, 1903).

For an ultimate purpose to be able to continue to satisfy indefinitely, it should "consist in that process of evolution whereby the existent comes more and more to embody those generals" (5.433, 1905), which Peirce called "reasonable" and which he regarded as "destined" (in the sense of being independent of accidental circumstances).[2]

Since the pragmaticist has made the end of reasoning the essential element, it becomes necessary to inquire into the logically good. This involves the morally good and ultimately depends on the nature of the *summum bonum* found out by aesthetics.

Peirce thought that the continual increase of idea potentiality is an ultimate end consistent with pragmaticism but he stipulated that an endless series of signs, which never get realized in action but are translated into nothing but signs, would not show any growth (283.103–4, 1905). Although the pragmaticist maintains that meaning is general and, as such, is of the nature of a sign, the importance of action must not be ignored. The most adequate way to convey the meaning of a concept, Peirce maintained, is to describe the habits of action that it will promote; and the only way to describe a habit is by giving a general account of the sort of action it will produce in specified circumstances (318.76[3], c. 1907). Peirce was unremitting. He claimed that mind (in the sense of representation) acts on matter in such a way as to impose upon it "conformity to certain peculiar Laws, called Purposes; and the manner of the reaction is that the Purposes themselves become modified and developed in being thus carried out. Logical analysis shows that it is essential to the nature of a representation that it should so develope itself by imposing purposes upon matter" (478.18[1], 1903). Consider how a law might operate on human conduct. The only reasonable way in which it might do so would be when awareness of that law creates reasonable expectations of some future occurrence. All that is needed is that such expectations should ordinarily be met (8.192, c. 1904). Yet if the anticipated reaction is not fulfilled, the resultant surprise might be a first step towards a new idea.

The interaction between the object and its representation, the law and its instantiation, is consistent with Peirce's view that an evolving *summum bonum* receives its impetus from all three normative sciences and from the interrelations between them.

While the *end* of reasoning indicates the secondary role of ethics and the primary role of aesthetics with regard to pragmaticism, reasoning itself testifies to the direct connection with ethics. Reasoning is controlled thought and the inquiry into the operation of self-control,

Peirce argued, is the business of ethics. Given the ethical principle that it is futile to criticize what one cannot control and that future facts are all that one can (in a measure) control, pragmaticism, which asserts that meaning refers to deliberate or controlled conduct, must maintain that the conclusion of a piece of reasoning refers to the future. According to Peirce, "a proposition describes a conceivable experiment. The subject (or antecedent) prescribes what is to be done, while the predicate (or consequent) tells what to expect will happen; and every proposition really relates to the future" (289.21-2, [c. 1905]).

If this is so, documents of the past must also relate to the future, for their only application can be to indicate what might be anticipated. (Peirce did not suggest that the past provides "lessons of history" but merely that it can effect future conduct [289.22, (c. 1905)]; for example, your next encounter with a discussion involving Peirce's understanding of logic and how it relates to the other normative sciences would be informed, perhaps, by your reading here.[3]) Thus the future-directedness of pragmaticism is borne out by ethics and endorses the conclusion derived from the recognition of real possibilities.

The relevance of ethics and aesthetics to logic and to pragmaticism makes the relations that obtain between the normative sciences of considerable moment to a clear understanding of pragmaticism. The pragmatic maxim allows that, given favourable circumstances, inquiry would ultimately attain the truth, wherever it may be found. When inquiry has achieved all that it can, three options remain: in the first, one course of action may be affirmed; in the second, it may be denied; in the third, virtue may be found in neither. Pragmaticism regards the first and second as asserting truth and falsity, respectively, while it considers the third meaningless (289.16-17, [c. 1905]).

Initially, Peirce maintained that truth is the opinion that adequate inquiry would confirm and fix for all time. He later modified this somewhat, since he saw no reason, with regard to any particular question, why opinion might not fluctuate for all time. If that were so, for those questions no *real* truth could be obtained (5.461, 1905; 288.170-3, 1905). This position was further qualified in 1905. "In such a case, (if such there be,)" he then said, "the real truth would be of an *indefinite* nature, that is, would in some measure violate the principle of contradiction, being as much *pro* as *con*, somewhat the one and somewhat the other" (300.7, 1905).

What explanation can be given for this statement? The ultimate end for pragmaticism is "a process of evolution whereby the existent comes more and more to embody a certain class of generals which in the course of the development show themselves to be reasonable" (329.20, c. 1904). Peirce seems to have suggested that both the external world and our knowledge of it are continually evolving. He argued that the objects of knowledge are independent of any particular mind, though not independent of thought in general. Experience is needed to pursue the pragmatic end, for without it people cannot advance to a new idea. With the impact of experience (which Peirce claimed constitutes the object as being exterior to the individual thinker) and the constant correction vouchsafed by the scientific method, there will be increasing uniformity of opinion. In the later stages of evolution, as the ultimately destined agreement is approached, the process advances increasingly through reason and so through self-control (329.20, c. 1904; 5.433, 1905). The final opinion, then, will no doubt be comprised of a set of general laws. Laws, of course, require only "an approach to uniformity in a decided majority of cases" (8.192, c. 1904). Peirce maintained that there is an element of chance in the universe that accounts for "sporting," or accidental variations. Consequently, there probably will be no definite answer to some questions. Furthermore, the propensity to take on habits is, evidently, not merely a law among laws but is also a law governing every law. That being so, the increasing instantiation of reasonableness will have an evolutionary effect on the external world also. It might continue to grow without surcease, confirming the possibility that there may be questions that never get decisive answers.

General laws are what render phenomena regular and intelligible. Peirce thought that they are the most thoroughly real things there are. Thus while they constitute the universe as intelligible, they simultaneously determine the opinion that culminates the investigations of the community of scientists, at which point the argument begins to encroach on metaphysics.

3. EFFECT ON METAPHYSICS

The application of the pragmatic principle to metaphysics and to the special sciences is warranted by the ordering of the sciences in terms of principle-dependence. The metaphysical doctrine with which the pragmatic method has most affinity, according to Peirce, is what he called "conditional idealism," a term that indicates its connection with, and correction of, Berkeley's theory (322.20 [c. 1907]; cf. 5.494, c. 1907).

If what is real does consist in a set of general laws that are expressed in the final opinion, it would seem plausible to conclude that reality is a third – such as the mind of objective idealism. Certainly monism is consistent with continuity which, Peirce maintained, is the guiding principle of his philosophy (6.202, 1898). (Recall his claim that continuity is the fundamental product of generality in the logic of relatives.) Moreover, a monistic theory follows from his view that metaphysics appeals to logic and phenomenology for principles. In 1896 Peirce wrote:

Metaphysics consists in the results of the absolute acceptance of logical principles not merely as regulatively valid, but as truths of being. Accordingly, it is to be assumed that the universe has an explanation, the function of which, like that of every logical explanation, is to unify its observed variety. It follows that the root of all being is One; and so far as different subjects have a common character they partake of an identical being. (1.487, c. 1896)

One of the merits of the pragmatic end is that it incorporates all three of the categories. But concluding that the final interpretant is mind is to collapse the three categories into thirds, for which Peirce reproved Hegel. On Hegel's doctrine, he maintained, everything is necessarily as it is by the logic of events, that is, by deduction; thus Hegel arrived at absolute idealism (6.218, 1898). As Peirce often remarked, this requires that the first and second categories be forsaken for, who has ever heard of three absolutes (308.51, 1903)?

The reasoning that led Peirce to accept objective idealism is found in "The Architecture of Theories" (6.7-34, 1891). He dismissed the Cartesian mind-body dualism summarily, but it nevertheless dictated the very way in which the question to be considered was phrased: whether physical laws and psychical laws are to be regarded:

(a)   as independent, a doctrine often called *monism*, but which I would name *neutralism*; or,
(b)   the psychical law as derived and special, the physical law alone as primordial, which is *materialism*; or
(c)   the physical law as derived and special, the psychical law alone as primordial, which is *idealism*. (6.24, 1891)

This manner of presenting the options makes (a) no choice at all; it merely restores the Cartesian dualism. Peirce remarked that "by placing the inward and outward aspects of substance on a par, it seems to render both primordial" (6.24, 1891). Thus Ockham's razor was employed to dismiss this non-alternative in favour of alternatives (b) and (c). Peirce maintained that laws are not rigid and so materialism is repugnant to his theory. There remains idealism and Peirce then accepted it as the only viable explanation of the universe: the only intelligible doctrine, he concluded, "is that of objective idealism, that matter is effete mind, inveterate habits becoming physical laws" (6.25, 1891).

If matter is reduced to effete mind, it is no longer recognizable as a separate category. Yet Peirce claimed that the categories are integral to a full understanding of pragmaticism (for example, at 8.256, 1902). Evidently he did not recognize the relation of metaphysics to logic and phenomenology at this juncture. Phenomenology, indeed, was not incorporated into his classification of the sciences in 1891.

Considering the changes that were effected throughout the development of the classification scheme, particularly with regard to phenomenology and the normative sciences, and given Peirce's view that any science depends on preceding sciences for principles, some modification in his post-classificatory metaphysical doctrine should be expected.

In his later writings Peirce actually suggested that pragmaticism does not conclude that mind is the final interpretant precisely. While the final agreement will be expressed in conditional propositions that can be grasped only by a mind, those propositions represent the real world in part; but they are *not* that world (735.12^1–13^1, n.d.). The final interpretant is not *thought* after all. The interpretant that is final in the logical sense of having attained its purpose is also final in the sense of halting translations into further signs, because it is *not* a sign. Peirce wrote that it "is to be regarded as the ultimate signification of the sign in the sense that looking through the others that is what one comes to see. It is the ripe fruit of thought. But this perfect fruit of thought can hardly itself be called thought, since it has no signification and does not belong to the faculty of cognition at all; but rather to the *character*" (298. Add 11, 1905);[4] that is, the character that is signified and that thought is intended to represent.

Even when it is granted that Peirce's philosophy does require a monism, characterizing the One as either mind or matter does not seem to explicate it further, and introducing half a dualism at the outset surely only complicates the issue. If Peirce had employed

Ockham's razor more rigorously, he might have been less quick to accept objective idealism. He might have realized that Descartes had already multiplied entities beyond necessity when he posited two substances. To accept this division into seconds and thirds and then to make one substance a derivative of the other (that is, seconds derivative of thirds) seems to be a very uncharacteristic procedure for Peirce to follow. Although thirds are not reducible to firsts and seconds, Peirce argued that there cannot be thirds without there being firsts and seconds. Had he stepped back to Aristotle, his choice might not have been dictated by Descartes and option (a) would have been an authentic monism. Aristotle's view does not unite a dichotomy; it merely recognizes unity. Peirce accepted the Aristotelian unity on occasion (for example, at 6.206, 1898), but moreover, what Peirce had to say about synechism coheres well with an original oneness in which neither matter nor mind is differentiated (7.565–78, c. 1892).[5]

Much can be said if the categories are permitted to explain how distinctions might arise from the undifferentiated One. It is, for example, whatever potentially is – whatever falls into the first category and is capable of becoming a second or a third (see 6.342–7, 1908). What being can laws have if not to regulate events that *will* occur under their governance? What else is signified by the representation of them as *conditional* propositions if not that future events *will* conform to formulation of the laws (see 5.48, 1903)? Moreover, the continuity, which Peirce claimed underscores his philosophy, is a third, but a third that has no being apart from firsts and seconds (6.202, 1898):

So, then, there are these three modes of being: first, the being of a feeling, in itself, unattached to any subject, which is merely an atmospheric possibility, a possibility floating *in vacuo*, not rational yet capable of rationalization; secondly, there is the being that consists in arbitrary brute action upon other things, not only irrational but anti-rational, since to rationalize it would be to destroy its being; and thirdly, there is living intelligence from which all reality and all power are derived; which is rational necessity and necessitation.
                                                                    (6.342, 1908)

This line of inquiry, however fascinating, reaches beyond the scope of my present project. I merely remark that neutral monism seems compatible with continuing evolution, and is also congruent with a continuum that returns to itself, such as Peirce suggested in his discussions on continuity (6.188, 1898; 6.210, 1898; 1.274, c. 1902). It does appear to be more in accord with a theory that aims at a continually increasing embodiment of those generals said to be destined as reasonable. Furthermore, the integrity of the categories is thus preserved and the ordering of the sciences is confirmed.

Peirce may have had some theory like this in mind when he cited "*conditional* idealism" as the metaphysical doctrine most appropriate to pragmaticism; but it would seem to require more amendment than a mere correction of Berkeley's idealism. Indeed, if this is the correct understanding of "conditional" in the context of pragmaticism, the term "idealism" might better be replaced by another expression. Idealism suggests that firsts and seconds are to be reduced to thirds in some way. Peirce does appear to have abandoned it finally; in 1908, while he assented to Berkeley's view that what is thought and the immediate thought-object are different aspects of the same thing, Peirce rejected the conclusion to idealism (or, at least, to Berkeley's idealism). Instead, he suggested that "the reason why different things have to be differently thought of is that their modes of metaphysical being are different" (6.339, 1908).

If Peirce's metaphysics does require some adjustment or reappraisal, it will more than likely receive its impulse from discontinuities recognized in the relations between the sciences as ordered in the classification scheme. This is just one indication of the value of the classification. Another indication is an increased understanding of what Peirce conceived logic to be. Insofar as the classification gives coherence to Peirce's philosophy, it has considerable value, for if the conclusions resulting from Peirce's own inquiries into mathematics, phenomenology, and the normative sciences are sound, pragmaticism is well grounded. But only if it is, indeed, a natural classification can it be of value to other sciences and philosophies; and this requires the confirmation of experience.

There can be only one natural classification and Peirce's claim to it cannot be refuted simply by discovering that anthropology, for example, does not rest in the assigned location. Sciences, conceived as the activity of the scientist, are not static. Peirce maintained that the members of the classification (the individual sciences) will be constantly evolving into the preceding sciences; that a similar evolutionary development occurs between corresponding disciplines in the three major divisions of the sciences; and that a third division concerning ideas might parallel the psychical and physical branches of the special sciences.

What I have called the "perennial" classification remained fundamentally the same over the last years of Peirce's studies, but he did not expect that it would endure, even if he had placed every existing science in the appropriate pigeon-hole. By its very nature, there can be no final scheme in that sense (unless it be the one in which mathematics is the sole member). But the *principles* governing the classification – the Comtean principle of hierarchical ordering according to principle-dependence, and the formal differentiating principle involving the three categories – do not change in the same way: throughout myriad transformations, the classification as such remains the same. Inquiry into the principles should not cease, Peirce would have insisted. Better or more refined principles may yet be discovered through the continued encounter with experience. Still, the principles governing Peirce's scheme must withstand the impact of experience if it is to be confirmed as the one natural classification of the sciences.

APPENDIX 1

Selective Terminology

Alternative Terms Used by Peirce for Major Divisions of the Sciences

CLASSIFICATORY SCIENCES
Sciences of kinds (675.11)
Systematic science (1345.48)

CRITIC
Critical logic (2.93)
Logic (4.9)

ESTHETICS [AESTHETICS]
Axiagastics (1334.Add38)
Callesthetic (633.1:5; 636.24)
Callics (633.1:5)

ETHICS
Antethics (1.573)
Critical ethics (1334.Add40)
Practics (1.573)

EXPLANATORY SCIENCES
Descriptive and explanatory sciences (675.11)
Descriptive sciences

Science of individual objects (675.11)

HEURETIC SCIENCES
Heurospude (1334.19)
Progressive science (427.122²)
Pure science (1334.23)
Sciences of discovery
Theoretic sciences

LOGIC
General semeiotic (634.15)
Normative semeotic (2.111)
Semeiotic (8.343)
Semiotic (2.227)

MATHEMATICS
Schematoscopy (1338.7)

METAPHYSICS
Empirothéory (1338.23)
Science of reality (675.11)
Trotoscopy (1334.35)

METHODEUTIC
Formal rhetoric (1.559; 4.116)
Heuristic (2.207)
Method (2.207)
Methodic (2.207)
Methodology (2.93)
Objective logic (1.444)
Pure rhetoric (2.229)
Speculative rhetoric (836.1)

NOMOLOGICAL SCIENCES
Sciences of laws (675.11)

NORMATIVE SCIENCES
Critical sciences (675.11)
Deuteroscopy (1334.35)

PHENOMENOLOGY
Empirics (1345.[1])
High philosophy (7.526)
Phanerochemy (1338.22)
Phaneroscopy
Protoscopy (1334.35)

PHILOSOPHY
Cenoscopy
Coenoscopy (1.573)

PHYSICS
Hyloscepsy (615.20)
Physical sciences
Physiognosy (1.242; 1340.[3–6])

PRACTICAL SCIENCES
Practic science (677.3)
Prattospude (1334.19)

PSYCHICS
Humanistic sciences (675.10)
Noescepsy (615.20)

Psychical sciences
Psychognosy (1.242; 1340.[3–6])

SCIENCES OF REVIEW
Digested science (677.2)
Digesting sciences (605.7)
Encyclopaedic sciences (605.17)
Encyclotactic (1338.4)
Exetastic science (677.2)
Retrospective science (283.9)
Science of science (675.10)
Systematic sciences (601.26[1]; 602.16)
Tactics (1334.19)
Tagmatic science (673.47; 677.2)
Taxospoud (1334.19)
Taxospude (1334.19)

SPECIAL SCIENCES
Idioscopy

SPECULATIVE GRAMMAR
Formal grammar (1.559; 4.116)
Hermeneutic (640.7)
Logical syntax (452.6)
Stecheotic (4.9)
Stechiology (5.446; 602.6)
Stoicheia (636.24)
Stoicheiology (4.9; 5.446)
Universal grammar (640.7)

APPENDIX 2

Brain Hemisphere Dominance in Peirce and Einstein

The study of the brain is still in its infancy and new discoveries constantly are being made. Nevertheless, information now available provides a plausible explanation for the seemingly incredible genius of persons who thought in images – persons who may not have excelled in school. Einstein fits into this category and I suggest that Peirce also qualifies.

Since the vast majority of adults are right-handed, language dominance normally resides in the left hemisphere of the brain, which controls speech, writing, mathematical, logical, and analytical activities, while the right hemisphere controls spatial relationships, creativity, music, and synthesizing activities. The tendency for speech to lateralize is correlated with structural differences in the two hemispheres, discernible even in the foetus.

For left-handed persons the situation is less sharply delineated. Those who write with the left hand, but who direct their pens from above the line pointing toward the lower edge of the paper, are found to have the same hemisphere specialization as right-handed persons. Left-handed persons (approximately 44 per cent) who write with the pen held in a more natural position have their hemispheres reversed such that the right hemisphere is language-dominant.[1] When such persons are obliged to use their right hands to write, shift gear levers, and so on, their imaging hemispheres must adapt to these atypical functions. Confusion, distress, and lack of co-ordination may occur in some. Others may acquire a visual/creative content in the extended linguistic use; that is, left-handed persons whose language dominant hemisphere is atypical and who have successfully converted to right-handedness may be able to make more facile connections between analytic and imaginative/creative activity than those who have not been so constrained. In some persons, it has been suggested, neither hemisphere is dominant and, without a definite left-to-right orientation, they may experience difficulty in learning to read and write.[2]

I have found nothing to indicate whether Einstein was right- or left-handed as a child. His parents were not strict, but he went to Luitpold Gymnasium from age ten and hated it for its rigidity. There, he may have been required to conform his handwriting. My guess is that he was one of those in whom neither hemisphere is dominant, for he did not learn to talk until age three and he still lacked fluency in speech at age nine.[2] There are, of course, alternative explanations for late speech development, however, my suspicion that Einstein had no dominant hemisphere has received some corroboration.[3]

Peirce also complained of language difficulties. English, he said, was no less foreign than Greek or German; diagrammatic thought was his natural mode of expression. He wrote: "One of the most extreme and most lamentable of my incapacities is my incapacity for linguistic expression" (632.5-6:1, 1909), and added in a note:

I will remark, by the way, that I am led to surmise that this awkwardness is connected with the fact that I am left-handed. For that my left handedness is not a mere accidental habit, but has some organic cause seems to be evidenced by the fact that when I left the last school where it had attracted attention, I wrote with facility with my right hand, but could not write legibly with my left; and yet when I ceased to make the effort to continue this habit of three years standing, I soon fell back to using my left hand, though I have always used knife, fork, and spoon, *at table*, just as others do.

(632.6:2, 1909)

The next sentence is crossed through but it reveals that Peirce knew that the left hemisphere normally controls speech: "Now supposing that my cerebral organ of speech is on the left side as in other people ..." (632.6:2, 1909). Peirce seems to have anticipated the modern view that the distribution of brain asymmetry may differ in left-handed persons. In the substituted sentence he wrote: "Now since my heart is placed as usual, it would seem that the connections between different parts of my brain must be different from the usual and presumably the best arrangement; and if so, it would necessarily follow that my thinking should be *gauche*" (632.6:2, 1909).

Peirce may have suspected that his facility with diagrammatic thought was connected to his proclivity to left-handedness, for he expressed frustration at right-handed people for their use of their eyes: they *look* with the right eye alone, he complained, though they *see* with both, and are unpractised at using the eye of the mind.[4]

Commentators have remarked that Peirce's penetrating analyses are in basic contrast with his speculative thought. But if Peirce was correct in surmising that he had an atypical brain hemisphere arrangement, the fact that he pursued both modes of thought is less surprising.

APPENDIX 3

Truth: Categorical or Conditional?

Father Vincent Potter has identified two passages in the *Collected Papers*[1] that appear to contradict one another: at 5.39 (1903) Peirce declared that logic asserts positive categorical truth, while at 2.65 (c. 1902) he maintained that logic "discovers and enunciates [laws that] are merely conditional, not categorical." Potter presents three suggestions as to how these two passages might be reconciled. The first two, although wanting, point in the right direction, I believe.

The purpose of Peirce's discussion at 5.39 is to distinguish phenomenology from the preceding science of mathematics. Hence he emphasized the fact that phenomenology is a positive science while mathematics is not. Logic and the normative sciences he also generally saw as positive sciences. The aim of the discussion at 2.65 is to overturn the view that logic is a psychological study. Accordingly, Peirce called attention to the idioscopic nature of psychology – its concern with special observations – in contrast to logic's cenoscopic aspect wherein observations are minimal and of a very general kind such as is available to all. In both contexts logic is said to be seeking positive knowledge, but in the first passage this positive aspect is underscored to distinguish it from the non-positive science, while in the second passage it is underplayed to distinguish it from the markedly positive special sciences. While an examination of the context serves to explain the different tones in the two passages, it is not adequate to resolve the apparent contradiction, and an explanation must be found elsewhere.

At 5.39 Peirce stated that logic asserts categorical *propositions*, while at 2.65 he denied that normative *laws* are categorical. It is of the nature of a law to be general, whereas categorical assertions refer to particular states of things; if it can be shown that categorical assertions are consistent with conditional laws, there need be no contradiction.

Peirce came to recognize that categorical and hypothetical propositions are essentially the same (3.439, 1896; 441.14, 1898; 751.2-3, n.d.; 817.3, n.d.; see also title of 787, c. 1895). To begin with, although the hypotheses of logic are designed to conform with facts and those of mathematics are indifferent to fact, it is not the task of either science to say what *is* the case (311.7, 1903). Yet if the conditionals of logic are *de inesse* (i.e., limited to actual states of things), then it would seem that every normative law would have to be a categorical assertion. Yet Peirce thought that he was mistaken in his view that it is important to ask what is the matter of fact expressed by the conditional proposition (839.13 [fragment], n.d.). He came to believe that to interpret every conditional judgment in this way was to deny the reality of an unactualized possibility. Indeed, only those possibilities known to be false need to be excluded (736.4, [1893?]; 817.3, n.d.). This connects with his altered view of pragmaticism (292.51, [c. 1906]).

The pragmaticist maintains that the intellectual purport of a concept is expressed in a conditional proposition that asserts that if the concept is applicable and if one has a certain purpose one would act in a certain way. Both purposes and habits (which are ways of acting) are general. The conditional proposition represents a universe of possibilities, but at the same time refers to possible acts, which are entirely individual. This would seem to pose a problem, but Peirce thought that it could be at least partly resolved if it is admitted that,

an endless series of experiences, each entirely consistent with those that precede it, cannot itself be experienced (*as* such endless series), but involves a first dose of ideality, or generality. It is not a perfect general, it is true; but the whole endless series of steps from this to true continuity (which is perfect generality elevated to the mode of conception of the Logic of Relations) are there described.[2] (5.528, c. 1905)

The conditional proposition that is said to constitute the intellectual purport of a concept represents the state of mind of one who has resolved or is about to resolve to act conditionally upon a certain purpose. But all resolves can only concern future acts and acts are altogether individual (288.191-2, 1905). Yet a concept itself, Peirce thought, is a kind of "hypostatic" abstraction.[3] Its meaning resides in the future possible instances. An actual resolve constitutes the categorical judgment; for example, saying that a piece of porcelain is soft before it is fired in a kiln amounts to saying that,

if anybody during that period tries to scratch it with a knife he will succeed, and to say this is again equivalent to saying that every experiment which is logically necessitated, if this be true, to turn out in a certain way, will turn out in that way; and this last statement has a corresponding equivalent, and so on endlessly. But of this endless series of equivalent propositions there is one which my situation in time makes to be the practical one for me, and that one becomes for me the primary meaning ... But after it has been baked, and nobody has taken occasion to try that experiment, it is a different experiment among the endless series of equivalents that now expresses my primary meaning. The nature of the fact does not change; but my relation to it and consequent mode of conceiving do change, although I all the time recognize the equivalence of the different meanings. (8.195, c. 1904)

Logic, as a normative science, disregards the particular state of things altogether and shows which method leads to the truth. Only thus can it recommend a procedure as leading invariably to the truth whatever the particular situation of the reasoner. Such reasoning is from pure hypotheses similar to those of the mathematician (693a. 102-4, [1904]). The logician's hypotheses retain their distinctive character in that they express real possibilities. These are the normative laws which, when applied to facts, yield categorical judgments.

APPENDIX 4

Concerning Objective Logic

Both Max Fisch[1] and Manley Thompson[2] have identified objective logic as a discipline linking normative semiotic to metaphysics: they have regarded it as either a separate discipline located between those two sciences, or as a study of metaphysics.

I find no mention of a science called "objective logic" in any of the schemes that follow upon the classification of logic as a normative science, and I am inclined to believe that Peirce's later view was that the logical systems needed in normative semiotic would be adequate to any application required by subsequent sciences.

Peirce used the term "objective logic" in several different ways during the course of his investigations. In 1893 he applied the term to second intentional logic, which is said to be a major part of formal logic (4.80, 1893); as such, it would be a mathematical study. In 1896 he declared that he had frequently and inaccurately used the term to designate speculative rhetoric or methodeutic (1.444, c. 1896; 3.430, 1896; 3.454, 1896) in order to indicate its connection with Hegel's logic.

1898 is the date of Peirce's manuscript "The Logic of Events," part of which is included in the *Collected Papers* under the heading "Objective Logic" (6.214-37, 1898). In an earlier portion of that manuscript, Peirce claimed that he was discussing the application of logic to metaphysics: his approach differed from Hegel's in that it was not limited to deductive inference but admitted hypothetic and inductive inference (6.5, 1898; 6.218, 1898). In this context, objective logic was set in contradistinction to subjective logic. Normative semiotic had not yet emerged as the third of the normative sciences and only the two universes of possibility and of actuality were included (6.189 and .192, 1898). Although Peirce had by then recognized the inadequacy of the Philonian conditional, the problem of representing the several modes of possibility in the system of existential graphs was still to be confronted.

In Peirce's application for aid from the Carnegie Institution (L75, 15 July 1902) section 33 of his proposed project was entitled "On Objective Logic." There Peirce adopted Hegel's expression to refer to the application of logical categories to the world. Logic had been listed as the third normative science in the classification of the sciences found in section 1 of the proposal, in which no mention is made of objective logic.

Thus far there was nothing to suggest that objective logic was a new science. The warrant for that opinion occurs in the "Minute Logic" of 1902. Peirce wrote:

With Speculative Rhetoric, Logic, in the sense of Normative Semeotic, is brought to a close. But now we have to examine whether there be a doctrine of signs corresponding to Hegel's objective logic; that is to say, whether there be a life in Signs, so that – the requisite vehicle being present – they will go through a certain order of development, and if so, whether this development be merely of such a nature that the same round of changes of form is described over and over again whatever be the matter of the thought or whether, in addition to such a repetitive order, there be also a greater life-history that every symbol furnished with a vehicle of life goes through, and what is the nature of it.   (2.111, c. 1902)

It is difficult to avoid concluding that Peirce had in mind a new discipline quite dissociated from normative semiotic. Yet objective logic seems to have the task of warranting both that there is a real world and "that there not only may be a living symbol, realizing the full idea of a symbol, but even that there actually is one" (2.114, c. 1902). According to Peirce, that hypothesis "involves the idea of a different mode of being from that of existential fact" (2.115, c. 1902). But the several modes of being and the validity of metaphysical conceptions, Peirce stated two paragraphs later, require only the *application* of principles of methodeutic.

Manley Thompson, however, thought that the two universes – of possibility and actuality – admitted in 1898 suffice only because of the assumption that the actual universe has an explanation. He considered that without that assumption a third universe is needed to portage between the two admitted universes. The general ideas or laws that comprise the third universe and necessitate objective logic enable that passage.[3]

The assumption that the actual universe has an explanation is fundamental to the normative study and does not seem to be supplanted by the introduction of a third universe.

The formalization of the third universe is facilitated by the introduction of tinctures to the system of existential graphs and was first elaborated in 1906.[4] Peirce called the three universes variously: the questionable and the possible, or things possible in themselves; the actual and the existent, or the actual and true, or actual fact; and the commanded and the compelled, or what is sure to be, or (later) what is resolved or intended.[5]

According to Don Roberts,

the tinctures were designed with more than formal logic in mind; they were meant to provide a structure in terms of which Peirce could apply his categories to propositions and inferences, to hypotheses, questions, and commands, to "all that ever could be present to the mind in any way or any sense" (Ms 499(s)) – and to do this with the same system that handled the formal logic as well. Indeed, once the tinctures were set up and in running order, a steady use of the graphs could be expected to turn up discoveries that would enrich and modify the theory of the categories, while continuing study of the categories would improve the classification of the tinctures.[6]

This accords with my own understanding that the system of existential graphs is required for speculative grammar (see p. 176 above). If it is correct, a logical system adequate to any application in metaphysics is antecedently developed.[7]

While the foregoing might not succeed in countering the interpretation that an independent science of objective logic is suggested in the passage quoted from the "Minute Logic," it does seem likely that the application of principles of methodeutic may answer in every case. If not, it is curious that objective logic does not appear in any of the classification schemes advanced by Peirce – not even in that of the "Minute Logic." Less cogent, but nevertheless worthy of note, is the fact that the inclusion of a new science of objective logic between the normative sciences and metaphysics would introduce a discrepancy into the categorial ordering of the sciences.

Notes

CHAPTER I

1 Weiss, "Charles S. Peirce," 402.
2 See appendix 2 for a discussion of Einstein and Peirce in connection with right- and left-handedness.
3 Einstein, *Autobiographical Notes*, 7–9.
4 Peirce described an incident that occurred when the family was dining: the dress of one of the ladies present caught fire; Peirce's younger brother extinguished it with singular alacrity. When he was later asked to explain the swiftness of his reflexes, young Herbert reported that he had mentally rehearsed appropriate action after Mrs Longfellow had died from just such an accident (5.487 note, 1907).
5 Peirce, *New Elements*, 3/1:191–2. In those days, before computer graphics, what apparatus would have been available to the pecunious Peirce?
6 See Roberts, *Existential Graphs*, chapter 6.
7 Biographical data on Peirce has been obtained from Brent, "Study in the Life of Peirce"; Eisele, "Peirce-Newcomb Correspondence" and *Studies in Scientific and Mathematical Philosophy*; Fisch, "Peirce and the History of Science" and "Was There a Metaphysical Club?"; Gallie, *Peirce and Pragmatism*; Lenzen, "Peirce as Astronomer" and "Peirce as Mathematical Physicist"; Manning "Peirce, Coast Survey, and Politics"; and Peirce, *New Elements*.
8 See note 15.
9 This is reported by W.B. Gallie, *Peirce and Pragmatism*, 36; see also note 35.
10 Peirce experienced paralysis under stress, which might have been a defense

mechanism triggered when the sufferer is unable to cope with material circumstances. Brent, "Study in the Life of Peirce," 215 note 45.

11 Ibid., 41–2; Brent's account of Peirce's life is impressively documented; however, it lacks balance and conveys a distorted impression of Peirce's philosophy.

12 Peirce, *Writings*, 1:xxvii.

13 Brent, "Study in the Life of Peirce," 41.

14 Lurie, *Louis Agassiz*, 182. The original Lazzaroni were street-loungers and beggars of Naples. Those associated with Peirce were neither idle nor mendicant: they were an informal alliance of eminent men in influential positions who aimed at controlling the institutional forums of science in America in order to promote scientific progress as they perceived it. The Lazzaroni (principally Louis Agassiz and Benjamin Peirce) overruled the reform proposals submitted by Charles William Eliot in his capacity as acting dean of the St. Lawrence School. They were powerful enough to block his appointment to the Runford professorship and the Scientific School deanship in 1863. In 1869 Agassiz, again supported by Benjamin Peirce, opposed Eliot's appointment to the Harvard presidency (ibid., 326–30, 362–3).

15 In her biography, Dorothy Ross hints that Peirce may have been prey to Hall's ambitions; *G. Stanley Hall*, 136 note 10. In 1882 Hall joined George S. Morris and Peirce in the philosophy department at Johns Hopkins. All three were eager to obtain tenure, but it was President D.C. Gilman's practice to appoint only one full professor. Ross portrays Hall as an opportunist given to underhand manoeuvres (ibid., 135–6). He would have recognized that the quiet temper of his long-time friend and idol, George Morris, was the lesser obstacle. Peirce would have presented more serious competition.

Newcomb was part-time faculty member at Johns Hopkins when he conveyed to Gilman the derogatory personal information provided by an "unknown informant" (J.E. Hilgard it seems) that led to Peirce's dismissal. Whether or not Hall instigated Newcomb's intervention is mere speculation. They must have been acquainted, however, because when Newcomb became president of the new American Society for Psychical Research in the fall of 1884, Hall was made on of the five vice-presidents (ibid., 162).

In April 1884 Hall was appointed full professor of psychology and pedagogy. When in 1885 Gilman suggested that Morris be invited back from Michigan to fill a chair in ethics, Hall responded by disparaging Morris's philosophical acumen. By 1888 Hall had become president of the new Clark University at Worcester, Massachusetts. In turning down Peirce's repeated applications for a teaching position or for a lecture series at Clark, Hall pleaded insufficient funds (certainly false at the outset) and obstructing trustees. (ibid., 198).

The incident which no doubt provided the basis for the report impugning Peirce's moral character occurred in the summer of 1878. While Peirce and Mme Pourtelai (who were then lovers) were holidaying in the White Mountains of New Hampshire, they "comported themselves in a way which led to something of a public scandal" (Brent, "Study in the Life of Peirce," 96; reference to the incident occurs in a letter written by Peirce's aunt, Charlotte Elizabeth Peirce, dated 20 October 1883).

16 *American Mathematical Society Semicentennial Publications* volume 1 (Eisele, *Studies in Scientific and Mathematical Philosophy*, 312).

17 Fisch, "Was There a Metaphysical Club?" 18.

18 Eisele, "Peirce's Philosophy of Education," 73.

19 Fisch, "Was There a Metaphysical Club?" 17; quoted from George P. Adams and William P. Montague, eds., *Contemporary American Philosophy: Personal Statements*, 2 vols. (New York: Macmillan 1930), 2.138. Enthusiasm is also expressed in a letter written by John Jay Chapman, quoted by Goudge, *Thought of C.S. Peirce*, 344-5.

20 See Manning, "Peirce, Coast Survey and Politics," 187.

21 Brent, "Study in the Life of Peirce," 52-8, 78-83.

22 Manning, "Peirce, Coast Survey and Politics," 188-9.

23 As far as unfinished work for the Survey is concerned, it seems that Peirce was discouraged by his troubled relations with that institution and he was preoccupied with other subjects.

24 Newcomb refused to recommend Peirce for the Survey post which must have been decisive because Peirce had written a brilliant exam; and Newcomb prevailed on the generally favourable executive committee of the Carnegie Institution to turn down Peirce's application for a grant, although it was probably the most intellectually profound research grant proposal ever submitted and it was supported by more than twenty impressive testimonials (Brent, "Study in the Life of Peirce," 168).

25 Brent reports that in order to escape his creditors Peirce would climb into his loft to work, hauling up the ladder behind him (ibid., 11, 253 note 68).

26 An exception is Paul Carus, editor of *The Monist* from 1890 to 1919, who did respond to Peirce's writings.

27 A sheriff's sale of Peirce's splendid library was ordered by the court to

cover his debts. James Mills Peirce purchased it for a mere $655.25 and returned it to Charles (ibid., 142).

28 Eisele, *Studies in Scientific and Mathematical Philosophy*, 26.

29 Along with the scholastic realists, Peirce defended the reality of abstract properties but, instead of regarding the most general properties as self-explanatory, he maintained that these could also be explained in terms of their relations, for example, to some law.

30 Peirce is not included in Robert Merton's list of those who had anticipated his thesis on multiple discoveries. See Merton, *Sociology of Science*, 353–4.

31 Peirce wrote approvingly of Whewell's work; in particular, he endorsed the view that advances in science depend upon observers equipped with appropriate ideas, for example, 6.604, 1893; 1.70, [c. 1898]; 2.761, c. 1905.

32 Familiarity and assurance in using words characterizes the first grade of clearness, while analytic definition marks the second grade. An account of these three grades of clearness is given in chapter 3.

33 See Ketner, *Comprehensive Bibliography*.

34 From the motto of this work, which concerns Plato's writings but is very relevant to Peirce's own writings.

35 For example, Manley Thompson acknowledges the importance of ethics and aesthetics to Peirce's logic, but he protests that the "development of this part of Peirce's philosophy is so slight as to make any detailed consideration of his fragmentary pronouncements on its problems seem singularly unpromising" (*Pragmatic Philosophy*, 197). Richard S. Robin writes that Peirce's "discussion of the normative sciences came at a time of life when Peirce was too old and too feeble to explore systematically more than a few facets of the subject, and so his writings on the normative sciences comprise only a relatively few pages amidst his vast philosophical output" ("Peirce's Doctrine," 271). The volume of writings discussing the normative sciences is altogether too considerable to be given perfunctory dismissal. That this was a later development in the evolution of Peirce's thought should enhance its significance rather than detract from it, because it represents his mature view. There is no evidence to support the hint that Peirce's mental capacity was waning. His inquiries into the normative sciences are more properly seen as the investigations of a philosopher rigorously attempting to develop a consistent system. Some of his more repugnant statements are apparently those of a logician following consistency where it leads him, rather than the aberrations of an "old and feeble" mind.

36 Flower and Murphey suggest that Klein's Erlanger program is a source for

the principle employed in Peirce's classification scheme in *History of Philosophy in America*, 2:607. Although I have not found any mention of the Erlanger program in Peirce, it is consistent with the Comtean principle he explicitly adopted and, therefore, it might well have confirmed him in his views. According to Klein, a given geometry can be seen as an instance of a more general geometry. Thus Euclidean geometry is a special case of affine geometry which, in turn, is a special case of projective geometry; Euclidean geometry would presuppose affine geometry.

37 See appendix 1; they are perhaps equal to "pragmaticism" in ugliness.

38 The studies more commonly pursued belong to the sciences of review or to the practical sciences. In a stereoscopic diagram, all three would relate directly to one another.

CHAPTER II

1 See Flint, *Philosophy as Scientia Scientiarum* and Richardson, *Classification*. Peirce recorded that, although there are many omissions, Richardson listed 146 theoretical classifications and 173 library classifications (1.203 and omission, see 427.3, 1902). The third edition (1930) lists 161 theoretical classifications and does not include Peirce's scheme.

2 Bacon, *Works*, 1 [*Philosophical Writings*]. 183-262.

3 Hobbes, *Leviathan*, chapter 9.

4 Standley, *Comte*, 31-7.

5 Comte, *Introduction to Positive Philosophy*, 37.

6 Standley, *Comte*, 57-9.

7 Comte, *Introduction to Positive Philosophy*, 48-66.

8 Spencer, *Reasons for Dissenting*, 15.

9 Mill, *Comte and Positivism*, 35 note.

10 Comte recognized that it was an anomaly in his scheme; see Comte, *Introduction to Positive Philosophy*, 50.

11 Hamilton, *Lectures*, 1:114.

12 Ibid., 1:125.

13 Whewell, *Novum Organon Renovatum*, book 2, chapter 9.

14 Flint, *Philosophy as Scientia Scientiarum*, 236-8.

15 Ibid., 271.

16 Pearson, *Grammar of Science*, 312-35.

17 Bowler, *Evolution*, 50-2.

18 Mayr, *Growth of Biological Thought*, 158-62, 171-7.

19 The image Agassiz unwittingly conveyed was that of an inept deity advancing by failed experiments.
20 Lurie, *Louis Agassiz*, 275–6.
21 Agassiz, "Agassiz on Origin of Species," 142–54.
22 At 1.205 and 1.205 note 1 Peirce discussed natural classes and remarked that he was influenced by Agassiz. At 1.229–31, 1902 he gave a qualified acceptance to Agassiz's definitions of classes and subdivisions. "No greater merit can a taxonomist have," he stated, " than that of having his eyes open to the ideas in nature; no more deplorable blindness can afflict him than that of not seeing that there are ideas in nature which determine the existence of objects. The definitions of Agassiz will, at least, do us the service of directing our attention to the supreme importance of bearing in mind the final cause of objects in finding out their own natural classifications" (1.231, 1902). Peirce recognized that Agassiz's *application* of his ideas was bound to fail because it would have required the taxonomist to have the perspective of the Creator (1.571, 1910).
23 See White, *Science and Sentiment*, 122–4. Wright must have been converted to Mill's philosophy already, e.g., by *A System of Logic* (1843), if Peirce's comment is to make sense; the *Examination of Sir William Hamilton's Philosophy* was published in 1865 – six years after the *Origins*.
24 Ruse, *Darwinian Revolution*, 185.
25 Ibid., 175.
26 Ibid., 180.
27 Ibid., 235–8.
28 Peirce explained:

Of every such substance there are two varieties . . . one of which twists a ray of light that passes through it to the right, and the other, by an exactly equal amount, to the left. All the ordinary physical properties of the right-handed and left-handed modifications are identical. Only certain faces of their crystals, often very minute, are differently placed. No chemical process can ever transmute the one modification into the other. And their ordinary chemical behaviour is absolutely the same, so that no strictly chemical process can separate them if they are once mixed. Only the chemical action of one optically active substance upon another is different if they both twist the ray the same way from what it is if they twist the ray different ways. There are certain living organisms which feed on one modification and destroy it while leaving the other one untouched. This is presumably due to such organisms containing in their substance, possibly in very minute proportion, some optically active body. Now I maintain that the original segregation of levo-molecules, or molecules with a left-handed twist, from dextro-molecules, or molecules with a right-handed twist, is absolutely incapable of mechanical explanation.   (5.65, 1903)

The reference indicates the source. Peirce probably came to these conclusions in the 1870s.

29 Skagestad, "Peirce on Biological Evolution," 108.

30 Mayr, *Growth of Biological Thought*, 149.

31 More recently Jean Piaget rejected a closed or linear classification and proposed a system based on a constantly growing spiral.

32 The manuscript breaks off here. It is a late manuscript since the term "pragmaticism" is used.

33 Bocheński, *History of Logic*, 4–5.

34 How Peirce perceived the contemporary situation is presented in the next chapter.

35 I am indebted to James Van Evra, "Richard Whately," 1–18, for bringing to my attention the larger significance of this first acquaintance with logic. His article is the source of the data included here.

36 Peirce granted that a classification that confines itself to actually existing sciences won't do for the next generation of scientists, even if it was satisfactory when it was devised. Conversely, if an early classification is useful now, it must have been useless when it was devised (1.203, 1902).

37 Flower and Murphey, *History of Philosophy in America*, vol. 2, chapter 10. This chapter reflects (but also corrects) Murphey's earlier work, *Development of Peirce's Philosophy*. In that work Peirce is depicted as engaged in a struggle to overcome difficulties in his early system. I think that Peirce was true to his conception of the scientist as one who strives to extend the indefinitely extensible boundaries of human knowledge. These two approaches to the Peirce opus are not incompatible of course, but the focus differs.

38 Flower and Murphey, *History of Philosophy in America*, 2: 588.

39 The term "relatives" refers to class relations rather than individual relations. This distinction remained unsatisfactory until 1883 when quantifiers were available to Peirce and he began to shape the logic of relations into its modern form.

40 The distinctions in parentheses are those Peirce identified retrospectively in order to show how these categories differed from his later formulation of monadic relations, dyadic relations, and triadic relations.

41 Flower and Murphey, *History of Philosophy in America*, 2.589.

42 What Peirce said of De Morgan in this passage might equally apply to himself: "No decent semblance of justice has ever been done to De Morgan, owing to his not having brought anything to its final shape. [It was] never sufficiently understood that his was the work of an exploring expedition, which every day comes upon new forms for the study of which leisure is, at the moment, lacking, because additional novelties are coming in and requiring note" (1.562, c. 1905). I am indebted to Josiah Lee Auspitz for bringing this to my attention.

43 Flower and Murphey, *History of Philosophy in America*, 2.593.

44 Developed by Peirce and one of his Johns Hopkins students, O.H. Mitchell; see 3.359–403, 1885. Although this was an independent discovery, it occurred six years after Frege's publication of *Begriffsschrift*.

45 Flower and Murphey, *History of Philosophy in America*, 2.597.

46 Peirce was never one to hesitate to adopt or discard a theory merely because he was alone in doing so. Infinitesimals were unfashionable then and only recently have been reconsidered.

47 According to Peirce, Kant made the mistake of confusing this with infinite divisibility (3.569, 1900; 6.168, 1903).

48 Flower and Murphey, *History of Philosophy in America*, 2: 605.

49 Ibid., 2:606.

50 This is not to say that Peirce expected to define all future sciences as he criticized others for attempting to do. Here I depart from Murphey, who evidently thinks that Peirce is obligated to show that the material aspect of his universal categories is necessary. He claims that Peirce "is proposing to predict nothing less than the direction in which future discovery must go" (Murphey, *Development of Peirce's Philosophy*, 330; see also Flower and Murphey, *History of Philosophy in America*, 2.607–8). The existence of the phenomenological categories cannot be asserted *a priori*.

CHAPTER III

1 However, he does not do that exactly.

2 As already mentioned, this sort of evolution in a science (here in the sciences of review) is one reason that a classification cannot remain static (see, for example, 1338.12, [c. 1905–6]).

3 This difficulty was subsequently resolved by defining a science in terms of the activity of the scientist.

4 Peirce also stated that "continuity is shown by the logic of relations to be nothing but a higher type of that which we know as generality. It is rela-

tional generality" (6.190, 1898); and "continuity is simply what generality becomes in the logic of relatives" (5.436, 1905).

5 See 175 below for an account of Peirce's confusion between these two modes of inference.

6 Consider the class "normative sciences" of which aesthetics, ethics, and logic are the members. The way in which logic differs from, or is similar to, ethics and aesthetics goes only a very small way towards augmenting our understanding of logic. (For example, they are similar in seeking what ought to be the case - in finding the conditions by which to determine what is good or bad in the particular areas of each. They differ in being concerned with feeling, action, and reasoning, respectively.) When this relation of similarity is supplemented by a whole network of relations, the importance of ethics and aesthetics to logic acquires a new dimension as will be seen in chapter 5.

7 Of course this is not the only point in the article that he subsequently criticized. By confining this exposition to his later remarks, I hope to avoid the difficulties not yet worked out in his early version and also to convey views that are contemporaneous with the classification of sciences which is, after all, a later development in his thought.

8 Nevertheless, it was implicitly expressed there. It required the later investigations (surveyed in chapter 2) before real possibility could be integrated into Peirce's philosophy.

9 E.J. Ashworth is not convinced of the justice of this criticism. See her *Language and Logic*.

10 Peirce listed eight different views on one occasion; or nine if medieval appeal to authority is included (2.208, 1901, from volume 2 of Baldwin's *Dictionary of Philosophy and Psychology*, endorsed by Mrs. C. Ladd-Franklin); and thirteen on another (2.18-78, c. 1902). In addition the more signifificant of these received treatment in various other passages. I propose to make use of all of these sources in an attempt to present a composite picture reflecting his more mature and careful accounts.

11 Reference to Schröder's *Exact Logic*, where these claims are made, may be found at 3.432, 1896.

12 Peirce addressed himself to that view (examined at 65-6).

13 Mill, *Hamilton*, chapter 21.

14 2.47, c. 1902. Peirce described the criterion of inconceivability: a proposition is found to be necessarily true or not on this criterion by asking if its denial is inconceivable. It is assumed that a necessary proposition must be true under all possible circumstances, whereas its denial need only attest that some circumstances may be imagined in which the proposition would

be false. The consequence seems to be that a proposition's necessity depends upon the imaginative powers of those involved (see Mill, *System of Logic*, 160). The problem is that usually we *are* able to imagine how a thing might be done if it ever will be possible for us to do it. The criterion can deceive us just because when we can't imagine a proposition to be false, neither can we imagine the way in which we might imagine it to be false. Even so, a new piece of information or some slight suggestion may, in the very next moment, enable us to imagine what no amount of thought would have permitted formerly (2.30, c. 1902).

Peirce cited Mill as saying that the history of science abounds with inconceivabilities that have been surmounted (see Mill, *System of Logic*, 157); Peirce gave an example from Euclid at 2.30, c. 1902. Hence a test of inconceivability would need to take into account not merely current imaginable possibilities, but also those possibilities conceivable after unlimited training and education. This, Peirce claimed, is that to which all reasonable disputants aim; that is, there would be no point to his dispute if he did not hope to reach agreement. But, Peirce continued:

what he aims at is the truth. Therefore, by the truth he means nothing more than a finally compulsory belief. If, then, you can prove to him that a necessary proposition is such that there will be a final, unshakable compulsion preventing him from imagining it to be false, you have proved to him that it has those characters which he expresses by saying that the proposition is true. Now to say that a necessary proposition is true is to say that it is necessarily true. The proposition is therefore true by defifinition, if by inconceivable is meant eternally inconceivable. But a definition is not a criterion. For a criterion is a method of experiment by which something is ascertained which is a sure indication of whether or not something different, and less easy otherwise to find out, is true.

(2.29, c. 1902)

15 Peirce pointed out that Mill does not base his own logic on associationalism but on a law of nature (see 75–7).

16 Peirce would admit that logic presupposes some truths commonly thought to belong to psychology: for instance, that repeated action produces habits; that people see things in spatial relations; and that one can recall past experiences (615.14–15, 1908). These experiences are not the discoveries of any special science, nor of any science in general. They are familiar experiences to any normally intelligent adult.

17 As the editors of the *Collected Papers* suggest, cf., Abbé Gratry, *La Logique* (Paris, 1855), 2.196–7. Peirce reported that it was forty years since he had read *La Logique*.

18 Earlier Peirce had rejected Gratry's explanation on the grounds that "an explanation should tell *how* a thing is done, and to assert a perpetual miracle seems to be an abandonment of all hope of doing that, without sufficient justification" (2.690, 1878).

19 Peirce noted that this is just the position taken in *Metaphysics*, 4.3, 1005b19. In this passage Peirce took up another mistake that he found in Aristotle, concerning first principles. It is the view that the process of reasoning must have had a beginning, so there must be a first premiss (see 2.26–7, c. 1902).

20 See Read, *Logic, Deductive and Inductive* (1898); Joseph, *An Introduction to Logic* (1906); Keynes in the last edition of his *Studies and Exercises in Formal Logic* (third edition, 1894); Jones, *Elements of Logic as a Science of Prepositions* (1890) and *An Introduction to General Logic* (1892).

21 Peirce noted that this illustrates the logical doctrine that the subject nominative is but an emphasized object.

22 Death to a society is not equivalent to the death of its members, of course. See Pearson, *Grammar of Science*, for example, 27–30 and 54–5.

23 At 2.81, c. 1902, Peirce included A.N. Whitehead.

24 On one occasion, Peirce made the claim that a part of the business of mathematics requires logic; that is, when "the mathematician is called in to consider a state of facts which are presented in a confused mass" (7.525, n.d.). Regardless of the function logic is required to perform (and Peirce did elaborate) we need notice only that this is clearly an *application* of mathematics. It is perfectly consistent to maintain both that pure mathematics has no need of logic, and that applied mathematics may require its assistance. One of the distinctive factors of pure mathematics is that it begins with arbitrary hypotheses that are absolutely distinct; unlike philosophy, for example, which must accept those forced upon it (1.443, c. 1896; 4.176, 1897).

25 Here Peirce gave the following droll illustration: "Thus a metaphysician who infers anything about a life beyond the grave can never find out for certain that his inference is false until he has gone out of the metaphysical business, at his present stand, at least."

26 The legitimacy of such an application is another question and one to which metaphysics should speedily address itself.

27 This is not simply the facile comment of a logician. Carolyn Eisele dem-

onstrates in *Studies* that there is ample evidence to qualify Peirce as one of America's foremost historians of science.

28 Mill, *System of Logic*, 206; 621.40, 1909.

29 Ernest Nagel credits Henri Poincaré with providing a proof for the proposition that "if one mechanical explanation for a phenomenon can be given, an infinity of others can also be constructed" in *Structure of Science*, 116 note 8.

30 Book 2, chapter 6.

31 Peirce illustrated these difficulties very nicely in 474, 1903 and in 647.17–20, 1910.

CHAPTER IV

1 Only at the end of the nineteenth century did Peirce understand science in this sense (339.267r, December 1905).

2 Peirce used "retrospective science" here, one of many terms he used. For the sake of clarity I have chosen to use one term throughout. A list of the several terms suggested for the major divisions of the sciences is given in appendix 1.

3 It is for the psychologist to determine whether or not scientists must do so. Peirce merely should have maintained that such extraneous considerations are not logically relevant. He would have been precluded from doing this only if he defined a science solely in terms of the activity of a social group; for if he had gone on to proscribe that activity it would need to be on the basis of some other criterion, namely, in terms of the purpose of science. Since the purpose of science is included in his definition, Peirce was able to make that move. And on one occasion, he did say that it is to the extent that scientists deviate from the search for truth for its own sake that they are not genuine scientists (1.235, c. 1902).

4 Peirce attributed the line to Pope, but it is by Pope's contemporary, Edward Young in *The Complaint: Night Thoughts*, Night IX, 1.769. Peirce's years at the Harvard College Observatory inform this statement.

5 Peirce thought there was inductive evidence to support his view.

6 Peirce notes that Whewell had recognized the need for suitable ideas (see also 6.604, 1893).

7 See chapter 2. Peirce would have had access to the 1901 edition.

8 If the business of developing a scheme is the task of logic and if metaphysics must be founded on logic, as Peirce maintained, then the scheme itself

will not be able to rest on metaphysics, not even if the metaphysics is saturated with realism.

9 Cows separated by colour have nothing but colour to distinguish them but, said Peirce, if red heads are attractive to men, classifying women by hair colour would be informative.

10 It might be said that Peirce's scheme serves to vindicate his own philosophy, but a scheme that receives its impetus from experience might equally have repudiated his philosophy and Peirce would have modified his philosophy if it could not accord with experience.

11 Peirce was often obscure, if not actually mystical, in some of his writings on final causation within the context of natural classification.

12 Consider the different routes whereby scientists have sometimes arrived at the same theory. Recall Peirce's belief that if a new idea is to emerge the science must have reached a certain stage of development. Peirce thought "the only source of the idea is the form of circumstance in which it was latent, and from the study of which it would infallibly be drawn" (426.6–7, 1902).

13 Peirce used the word "habit" in its Aristotelian sense (as in *Metaphysics* 5.20) meaning "any lasting state whether of a person or a thing, this state consisting in the fact that on any occasion of a certain kind that person or thing would, either certainly or even only probably behave in a definite way" (673.14–15, c. 1911; see also 5.477–80, c. 1907; 681.20–2, 1913; s104.12–13, n.d.).

14 Final causation must not be thought to supplant efficient causation. Each complements and is indispensable to the other. The law of habit, Peirce continued, is also "a simple formal law, a law of efficient causation."

15 Ultimately, Peirce considered this to be a phenomenological study of the material aspect of his formal categories.

16 He remarked on a difficulty with the relations between sodium and gold (1344.12, n.d.); see 7.222, 1901 for the table according to atomic weights as Peirce knew it; see also 693b.432–42, [1904] for further remarks.

17 The reason for developing a classification of the sciences is not to be confused with the final cause that governs the classification.

18 Comte does include geometry within concrete mathematics (see Comte, *Introduction to Positive Philosophy*, 66). More will be said of Peirce's views on Comte's principle of classification in section 4.

19 The six months spent learning classificatory techniques from Louis Agassiz in the early 1860s undoubtedly provided Peirce with a good basis for these investigations.

20 Peirce did not always present his classifiifications in tabular form, so that many of the schemes presented below are compilations from the texts. I have taken the additional liberty of amalgamating where more than one scheme (essentially the same) in the same manuscript gives different divisions more adequate treatment. On the other hand, I have omitted portions when Peirce pursued elaborations that are of no interest to the main line of development but that might obscure basic points of comparison.

21 Peirce later reconsidered the assessment of the relation between hypothesis and induction given at 2.623, 1878 (see the discussion of speculative grammar in chapter 5).

22 Compare a classification of laws at 1.514, c. 1896.

23 This depends on my chronology being correct. It must be admitted, however, that the foregoing assumption is one of the bases for dating certain manuscripts.

24 In Auguste Comte, *Cours de philosophie positive*, deuxième leçon, (1830). Peirce did not emulate Comte's scheme, however. That sequence was: mathematics, astronomy, physics, chemistry, biology, sociology.

25 At 2.198, c. 1902, Peirce wrote that it "has only been *within* five or six years that all the intimacy of its [ethics'] relation to logic has been revealed to me" (my italics). Vincent Potter maintains that Peirce was *firmly* convinced of the relationship between these two sciences about 1894, but I have not found the evidence for this. See Potter, *Peirce on Norms and Ideals*, 52. Yet in his application to the Carnegie Institution in 1902 Peirce made the claim that he had recognized the dependence of logic on ethics (albeit in a general and vague way) as early as 1869 (L75.160-1, 230-2, and 358 [in a pagination established by Don D. Roberts], 1902); reference is to *The Journal of Speculative Philosophy* 2:207, 208, see 5.354-7, 1869. For an account of elements in Peirce's early writings that suggest the beginnings of that relationship, see Pfeifer, "*Summum Bonum* in Peirce," chapter 2.

26 Fisch, "Peirce's Progress," 172; see also chapter 2, section 2 above.

27 In the actual scheme, groups of three do predominate, but this is not the only warrant for claiming that the categories were surfacing in Peirce's thinking here. Other passages in this manuscript refer to triads and to the "three formal points of view."

28 Sketches of a triadic classification system (of ideas, not of sciences) occur on a page marked "*important*" at 900(s).[3], c. 1896, omitted from 1.417-520. Degenerate forms of the categories (see section 6) are assigned to the first subdivisions but not to succeeding ones.

29 Murphey contends that Peirce could continue to base his theory of the categories on logic if the sciences (specifically the normative sciences) that precede logic in his classification scheme are ordered in accordance with the categories. Peirce solved his dilemma, Murphey argues, by intro-ducing phenomenology, the sole purpose of which is to furnish a founda-tion for the categories (Murphey, *Development of Peirce's Philosophy*, 366–7). But if Murphey is correct in his assessment of a dilemma, the pro-posed solution would only push the problem one stage further up the ladder: since the divisions of mathematics are in accordance with the cate-gories, Peirce would not be able to found his theory of the categories on phenomenology. Mathematics is, as a matter of fact, the first science to determine the (formal) categories but Murphey's argument would require that the principles of a classification scheme should be worked out before any science could be developed, which is to say the system would have to be of *possible* sciences – anathema to Peirce (ibid., 330). The problem is deflected when it is recognized that ordering by the categories is not con-fined to the normative sciences. Furthermore, the categories have emerged as the differentiating principle. And that principle was not imposed (ostensibly at least). Here it is provisional.

30 Such a suggestion should not go unquestioned. The context here is a draft and one not polished for publication. Peirce may simply have been con-trasting his earlier scheme with those just compiled.

31 At 1.618 Peirce aligned himself with Aristotle in separating both ethics and aesthetics from the theoretical sciences.

32 The *logisches Gefühl* of the German logicians.

33 *Nation* 69 (1899): 356.

34 A version of this scheme is found at 1.589–90, c. 1900.

35 *Nation* 70 (1900): 481.

36 *Science* 40 (1900): 620–1.

37 See 5.533, c. 1905 where Peirce cited the Lowell lectures of 1903 as the first occasion on which a pragmatist argued that logic might be based on ethics. That was "maintained on the ground that reasoning is thought subjected to self-control."

38 Here phenomenology is called "the categories" and this might indicate that the scheme post-dates an entry in the Logic Notebook of 22 July 1902 (339.222r) in which Pierce cited a new science, "categoric," which is to precede mathematics. Fisch has characterized this as a "momentary aberra-tion" in Fisch, "Hegel and Peirce," 182 note 25.

39 Comte was given credit in the second section of chapter 2 of the "Minute Logic" (2.119, c. 1902).

40 An exception is an oblique reference at 1.223, c. 1902.

41 Later in this manuscript orders are said to be distinguished by the different governing conceptions (7.374 note 10, c. 1902). Since the dominant governing conception is Comte's principle, these could be one and the same.

42 Later, families are said to be distinguished by their different methods of investigation (7.374 note 10, c. 1902). It is not clear that this is what distinguishes the families of the normative sciences, however they are ordered. See comment below.

43 This makes use of the scheme that occurs at the end of manuscript 427, various other parts of the manuscript, as well as that segment published in the *Collected Papers*.

44 Branches, classes and other divisions do appear in some later manuscripts, however, for example, 615.18–29, 1908.

45 The earliest commentator to urge the importance of understanding Peirce's logic as a normative science is Arthur W. Burks in "Peirce's Conception of Logic;" but his interpretation depends largely on this 1902 formulation in which the relationship between ethics and logic is sometimes imbued with an ethics of logic. He overlooks later developments in both the manuscripts and the published material. Manley Thompson (in *Pragmatic Philosophy*) is another who concentrates on the position expressed in the "Minute Logic" and finds it (naturally enough) beset with uncertain assertions.

46 This is one of the difficulties that led Maryann Ayim to conclude that the hierarchy of the normative sciences is mistaken ("Peirce's View," 36).

47 Increasingly, the role of self-control in logic is recognized, however (see 2.123; 2.144; 2.165; and 2.182–3, all from "Minute Logic", c. 1902).

48 In subsequent alternative pages the normative sciences are said to be a kind of final cause in that they are concerned with what ought to be, while metaphysics investigates "what at bottom is (tracing, as it were, efficient causes, or something analogous)." Accordingly, orders 2 and 3 more or less parallel the two divisions of the special sciences. Yet this is thought to be an "external" or an "arbitrary" consideration, which it would not be appropriate to include, so again nothing follows (427.98²–9², c. 1902).

49 Peirce was trying to promote interest in order to get critical comments.

50 Murphey, *Development of Peirce's Philosophy*, 358–9.

51 Since the normative sciences are ordered according to the categories, Murphey thought Peirce could "no longer rest his theory of the categories on logic" in *Development of Peirce's Philosophy*, 366. Peirce's answer, according to Murphey, was to introduce a "new science," phenomenology.

We have already examined the problems with that move; but phenomenology had been included in the classification when philosophy was limited to logic and metaphysics. Hence that could not have been the *reason* for its introduction.

52 I believe the editorial inserts distort the sense of this passage.

53 Nonetheless, the differentiating idea of the heuretic sciences is in terms of objects of observation and this reflects the fact that all divisions of philosophy require the experience of mature adults.

54 Boston: Alfred Mudge & Son 1903.

55 Peirce refrained from using the expression "natural priority" only to avoid importing the *whole* of Aristotle's theory of priority.

56 It may well have some connection with the material categories (discussed below), which are also thought to have little importance.

57 He reported that he made "long and arduous studies of this matter" (5.38, 1903); that his three categories "resulted from two years incessant study in the direction of trying to do what Hegel tried to do. It became apparent that there were such categories as his. But bad as his are [he] could substitute nothing radically better" (L463, July 1905 – draft letter to Lady Welby, quoted in Fisch, "Hegel and Peirce," 176); that "he has had another list under active advisement for more than forty years" (283.3⁴, 1905); that when he was in his twenties he "devoted more than two years with all the passion of that age to the study of phanerochemy, in almost every waking hour and dreaming of nothing else" (1338.25, [c. 1905–6]); and that "the two most passionately laborious years of [his] life were exclusively devoted to trying to ascertain something for certain about [them]" (1.288, [c. 1906]).

58 Fisch, "Hegel and Peirce," 177; see also 1.525, 1903; and consider Peirce's conclusions about any *a priori* use of the categories in classifying the sciences. Hereafter, the term "categories" must be understood to refer to the universal categories.

59 See also 4.317-23, c. 1902; 602.12-13, 1903-8; 8.297, 1904; 1.350, c. 1905; 908.5, n.d. This is a task for formal logic, which Peirce held to be singularly related to mathematics. If this is the study in which Peirce first described the categories (cf. 1.553-9, 1867), then perhaps their discovery was synchronized with the proper logical sequence after all.

60 See chapter 2, section 2 for earlier versions of the categories.

61 Peirce elucidated the expression "unnecessarily imported" in a footnote: "This term is borrowed from the geometers, who speak of a pair of complanar rays as a 'degenerate conic.' That is, the idea of their being a conic is unnecessarily imported" (478.29 note, 1903).

62 They are mentioned again in a letter to Lady Welby dated 12 October 1904
   (8.330–1) and still later (1338.34–9, [c. 1905–6]); and they were mentioned
   earlier (1.473–81, c. 1896).

63 Although Vincent Potter has given an insightful account of the categories,
   he regards his own attempts to relate them to the classification as speculative. Moreover, he seems unaware of the central idea of principle-
   dependence which governs the ordering of the sciences.

64 This should be so, that is, if that classification is indeed natural and if triads are pervasive as Aristotle, Kant, Hegel, and Peirce believed.

65 I employ the numbering system used by Peirce in manuscript 1135 to indicate each level of discrimination.

66 He claimed to have worked out more than 300 branches.

67 Compare the general divisions governing the special sciences.

68 The following manuscripts (all post 1902) more or less follow this pattern
   with varying degrees of completeness: 1.180–201, 1903; 602.14–16, [1903–
   8]; 693a.70–6, [1904]; 283.9–31, 1905; 328.20–2, c. 1905; 1334.16–40, 1905;
   605.6–17, [1905–6]; 1338.3, [c. 1905–6]; 601.20–31, [1906]; 615.18–29, 1908;
   655.17–26, 1910; 673.47, c. 1911; 675.10, [c. 1911]; 677.2, [c. 1911]. An exception is found in a 1905 manuscript in which the heuretic sciences are
   divided into mathematics, positive science, and the natural history of
   thought; the positive sciences are subdivided into cenoscopy and idioscopy
   (1334.24). Yet Peirce made it clear that this was no more than a prediction.
   This natural history of thought would not be the "logic" that Dewey described as a "natural history of thought" and that elicited severe criticism
   from Peirce (see 8.190, 1904; 8.239, 1904).

CHAPTER V

1 In *The Development of Peirce's Philosophy*, Murray G. Murphey seems to
   confine the role of the categories in Peirce's classification scheme to the
   divisions of the normative sciences and he claims that they subvert the
   architectonic. Thus, he says, "since logic is only one of the normative
   sciences, and since the divisions of the normative sciences are themselves
   obviously based on the categories, it is clear that Peirce can no longer rest
   his theory of the categories on logic" (ibid., 366). Such an argument presupposes that the principles of a classification scheme must be determined
   before any science can be embarked upon – which is to say that the system
   must be of possible sciences. That, of course, is what Murphey accuses
   Peirce of doing. Since Peirce addressed himself to the dilemma of pursu-

ing a science of logic without employing principles of its own investigations, that discussion, together with his rejection of a procedure that proposes to classify *possible* sciences, resolves Murphey's quandary.

2 Peirce thought that it was a mistake to view mathematics as a wholly quantitative study since that would limit it to strictly linear arrangements with which to compare other linear arrangements. The relations of cause and effect, reason and consequent, are of this kind. Peirce granted their importance but reminded us that mathematics extends to the theory of all groups (328.23–5, c. 1905). By "group" he meant "the whole of any system of relationship, regarded in a certain abstract way" (328.26, c. 1905). And not all relations are quantitative.

3 Peirce frequently used Jeremy Bentham's terms for philosophy and the special sciences since they express the distinction he wished to emphasize: "Cenoscopy" is the "watch tower of the common" and "idioscopy" is the "watch tower of the peculiar" (778.8, [c. 1909]).

4 Peirce was not totally consistent in that opinion. In one manuscript the classification of the elements of the phaneron appears to spill over into the province of the normative sciences. There, phenomenology is said to study, not the universal phenomena in their firstness, but rather the categories in their forms of firstness. This appears to limit phenomenology to the study of the ideas of firstness, secondness, and thirdness. The categories in their forms of secondness (as they present themselves in common experience) are topics for a new science, Encyclopedeutics, which is to examine the material categories. The categories in their forms of thirdness, Peirce here maintained, concern the ideas of signs of firstness, secondness, and thirdness and are topics for the normative sciences. This appears to be inconsistent with his usual view that the normative sciences are to examine the phenomena in their secondness; it reduces the role of phenomenology to what seems to be its mathematical part and it distorts the symmetry of the divisions of philosophy. Moreover, in the same manuscript Peirce recognized that the task of logic is to examine the general theory of signs, and *that* science is the third of the normative sciences (478.40–2, 1903).

5 Peirce went so far as to say that phenomenology "can hardly be said to involve reasoning" (2.197, c. 1902). However, I do not believe that he would deny the need of a *logica utens*. Rather, he seems to have been denying that its conclusions are positive assertions about the world.

6 To avoid the inclusion of such distinctions within the province of ethics on the heuretic level, Peirce was prompted to refer to that science as prenormative on one occasion (1.577, c. 1902).

7 See also Goudge, *Thought of C.S. Peirce*, 349.

8 This is his expressed opinion of both logic and aesthetics on occasion (see for example, 675.12–14, [c. 1911]).

9 Potter has developed a chronological exposition. He has remarked the confusion and has revealed many of Peirce's contradictory assertions; see particularly Potter, *Peirce on Norms and Ideals*, 127 note 12.

10 In another context some argument would be needed to support that claim. Almost anything said concerning the evolution of Peirce's thought in the present discussion could be adduced to substantiate that point. I merely note that mention of a fourth grade of clearness (5.3, 1901; 8.176 note 3, 1902; L75.68, 1902) and more ambiguous mention of an additional (that is, a fourth) grade of meaning are limited to the years 1901–3, while in later manuscripts (for example, 620.18, 1909; 649.1–2, 1910) Peirce admitted only three grades, commenting that he was late in coming to a definite conception of the third grade.

11 It is the requirement of universalization that creates the ethical egoist's dilemma; Peirce seemed to dispense with that requirement here.

12 On another occasion, God's purpose is thought to be the creation of "an answering mind" which is "God's movement toward self reproduction." Here Peirce maintained that the theoretical scientists recognize that the lot of the human race is inconsequential once it has "subserved its purpose of developing a new type of mind that can fear and worship God better" (1334.20–1, 1905).

13 Here Peirce attempts to give expression to the phenomenological requirements (that the ideal should reflect all three categories) while at the same time positing an ideal that is an immediate quality. The evolutionary character of the ideal asserts itself nonetheless.

14 This is somewhat ambivalent. I do not think that Peirce was expressing the hope that boundless reason should turn out to be utterly helpless, nor do I believe that he was expressing a conviction that it inevitably would be so. I think that he intended to indicate that, because of the limitations of his present experience, boundless reason could not (by the very nature of the case) reveal a meaning that has not yet materialized and so is not accessible to thought.

15 The footnote at 5.402 is examined by Walter P. Krolikowksi in "The Peircean *Vir*," 257–70.

16 Peirce quoted a minister of the church as saying that anaesthetics were "a decoy of Satan which though speciously offering to bless women, will in the end rob God of the deep and earnest cries for help that rise to Him in the time of their trouble" (649.30–1, 1910).

17 Peirce could not have intended both of his two inserts to remain standing in the text. I have deleted the less legible "some things left[?]" and allowed "End" to stand.

18 Perhaps this ties in with what Peirce had in mind when he equated phenomenology with "pragmaticistic ideology."

19 This was the difficulty that prompted Peirce to subsume aesthetics under ethics; but that does not resolve the problem.

20 Only in one late manuscript do I find a discrepancy. There, Peirce linked ethics (with metaphysics and psychology) as sciences that have more than usual need to appeal to principles of logical analysis. It could not be an oversight, since he went on to say that logical critic obtains its principles from mathematics, phenomenology, and aesthetics (there called "callesthetics") and from no other source (633.1:4–5, 5 September 1909). Yet, a few weeks later, when he was again writing on the same topic, the science of logic is said to depend on phenomenology, callesthetics, and ethics – and mathematics is omitted since he was citing positive sciences only (636.24, 25 September 1909).

21 At one point Peirce limited the "others" to those one has a *duty* to control. The inclusion of duty might augment the province of criticism; e.g., I could construe it as my duty to criticize the nuclear powers for pursuing policies that increase the risk of nuclear winter on our planet, even though effecting a change in those policies is beyond my control. Peirce would respond that such criticism is reasonable only so far as it may affect the targeted conduct and no further (329.12, c. 1904). Just so, if we could repress our feelings of revulsion at the actions of a Hitler without detriment to moral sensibility, there would seem to be no need to form judgments about historical figures (598.6, [c. 1902]). And while Peirce granted that society needs to protect itself, he thought that subsequent wrongs done to offenders are misguided. Offenders, he urged, should be placed in "an environment as elevating to them" as possible (288.163, 1905). Yet Peirce was premature in introducing the term "duty" before he had determined what constitutes duty.

22 I have suggested earlier (in chapter 3, section 5) that this very dissatisfaction was an important factor in prompting Peirce to relate logic to other sciences by means of a classification scheme.

23 Vincent Potter sees a contradiction between two passages in the *Collected Papers*, in *Peirce on Norms and Ideals*, 25, which is pertinent to the present discussion. I address his concern in appendix 3 below.

24 Don Roberts refers to the program suggested by Peirce's tinctures as "the analysis of the conceptions of logic in terms of the categories" (Roberts,

Existential Graphs, 102–3). He cites 670.20 and .29, 1911 and 674.14, c. 1911 as evidence that Peirce had been pursuing that program.

25 Prior to any systematic study, the rudimentary classification of arguments implied by such a general method belongs to the reasoner's *logica utens*.

26 This term was introduced by Richard S. Robin in "Peirce's Doctrine," 271–2.

27 Speculative grammar is the subject of volume 2, book 2 of *Collected Papers*.

28 The first reference follows from 5.145; the versos of those pages are published as 5.146–50. Both sources list published occurrences of the confusion.

   Peirce frequently referred to hypothetical inference as "abduction" but that term is derived from his conjecture concerning an interpretation of an obliterated word in Aristotle's *Prior Analytics* 2.25. Because his opinion was unconfirmed he thought it wiser to use the term "retroduction" "to imply that it turns back and leads from the consequent of an admitted consequence to its antecedent" (857.5, n.d.; see also 8.209, c. 1905).

29 The view expressed by Ayim ("Peirce's view," 197–9), that the reverse ordering is equally legitimate, seems mistaken. In the first place, her warrant for the alternative occurs in the same series of lectures in which Peirce had pronounced for retroduction as first, induction as second, and deduction as third (she herself cites 5.171, 1903). Her references for the alternative ordering index Peirce's attempts to see how the pragmatic maxim (here called the "logic of abduction") might be related to thirdness – not to *make* it a third (5.206–8, 1903). This was in 1903, when Peirce was trying to restate his pragmaticism in contradistinction to James's popularized version. He had recognized the reality of possiblity and the future-directedness of pragmaticism, and was eager to correct the blunder of his early pronouncement regarding the hardness of an unexamined diamond. The connection of the pragmatic maxim with the experimental method has tended to lay emphasis on its inductive character, although Peirce had never meant experimentation in the narrow sense (see 315.21 verso [omission between 5.195 and 5.196], 1903). He was not denying the role of induction on this occasion but was merely shifting the emphasis and he may have been guilty of over-compensating in a way reminiscent of his flirtation with a fourth grade of clearness. All three modes of inference are involved in the pragmatic method just as are all three categories. Here, Peirce had drawn attention to the conditional/possibility aspect of the maxim but he was also anxious to retain sight of its element of thirdness.

30 See also Roberts, *Existential Graphs*.

31 Critic is the subject of volume 2, book 3 of *Collected Papers* where the categories once again predominate.

32 Peirce intended the parenthetical additions to the original pronouncement to supply clarification without substantial modification.

33 Max Fisch had remarked that this does not seem to cohere with another statement of Peirce's, namely, that "the maxim of pragmatism, if true, fully *covers* the entire logic of abduction" (5.196, 1903). The difficulty Fisch recognizes is that if, as I have indicated, the "logic of abduction" or retroduction is pursued in all three departments of logic, how can a maxim that is the product of methodeutic cover the entire logic of abduction? What could Peirce have meant by the term "cover"? If he meant no more than that the pragmatic maxim allowed the inclusion of all hypotheses appropriate to retroductive inference, he would seem to be making a point of consistency and there need be no incoherence between the two statements. If, on the other hand, Peirce was maintaining that investigation into retroductive inference depended on the pragmatic maxim as a principle or, that the pragmatic maxim and retroductive inference were identical, it would be difficult to reconcile the two statements in question. The remark that "the maxim of pragmatism cannot cut off any kind of hypothesis which ought to be admitted" (5.196, 1903) might be adduced to support the former view. Since retroductive inference requires *testable* hypotheses and since it is an essential contributor to the maxim, it is not altogether surprising that there is a similitude with hypotheses yielding possible practical consequences such as are warranted by the pragmatic maxim.

34 This has its analogue in induction, where a controlled inference is not possible from any one of the individuals that together provide its basis.

35 Peirce reconstructed the series of guesses, punctured by experiments, involved in Archimedes' discovery of the properties of the lever (692.31–5, 1901).

36 Ayim provides a comprehensive account of that system in "Peirce's View," 146–9.

37 A more extensive list of problems is to be found in the *Collected Papers* (6.6, c. 1903 = 283.25–30, 1905).

38 Max Fisch and Manley Thompson both think that Peirce intended that objective logic should link normative semiotic to metaphysics. This is discussed in appendix 4.

39 Nonetheless I am convinced that any such study must be preceded by a propaedeutic such as is attempted in this volume.

40 The ordering of the branches differs at 1.192 in that physical metaphysics is placed after the next branch.

41 Peirce thought this might be construed as an exception to his ordering of the sciences but such aid is in the form of data and no contravention to the hierarchy of principle-dependence is involved.

42 Probably that same innovation inspires an alternative ordering in which Peirce ventured the opinion that the heuretic sciences might divide into mathematics, positive sciences, and the natural history of thought. The positive sciences would then be assigned the two divisions of philosophy and special sciences, and the special sciences would retain the usual two divisions (1334.24, 1905). But the result in this case is a further *decrease* in symmetry.

43 These references cover all three divisions of the special sciences. Divisions vary somewhat between references (cf. 8.192, c. 1904).

44 For a sample list see 1.243, c. 1902.

45 In the pages omitted at 1.645 this idea is linked with the classification scheme (see particularly 437.18-19, 1898). Space, time, and law were the really continuous and eternal things for Peirce. I suspect that the foregoing is consistent with pragmaticism but I do not intend to pursue the question.

CHAPTER VI

1 See *The Will to Believe* (1896), and James's lecture "Philosophical Conceptions and Practical Results" delivered at the University of California in 1898, published in his *Pragmatism*.

2 Recall that this end fulfils the phenomenological requirement of incorporating the three cenopythagorean categories. To underscore that particular character of his revised theory, Peirce on one occasion called his doctrine "Cenopythagorean Pragmaticism" (5.555 note*, c. 1906).

3 This is not to lose sight of the fact that, for Peirce, *meaning* is open ended and hence cannot be completely specified. It is not your experience or mine that is pertinent; rather it is every possible future experience of an unlimited community of reasoners.

4 This is from omission at 4.8. The "looking" is done through the mind's eye, of course (see 298. Add 11, 1905; cf. 5.491, c. 1907; 322.10-11, [c. 1907]).

5 Curiously, his choice of the word "synechism" suggests that a Cartesian dualism is presupposed for, as he himself noted, "the Greek word means continuity of parts brought about by surgery" (7.565 note 28, c. 1892) i.e.,

severed (or at least "discrete") elements are united. Yet the synechist (and Peirce counted himself as one) "will insist that all phenomena are of one character" (7.570, c. 1892).

APPENDIX 2

1 Restack, *The Brain*, chapter 10.
2 French, *Einstein*, 155.
3 Tony Buzan on U.S. National Public Radio Morning Edition Series. *Expanding Human Intelligence*, 13 August 1984.
4 298. Add 11, 1905. Our eyes involve cerebral specialization but Peirce was speaking metaphorically (although insightfully) here.

APPENDIX 3

1 See Potter, *Peirce on Norms and Ideals*, 25 and Appendix 1, 207–8.
2 Presumably it would be a difficulty for James and Schiller who, according to Peirce, were of the opinion that an infinite series could not be completed nor the concept fully formed; see 195 above.
3 By "hypostatic" abstraction Peirce meant "the act of metamorphosing a predicate or verb-idea into a subject (or grammatical object which is a secondary subject)" (288.41, 1905).

APPENDIX 4

1 Fisch, "Hegel and Peirce," 181–6.
2 Thompson, *Pragmatic Philosophy*, particularly 179–94; and "Review," 244.
3 Thompson, *Pragmatic Philosophy*, 193; he cites 6.455, 1908.
4 For an account of developments relating to the introduction of the third universe see Roberts, *Existential Graphs*, section 6.
5 Ibid., 90–2, 102.
6 Ibid., 100.
7 Notice the interaction between inquiries, which Roberts has remarked here.

Selected Bibliography

I WORKS BY CHARLES SANDERS PEIRCE

Peirce, Charles Sanders. The Charles S. Peirce Papers. Houghton Library, Harvard University, Cambridge, Mass. Microfilm.

– *Collected Papers*. 8 vols. Vols. 1–6 edited by Charles Hartshorne and Paul Weiss. Cambridge, Mass.: Harvard University Press 1931–5. Vols. 7–8 edited by Arthur Burks. Cambridge, Mass.: Harvard University Press 1958.

– *The New Elements of Mathematics*. Edited by Carolyn Eisele. 4 vols in 5. The Hague: Mouton 1976.

– *Writings of Charles S. Peirce: A Chronological Edition*. Vol. 1, *1857–66*. Vol. 2, *1867–71*. Bloomington, Ind.: Indiana University Press 1982–.

II OTHER SOURCES

Agassiz, Louis. "Professor Agassiz on the Origin of Species." *American Journal of Science and Arts*, 2d ser., 30 (1860):142–54.

Ashworth, E.J. *Language and Logic in the Post-Medieval Period*. Dordrecht: D. Reidel Publishing 1974.

Ayim, Maryann. "Peirce's View of the Roles of Reason and Instinct in Scientific Inquiry." PH D diss., University of Waterloo 1972.

Bacon, Francis. *Works*. 2 vols. Boston: Houghton Mifflin n.d.

Bocheński, I.M. *A History of Formal Logic*. Notre Dame, Ind.: University of Notre Dame Press 1961.

Bowler, Peter J. *Evolution: The History of an Idea*. Berkeley, Cal.: University of California Press 1984.

Brent, Joseph Lancaster, III. "A Study in the Life of Charles Sanders Peirce." PH D diss., University of California 1960.

Burks, Arthur W. "Peirce's Conception of Logic as a Normative Science." *Philosophical Review* 52 (1943):187–93.

Butts, Robert E., ed. *William Whewell's Theory of Scientific Method*. Pittsburgh: University of Pittsburgh Press 1968.

Cadwallader, Thomas C. "Peirce as an Experimental Psychologist." *Transactions of the Charles S. Peirce Society* 11 (1975):167–86.

Comte, Auguste. *Introduction to Positive Philosophy*. Edited and translated by Frederick Ferre. Indianapolis: Bobbs-Merrill 1970.

Einstein, Albert. *Autobiographical Notes*. Edited and translated by P.A. Schlipp. La Salle, Ill.: Open Court 1979.

Eisele, Carolyn. "C.S. Peirce's Search for a Method in Mathematics and the History of Science." *Transactions of the Charles S. Peirce Society* 11 (1975):149–58.

- "The Charles S. Peirce-Simon Newcomb Correspondence." *Proceedings of the American Philosophical Society* 101 (1957):409–33.

- "Peirce's Philosophy of Education in his Unpublished Mathematics Textbooks." In *Studies in the Philosophy of Charles Sanders Peirce*. Edited by Edward G. Moore and Richard S. Robin. 2d. ser. Amherst, Mass.: University of Massachusetts 1964. Pp. 51–75.

- *Studies in the Scientific and Mathematical Philosophy of Charles S. Peirce*. Edited by R.M. Martin. The Hague: Mouton 1979.

Fisch, Max H. "Hegel and Peirce." In *Hegel and the History of Philosophy*. Edited by J.J. O'Malley, F.G. Weiss, and K.W. Algozin. The Hague: Martinus Nijhoff 1974. Pp. 171–93.

- "Peirce and the History of Science." *Transactions of the Charles S. Peirce Society* 11 (1975):145–8.

- "Peirce's Progress from Nominalism toward Realism." *Monist* 51 (1967):159–78.

- "Was There a Metaphysical Club in Cambridge?" In *Studies in the Philosophy of Charles Sanders Peirce*. Edited by Edward G. Moore and Richard S. Robin. 2d ser. Amherst, Mass.: University of Massachusetts Press 1964. Pp. 3–22.

Fitzgerald, John J. *Peirce's Theory of Signs as a Foundation of Pragmaticism*. The Hague: Mouton & Co. 1966.

Flint, Robert. *Philosophy as Scientia Scientiarum; and a History of Classification of the Sciences*. New York: Charles Scribner's Sons 1904.

Flower, Elizabeth amd Murray G. Murphey. *A History of Philosophy in America*. 2 vols. New York: G.P. Putnam's Sons 1977.

French, A.P. *Einstein, a Century Volume*. London: Heinemann 1979.

Gallie, W.B. *Peirce and Pragmatism*. Harmondsworth: Penguin Books 1952.

Goudge, Thomas A. *The Thought of C.S. Peirce*. New York: Dover Publications 1969.

Hamilton, William. *Lectures on Metaphysics and Logic*. 4 vols. Edinburgh: 1861–6. Facsimile reprint. Stuttgart-Bad Connstatt: Friedrich Frommann Verlag 1970.

Hobbes, Thomas. *Leviathan, or the Matter, Forme and Power of a Commonwealth, Ecclesiasticall and Civil*. Edited by Michael Oakeshott. Oxford: Basil Blackwell n.d.

James, William. *Pragmatism, a New Name for Some Old Ways of Thinking*. New York: Longmans Green 1907.

Kent, Beverley E. "Logic in the Context of Peirce's Classification of the Sciences." PHD diss., University of Waterloo 1975.

– "Objective Logic in Peirce's Thought." *Transactions of the Charles S. Peirce Society* 13 (1977):142–6.

– "Peirce's Esthetics: A New Look." *Transactions of the Charles S. Peirce Society* 12 (1976):263–83.

Ketner, Kenneth Lane and others, eds. *A Comprehensive Bibliography and Index of the Published Works of Charles Sanders Peirce with a Bibliography of Secondary Studies*. Greenwich, Conn.: Johnson Associates 1977.

Krolikowski, Walter P. "The Peircean *Vir*." In *Studies in the Philosophy of Charles Sanders Peirce*. Edited by Edward G. Moore and Richard S. Robin. 2d ser. Amherst, Mass.: University of Massachusetts Press 1964. Pp. 257–70.

Lenzen, Victor F. "Charles S. Peirce as Astronomer." In *Studies in the Philosophy of Charles Sanders Peirce*. Edited by Edward G. Moore and Richard S. Robin. 2d ser. Amherst, Mass.: University of Massachusetts Press 1964. Pp. 35–50.

– "Charles S. Peirce as Mathematical Physicist." *Transactions of the Charles S. Peirce Society* 11 (1975):159–66.

Lurie, Edward. *Louis Agassiz: A Life in Science*. Chicago: University of Chicago Press 1960.

Manning, Thomas G. "Peirce, the Coast Survey, and the Politics of Cleveland Democracy." *Transactions of the Charles S. Peirce Society* 11 (1975):187–94.

Mayr, Ernst. *The Growth of Biological Thought: Diversity, Evolution, and Inheritance*. Cambridge, Mass.: Belknap Press of Harvard University Press 1982.

Merton, Robert K. *The Sociology of Science: Theoretical and Empirical Investigations*. Chicago: University of Chicago Press 1973.

Mill, John Stuart. *Auguste Comte and Positivism*. Ann Arbor: University of Michigan Press, Ann Arbor Paperbacks 1961.

– *An Examination of Sir William Hamilton's Philosophy, and of the Principal Philosophical Questions discussed in his Writings*. 2 vols. Boston: W.V. Spencer 1865.

– *A System of Logic*. London: Longmans 1965.

Moore, Edward G. and Richard S. Robin, eds. *Studies in the Philosophy of Charles Sanders Peirce*. 2d ser. Amherst, Mass.: University of Massachusetts Press 1964.

Murphey, Murray G. *The Development of Peirce's Philosophy*. Cambridge, Mass.: Harvard University Press 1961.

Nagel, Ernest. *The Structure of Science: Problems in the Logic of Scientific Explanation*. New York: Harcourt Brace 1961.

Pearson, Karl. *Grammar of Science*. London: J.M. Dent and Sons 1892.

Perry, Ralph Barton. *The Thought and Character of William James*. 2 vols. Boston: Little, Brown 1935.

Pfeifer, David Elmer. "The *Summum Bonum* in the Philosophy of C.S. Peirce." PH D diss., University of Illinois 1971.

Potter, Vincent G. *Charles S. Peirce on Norms and Ideals*. Amherst, Mass.: University of Massachusetts Press 1967.

Restak, Richard M. *The Brain: The Last Frontier*. Garden City: Doubleday 1979.

Richardson, Ernest Cushing. *Classification: Theoretical and Practical*. Hamden, Conn.: Shoe String Press 1964.

Roberts, Don Davis. *The Existential Graphs of Charles S. Peirce*. The Hague: Mouton 1973.

Robin, Richard S. *Annotated Catalog of the Papers of Charles S. Peirce*. Amherst, Mass.: University of Massachusetts Press 1967.

– "The Peirce Papers: A Supplementary Catalog." *Transactions of the Charles S. Peirce Society* 7 (1971):37–57.

– "Peirce's Doctrine of the Normative Sciences." In *Studies in the Philosophy of Charles Sanders Peirce*. Edited by Edward G. Moore and Richard S. Robin. 2d ser. Amherst, Mass.: University of Massachusetts Press 1964. Pp. 271–88.

Ross, Dorothy. *G. Stanley Hall: The Psychologist as Prophet*. Chicago: University of Chicago Press 1972.

Ruse, Michael. *The Darwinian Revolution*. Chicago: The University of Chicago Press 1979.

Schlaretzki, W.E. "Scientific Reasoning and the Summum Bonum." *Philosophy of Science* 27 (1960):48–57.

Skagestad, Peter. "C.S. Peirce on Biological Evolution and Scientific Progress." *Synthese* 41 (1979):85–114.

Spencer, Herbert. *Reasons for Dissenting from the Philosophy of M. Comte and other Essays*. Berkeley: Glendessary Press 1968.

Speziale, Pierre. "Classification of the Sciences." In *Dictionary of the History of Ideas: Studies of Selected Pivotal Ideas*. New York: Charles Scribner's Sons 1968.

Standley, Arline Reilein. *August Comte*. Boston: Twayne Publishers 1981.

Thompson, Manley. *The Pragmatic Philosophy of C.S. Peirce*. Chicago: University of Chicago Press 1953.

- "Review of *Charles S. Peirce on Norms and Ideals*, by Vincent G. Potter." *Ethics* 79 (1969):244–6.

Van Evra, James. "Richard Whately and the Rise in Modern Logic." *History and Philosophy of Logic* 5 (1984):1–18.

Weiner, Phillip P. and Frederic H. Young, eds. *Studies in the Philosophy of C.S. Peirce*. Cambridge: Harvard University Press 1952.

Weiss, Paul. "Biography of Charles S. Peirce." In *Dictionary of American Biography*. Vol. 14, 398–403.

Whewell, William. *Novum Organon Renovatum*. London: 1858.

White, Morton. *Science and Sentiment in America: Philosophical Thought from Jonathan Edwards to John Dewey*. New York: Oxford University Press 1972.

Index